Sexology Uncensored

Sexology Uncensored

The Documents of Sexual Science

Edited by Lucy Bland and Laura Doan

The University of Chicago Press

Lucy Bland is senior lecturer in Women's Studies, University of North London. She publishes extensively on the history of sexuality. Her most recent book, *Banishing the Beast: English Feminism and Sexual Morality, 1885–1915*, was published in 1994.

Laura Doan is professor of English at the State University of New York, Geneseo. She is the editor of *The Lesbian Postmodern* (1994) and *Old Maids to Radical Spinsters* (1991).

The University of Chicago Press, Chicago 60637
Polity Press, Cambridge CB2 1UR, UK
First published in 1998 by Polity Press in association with
Blackwell Publishers Ltd.
© Polity Press 1998
All rights reserved. Published 1998

07 06 05 04 03 02 01 00 99 98   1 2 3 4 5 6

ISBN: 0-226-05668-6 (cloth)
ISBN: 0-226-05669-4 (paper)

Library of Congress Cataloging-in-Publication Data

Sexology uncensored : the documents of sexual science / Lucy Bland and
    Laura Doan, co-editors.
        p.   cm.
    Companion volume to: Sexology in culture.
    Includes bibliographical references.
    ISBN 0-226-05668-6 (cloth : alk. paper). — ISBN 0-226-05669-4
(pbk. : alk. paper)
    1. Sexology—History—Sources.   I. Bland, Lucy.   II. Doan, Laura
L., 1951– .

    HQ60.S4965   1998
    306.7'09—dc21   98-16624
                                                                          CIP

This book is printed on acid-free paper.

Contents

3/24 ✓

Editors' Note

Omissions from the material as originally published are indicated by ellipses within square brackets, thus: [. . .]. Where a paragraph or more has been excluded, there is a line space above and below such ellipses. All others are as in the original publication. Apart from minor amendments, the few editorial interventions necessitated by publishing these documents in a single volume also appear in square brackets. The original spelling, capitalization and emphases have been adhered to.

Acknowledgements

The editors would like to thank the following for their generous and efficient help in the preparation of this manuscript: Marlene Mussell, Marisa Burkhardt, Gail English, Marie Henry and Lesley Hall. Thanks to Simon Shepherd for the idea of the sourcebook. We owe a special debt of thanks to the generosity of Professor François Lafitte.

The following list cites the original sources for the extracts used in this volume. The editors and publishers are grateful for permission to use copyrighted material where indicated.

Part I
From *The Evolution of Sex* by Patrick Geddes and J. Arthur Thomson (Walter Scott, London, 1889), pp. 267–71.
    From *The Criminal* by Havelock Ellis (Walter Scott, London, 1890), pp. 216–18, 219–20. Copyright © François Lafitte.
    From *The Female Offender* by Cesare Lombroso and Guglielmo Ferrero [1893] (T. Fisher Unwin, London, 1895), pp. 107, 108–9, 110, 150–2. Copyright © Peter Owen Ltd, London.
    From *Man and Woman: A Study of Human Secondary Sexual Characteristics* by Havelock Ellis (A. & C. Black, London, 1894), pp. 250–3, 408, 424, 425, 438–9, 440–1, 448, 495, 496–7, 522, 523. Copyright © François Lafitte.
    From *Sex and Character* by Otto Weininger [1903] (translation of the sixth edition, W. Heinemann, London, 1906), pp. 88–9, 90–1, 248–9, 250, 292–3, 300.

From *The Sexual Question: A Scientific, Psychological, Hygienic and Sociological Study* by August Forel [1906] (William Heinemann (Medical Books), London, 1908), pp. 92, 93–4.

From *The Sexual Life of Our Time in Its Relations to Modern Civilization* by Iwan Bloch [1907] (translation of the sixth edition, W. Heinemann, London, 1908), pp. 55, 56–7, 58–9, 60, 62–3, 64, 76–7, 83–4, 85, 86.

From *Studies in the Psychology of Sex*, vol. I: *The Evolution of Modesty, The Phenomena of Sexual Periodicity, Auto-Erotism* by Havelock Ellis [1899] (F.A. Davis, Philadelphia, 1900), pp. 1, 29, 43–4. Copyright © François Lafitte.

From *Problems of the Sexes* by Jean Finot (David Nutt, London, 1913), pp. 130, 132, 133, 135–6, 193–5, 196, 209, 228–9, 390–1.

Part II

From *Psychopathia Sexualis: With Especial Reference to the Antipathic Sexual Instinct. A Medico-Forensic Study* by Richard von Krafft-Ebing [1886] (translation of the twelfth edition, F.A. Davis, Philadelphia, 1903), pp. 395–7, 399.

From *The Intermediate Sex* by Edward Carpenter [1896] (London: George Allen & Unwin Ltd, 1916), pp. 16–18, 19–20, 21–2, 22–3, 26, 27, 29–32, 37–8.

From 'Editorial on the publication of Havelock Ellis's *Sexual Inversion*', *The Lancet*, 19 November 1896, pp. 1344–5.

From *Studies in the Psychology of Sex*, vol. II: *Sexual Inversion* by Havelock Ellis [1897] (third edition, F.A. Davis, Philadelphia, 1915), pp. 91, 107–8, 222–3, 226–9, 302, 304, 322, 327, 329. Copyright © François Lafitte.

From *Sex and Character* by Otto Weininger [1903] (translation of the sixth edition, W. Heinemann, London, 1906), pp. 47, 48–9, 49–50, 51.

From 'Homosexuality' by C. Stanford Read, *The Journal of Mental Science*, vol. 67, January 1921, pp. 8–10.

From 'Studies in Feminine Inversion' by F.W. Stella Browne, *Journal of Sexology and Psychanalysis* [*sic*], 1923, pp. 51–8.

From 'A Case of Homosexual Inversion' by T[homas] A[rthur] Ross, *The Journal of Neurology and Psychopathology*, vol. 7, April 1927, pp. 314–19, 321.

From *Report on the Psychological Treatment of Crime* by W[illiam] Norwood East & W. H. de B. Hubert (HMSO, London, 1939), pp. 85, 86–7, 91, 98–9, 100.

Part III

From *Psychopathia Sexualis: With Especial Reference to the Antipathic Sexual Instinct. A Medico-Forensic Study* by Richard von Krafft-Ebing

[1886] (translation of the twelfth edition, F.A. Davis, Philadelphia, 1903), pp. 289, 294–6, 297, 304, 328, 335–7, 352–3, 354, 401–4, 428–39.

From *Studies in the Psychology of Sex*, vol. II: *Sexual Inversion* by Havelock Ellis [1897] (third edition, F.A. Davis, Philadelphia, 1915). pp. 235–6, 237, 239–44. Copyright © François Lafitte.

From *Transvestites: The Erotic Drive to Cross-Dress* by Magnus Hirschfeld [1910] (translation by Michael A. Lombardi-Nash, Prometheus Books, Amherst, NY, 1991), pp. 219–20, 221, 222–7, 233, 234. Copyright © Prometheus Books, 1991. Reprinted by permission of the publisher.

Part IV

From *Studies in the Psychology of Sex*, vol. III: *Analysis of the Sexual Impulse, Love and Pain, The Sexual Impulse in Women* by Havelock Ellis (F.A. Davis, Philadelphia, 1903), pp. 27–8, 56–9, 69–71, 88, 180–1, 185–9, 196–7, 203. Copyright © François Lafitte.

From *Married Love: A New Contribution to the Solution of Sex Difficulties* by Marie Carmichael Stopes (A.C. Fifield, London, 1918), pp. 19–22, 46–50. Copyright © Victor Gollancz.

From *Men, Women and God* by A. Herbert Gray (Student Christian Movement, London, 1923), pp. xi, xii-xiii, xiv-xv, xvii-xviii.

From *Hypatia or Woman and Knowledge* by Dora Russell (Kegan Paul, Trench, Trubner & Co., London, 1925), pp. 31–5, 36, 37. Copyright © Routledge.

From *Ideal Marriage: Its Physiology and Technique* by Theodore Van de Velde (William Heinemann (Medical Books), London, 1928), pp. 7–8, 9, 144–5, 169–71.

From *The Sex Factor in Marriage: A Book for Those Who Are or Are About to Be Married* by Helena Wright (Williams & Norgate Ltd, London, 1930), pp. 68–77. Copyright © A. & C. Black.

Part V

From *The Problem of Race-Regeneration* by Havelock Ellis (Cassell and Company Ltd, London, 1911), pp. 62–5, 70–1. Copyright © François Lafitte.

From *A Letter to Working Mothers on How to Have Healthy Children and Avoid Weakening Pregnancies* by Marie Carmichael Stopes (Mother's Clinic for Constructive Birth Control, London, 1919), pp. 3–6. Copyright © The Galton Institute.

From *Men, Women and God* by A. Herbert Gray (Student Christian Movement, London, 1923), pp. 149–54.

From *Parenthood: Design or Accident? A Manual of Birth-Control* by Michael Fielding (The Labour Publishing Company, London, 1928), pp. 13–14, 18–23, 35–7, 68–9, 76–7.

From *Comments on Birth Control* by Naomi Mitchison (Faber and Faber, London, 1930), pp. 10–15. Copyright © Faber and Faber Ltd.

From 'The Right to Abortion' by F.W. Stella Browne in *Abortion (3 Essays)* edited by F.W. Stella Browne, A.M. Ludovici and Harry Roberts (George Allen & Unwin, London, 1935), pp. 29–34.

From 'The Case Against Legalized Abortion' by A.M. Ludovici in *Abortion (3 Essays)* edited by F.W. Stella Browne, A.M. Ludovici and Harry Roberts, (George Allen & Unwin, London, 1935), pp. 58–61, 101–4.

Part VI

From *The Sexual Question: A Scientific, Psychological, Hygienic and Sociological Study* by August Forel [1906] (William Heinemann (Medical Books), London, 1908), pp. 510, 511, 512–13.

From *The Scope and Importance to the State of the Science of National Eugenics* by Karl Pearson (Dulau and Co., London, 1909), pp. 9–12.

From *The Family and the Nation: A Study in Natural Inheritance and Social Responsibility* by William Cecil Dampier Whetham and Catherine Durning Whetham (Longmans, Green and Co., London, 1909), pp. 197–201.

From *Woman and Labour* by Olive Schreiner (T. Fisher Unwin, London, 1911), pp. 225–6, 227–30, 231–3.

From *The Problem of Practical Eugenics* by Karl Pearson (Dulau and Co., London, 1912), pp. 36–9.

From *The Task of Social Hygiene* by Havelock Ellis (Constable and Company Ltd, London, 1912), pp. 31, 40–1, 42–3, 44–7. Copyright © François Lafitte.

From *The Eugenic Prospect: National and Racial* by C[aleb] W. Saleeby (T. Fisher Unwin Ltd, London, 1921), pp. 34–8.

From 'Notes of the Quarter [on Nazism]', *The Eugenics Review*, vol. 25, April 1933–January 1934, pp. 76, 77. Copyright © The Galton Institute.

From 'Aims and Objects of the Eugenics Society', *The Eugenics Review*, vol. 26, April 1934–January 1935, pp. 133–5. Copyright © The Galton Institute.

From 'Eutelegenesis' by Herbert Brewer, *The Eugenics Review*, vol. 27, April 1935–January 1936, pp. 121–5, 126. Copyright © The Galton Institute.

From 'Eugenics and Society' by Julian Huxley, *The Eugenics Review*, vol. 28, April 1936–January 1937, pp. 26–29, 30–31. Copyright © The Galton Institute.

Part VII

From *The Sotadic Zone* by Sir Richard Burton [1886] (The Panurge Press, New York, 1930), pp. 17–18, 20, 23.

From *Psychopathia Sexualis: With Especial Reference to the Antipathic Sexual Instinct. A Medico-Forensic Study* by Richard von Krafft-Ebing [1886] (translation of the twelfth edition, F.A. Davis, Philadelphia, 1903), pp. 199–200.

From *The Female Offender* by Cesare Lombroso and Guglielmo Ferrero [1893] (T. Fisher Unwin, London, 1895), pp. 111–13. Copyright © Peter Owen Ltd, London.

From *Studies in the Psychology of Sex*, vol. II: *Sexual Inversion* by Havelock Ellis [1897] (third edition, F.A. Davis, Philadelphia, 1915), pp. 8–9, 13–14, 16–18, 21, 23–5, 26–8, 57–9, 264. Copyright © François Lafitte.

From 'Sexual Inversion Among Primitive Races' by C.G. Seligmann, *Alienist and Neurologist*, vol. 23, 1902, pp. 11–13.

From *Sex and Character* by Otto Weininger [1903] (translation of the sixth edition, W. Heinemann, London, 1906), pp. 302–4, 306, 308–12, 316–17, 319–20, 329–30, 345.

From *The Sexual Question: A Scientific, Psychological, Hygienic and Sociological Study* by August Forel [1906] (William Heinemann (Medical Books), London, 1908), pp. 189, 507–9.

From 'A Perversion Not Commonly Noted' by Margaret Otis, *Journal of Abnormal Psychology*, vol. 8, June–July 1913, pp. 113–16.

From *Men and Women: The World Journey of a Sexologist* by Magnus Hirschfeld [1933] (translation by O.P. Green, G.P. Putnam's Sons, New York, 1935), pp. xviii–xix.

From *Racism* by Magnus Hirschfeld (translated and edited by Eden and Cedar Paul, Victor Gollancz Ltd, London, 1938), pp. 150–4, 160–2, 169–72. Copyright © Victor Gollancz.

Part VIII
From *Psychopathia Sexualis: With Especial Reference to the Antipathic Sexual Instinct. A Medico-Forensic Study* by Richard von Krafft-Ebing [1886] (translation of the twelfth edition, F.A. Davis, Philadelphia, 1903), pp. 216–24, 561–70.

From *The Female Offender* by Cesare Lombroso and Guglielmo Ferrero [1893] (T. Fisher Unwin, London, 1895), pp. 115, 116–18, 121–2. Copyright © Peter Owen Ltd, London.

From *Studies in the Psychology of Sex*, vol. I: *The Evolution of Modesty, The Phenomena of Sexual Periodicity, Auto-Erotism* by Havelock Ellis [1899] (F.A. Davis, Philadelphia, 1900), pp. 111–15. Copyright © François Lafitte.

From *The Sexual Life of Our Time in Its Relations to Modern Civilization* by Iwan Bloch [1907] (translation of the sixth edition, W. Heinemann, London, 1908), pp. 652–3.

From *Studies in the Psychology of Sex*, vol. VI: *Sex in Relation to Society* by Havelock Ellis (F.A. Davis, Philadelphia, 1910), pp. 266–73, 277–80. Copyright © François Lafitte.

From *Sadism and Masochism: The Psychology of Hatred and Cruelty* by Wilhelm Stekel, vol. 1 [1924] (translated by Louise Brink, John Lane, The Bodley Head, London, 1935), pp. 57–60. Copyright © Random House UK Limited.

From *Studies in the Psychology of Sex*, vol. VII: *Eonism and Other Supplementary Studies* by Havelock Ellis (F.A. Davis, Philadelphia, 1928), pp. 26–30. Copyright © François Lafitte.

From *Sexual Anomalies and Perversions: Physical and Psychological Development and Treatment* by Magnus Hirschfeld (Torch Publishing Company Ltd, London, 1936), pp. 601–3.

Every effort has been made to trace the copyright holders, but if any have been inadvertently overlooked, the publisher will be pleased to make the necessary arrangements at the first opportunity.

General Introduction

Lucy Bland and Laura Doan

Sexology: the word itself confounds many readers, its meaning obscure or its objectives sinister. Simply put, sexology is the study and classification of sexual behaviours, identities and relations. In the last third of the nineteenth century, the discipline emerged in Western modernity as part of a wider concern with the classification of bodies and populations, alongside other new sciences, such as anthropology, sociology, psychology and criminology. Frequently, however, misunderstanding, scepticism, and even hostility towards sexology's taxonomies and categories, and towards the way in which sexological theories have been applied (or might have been applied), cloud our understanding of what early sexologists actually said or did. We would attribute such apprehensions and preconceptions in part to a heavy reliance by readers on secondary sources rather than on an immersion in primary material. This is hardly surprising since a majority of the documents reprinted in this volume have been 'censored' in the sense that they have been difficult to obtain, subject to restricted circulation, or available only in medical archives. As Roy Porter and Lesley Hall explain, for years readers with a legitimate interest in the subject of sex had to seek out 'serious and reputable books ... from insalubrious sources'.[1] The central texts of sexual science were reputedly stored among the 'pornographic' materials in the British Library's infamous 'little cupboard'.[2] *Sexology Uncensored: The Documents of Sexual Science* contains for the first time in a single volume extracts drawn from a rich variety of sources covering the period 1880 to World War II. We aim to make readily accessible the ideas of individual sexologists in their own words, so that readers are better informed about this pioneering body of knowledge and more adequately equipped to construct an informed critique of its achievements and shortcomings.

Although this radical, new discipline developed throughout Britain, Europe and North America from the 1870s, the actual term 'sexology' was not coined until the early twentieth century, and it was not recognized as a legitimate branch of science until the interwar years. Sexology, it is commonly assumed, displaced the old view of sexual practices as sinful – and hence under the jurisdiction of the church – and imposed a new view of sexual perversions as disease and/or manifestations of degeneracy, and thus under the jurisdiction of medicine. The founders of modern sexology – men such as Richard von Krafft-Ebing, Havelock Ellis and Magnus Hirschfeld – sought to produce an exhaustive classification of the multiple aspects of sexuality by tracing its etiology, scrutinizing its fantasies, its fetishes and the numerous pleasures of the body, and constructing new pathologized individual identities, such as the homosexual, pervert, sadist, masochist, and frigid woman. While sexology sought to label bodies and desires, it was also concerned with populations as an object of study and set about delineating the criteria for human and 'racial' betterment through the regulation of procreation and biological heredity. Sexology's novelty was not simply its subject matter but its assumption that sexuality had an importance for all aspects of the lives of individuals and society as a whole. Sexologists generally combined biological, anthropological and historical data with the 'case study' in which individual experience itself, as narrated to the investigator, was taken as evidence of sexual phenomena. Indeed, sexological labels often emerged as a unique and active collaboration between the sexologist and the patient or informant, as in the case of the homosexual, rather than as an unwelcome imposition on a passive community. In other instances, sexologists compiled ethnographic information from all parts of the globe, uncritically incorporating into their studies the observations of anthropologists and social observers, as seen in the work, for example, of Iwan Bloch, August Forel, Theodore Van de Velde and Cesare Lombroso.

Critical assessment of the sexological project often focuses on the question of whether sexology constituted a boldly innovative and emancipatory investigation into human sexuality or whether it was merely another tool of social repression. Any consideration of sexology's impact, however, must first take into account exactly who had access to sexological literature and when. Since sexual knowledge was perceived as dangerous, some early sexologists were pressured to ensure that their 'forbidden' work did not circulate beyond a small group of experts in the fields of medicine and law, as typified by Krafft-Ebing, who wrote *Psychopathia Sexualis* as a handbook to assist courts in understanding sexual crime. Yet such was the demand for information as basic as human physiology and the 'facts of life' that attempts to withhold this literature from a larger readership frequently failed. The feminist readers of the pre-World War I journal *The Freewoman*, for instance, exchanged texts and extracts among themselves, and held discussion groups on sexological topics. Just after the war Marie Stopes's best-seller *Married Love* popularized many of Ellis's ideas on heterosexuality, and later others, such as Dora Russell, Van de Velde and Helena Wright, extended sexual knowledge still further. As the readership grew, so did sexology's deployment – specialists (physicians and lawyers) and non-specialists (journalists and politicians) alike drew on its theories and findings for purposes unanticipated by sexologists themselves.

Not only did sexology seem to lend scientific or medical 'legitimacy' to a variety of causes, but its claims could be taken up and applied by individuals or groups with very different agendas, ranging from feminists, socialists and liberals to the extreme political and moral right. In the case of eugenics, for example, some socialists believed that it could form an important component in their programme of social reform, yet many on the political right likewise looked to eugenics as a means to a future congruent with their ideology. The sexological construction of female sexual inversion too was deployed strategically for both the enemies and champions of lesbians. In 1918 right-wing Member of Parliament Noel Pemberton-Billing selectively used the work of Krafft-Ebing to proclaim sexual deviance in his accusation of lesbianism against the well-known dancer Maud Allan. A decade later novelist Radclyffe Hall found both Krafft-Ebing's and Ellis's work on sexual inversion useful in her crusade for the social acceptance of lesbianism. Sexology could thus be simultaneously empowering and disempowering, for it offered not a homogeneous ideology but the potential to be all things to all people.

The historiography of sexology typically casts sexual science as either progressive or repressive. In the 1960s, sexology was widely regarded as liberatory: practitioners were thought to have broken the 'conspiracy of silence' which had supposedly surrounded the subject of sex throughout the Victorian era, and to have pointed the way to an enlightened sexuality. However, since the 1970s, with the writings of Michel Foucault, especially his *History of Sexuality*, and the political astuteness of feminists and lesbian and gay theorists, this view of sexology has been fundamentally questioned. Not only have the Victorians been revealed as far from silent in matters of sex, but the forward march of sexual modernism has been exposed as a myth (the 1960s' so-called sexual revolution did not put an end to women's sexual subordination, and the 1967 Sexual Offences Act, which decriminalized male homosexuality, unfortunately did not eliminate homophobia). The gay rights movement of the late 1960s and 1970s sparked a renewed interest in early sexology, as gay historians sought to discover the origins of the 'modern homosexual'. Work by scholars such as Jeffrey Weeks has been crucial to this endeavour. Weeks presents an insightful overview of sexology's development and offers cogent synopses of the key ideas of major sexologists, positioning each within a specific socio-historical context.[3] While largely positive about sexology's accomplishments, Weeks does not neglect the contradictory nature of much sexology, such as the tension within Ellis's work between a radical and a conservative orientation.

The feminist critique of sexology has been spearheaded by Sheila Jeffreys, who argues: 'It is clear from the writings of the sexologists that they were far from enthusiastic about feminism, and particularly its lesbian manifestations. An attack upon passionate emotional involvement between women seemed to undermine the link between them and dilute their potential strength.'[4] For Jeffreys, sexology's anti-feminism and anti-lesbianism represented a substantial threat to all women. Lillian Faderman, in a ground-breaking study of lesbian history, is also highly suspicious of what she terms the sexologists' conscious or unconscious 'hidden agenda', which aimed to 'discourage feminism and maintain traditional sex roles by connecting the women's movement to sexual abnormality'.[5] This sharp critique is echoed by Margaret Jackson, who also reminds readers of the important contributions made by women in this field. She charges that 'the sexological model of sexuality' was fundamentally 'anti-feminist': 'Ellis, Bloch and Forel all expressed their theoretical support for the emancipation of women but were in fact highly selective about the forms of feminism they would support, and often attacked the Women's Movement for turning women away from what they considered to be the "laws of their nature", which were heterosexuality, marriage and motherhood.'[6]

These feminist historians correctly challenge the way in which some sexologists reinforced 'hetero-patriarchy' as normative at the expense of women, rendering what was culturally inscribed as 'natural'. This critique, however, is also problematic in that it glosses over significant differences between sexologists and ignores the shifts in individual sexologists' theoretical perspectives. Such readings rely on a misleading construction of sexology by assuming that 'the sexologists' formed a united front, and that diverse and contradictory theoretical positions were monolithic, coherent and unified. Further, although sexology may not have engendered universal sexual 'emancipation', we would suggest that it is equally wrong to conclude, as have some historians, that sexology has been simply harmful in its effects. It is clearly the case that sexology has contributed to the control of certain sexual behaviours and sexual subjectivities, but it has also proved positive for many in its offer of identities and a language of expression.

Emerging academic disciplines (gender studies, queer theory, and gay and lesbian studies) are poised to launch a sophisticated and rigorous reexamination of the medical models and theories of early sexology. Several of the essays in *Science and Homosexualities*, edited by Vernon Rosario, map out new ways of reading and assessing the achievements of such sexologists as Karl Heinrich Ulrichs, Krafft-Ebing and Hirschfeld. Harry Oosterhuis, for example, offers a careful analysis of Krafft-Ebing's career that traces crucial shifts in his position: 'Krafft-Ebing's views were far from static or coherent, and in several ways his scientific approach to sexuality was ambivalent.'[7] We hope that the companion volume to *Sexology Uncensored*, entitled *Sexology in Culture: Labelling Bodies and Desires*, will make an important contribution to ongoing debates concerning the role of sexology in relation to homosexuality and feminism, as well as in new areas of historical investigation that have thus far received little scholarly attention, such as transsexuality and bisexuality.

Although no sourcebook can be exhaustive or comprehensive, some readers will inevitably note the absence of particular sexologists. All of our editors have attempted throughout the selection process to adhere to two guiding principles: first, that the work in question was influential at the time of its publication, and second, that the selection is difficult to obtain today. Thus Sigmund Freud's work, although enormously influential, has been excluded, not because he is not a sexologist in certain respects, but because his writings are widely available. To say that these texts were 'influential at the time of their publication' begs the question, influential for whom? Some extracts clearly had a wide popular readership and a huge direct impact, the work of Stopes being an obvious example. Other extracts, although not necessarily available to the wider public, nevertheless contributed to general 'knowledge' via the writings of popularizers or the declarations and actions of policy-makers. Our choices therefore have been strategic, and we have even included certain writers who might not have perceived themselves as sexologists at all, such as Naomi Mitchison, Dora Russell and Herbert Gray. The concerns of such writers, however, dovetailed with those of mainstream sexologists, be they reproductive control or ideal marriage.

Each part of this volume opens with a short introduction. We have tried to avoid being monolithic ourselves in our interpretation of sexology in that our introductory commentaries are not all of one mind. On the one hand, Lucy Bland, in her brief comments on Ellis and heterosexuality in part I, suggests that Ellis's ideas on the male's sexual aggressiveness and the female's 'primordial urge' to be conquered reinforced the supposed 'naturalness' of heterosexuality, as well as a rather narrow and oppressive view of heterosexual relations. Lesley Hall, on the other hand, claims in part IV that early sexologists, including Ellis, destabilized assumptions about heterosexuality's 'naturalness' by emphasizing that 'normal' sexual intercourse was not natural but problematic, in particular for the achievement of female sexual pleasure. The contradiction between Bland's and Hall's positions is more apparent than real, for it illustrates not only the potentially different readings of sexology, but also the co-existence within any sexological text of contrasting claims and implications.

Within each part the excerpts are organized chronologically so that the reader will get a sense of how each topic developed and shifted over time. This volume opens with 'Gender and Sexual Difference' because sexologists, in response to the contemporary topicality of feminism, frequently took the question of what constituted sex difference as their starting point. The next three parts ('Homosexualities', 'Transsexuality and Bisexuality', and 'Heterosexuality, Marriage and Sex Manuals') trace the etiology and categorization of identities, sexual orientations and practices.

As with any so-called objective scientific method, sexology was rooted in the cultural beliefs and values of its practitioners, primarily white, middle-class men, who often conceptualized their subjects in terms of the constructed binaries which inscribed the dominant power relations (female against male, deviant or pervert against norm, homosexual against heterosexual, primitive against civilized). The parts on 'Reproductive Control', 'Eugenics' and 'Race' deal, directly or indirectly, with procreative behaviour and the implications for individuals and society as a whole. The part entitled 'Race' is perhaps the anomaly of the sourcebook, for clearly 'race' as such cannot be seen as a branch of sexology. We include it to indicate how sexologists' pronouncements on sex were crucially interconnected with pronouncements on 'race' in ways that have too often been overlooked. The final part on 'Other Sexual Proclivities' contains material not easily subsumed under a single heading, in order to demonstrate the far-reaching gaze of the sexologist.

At the outset we posited that the inaccessibility of sexological literature has played a part in generating apprehension among readers who, unable to obtain primary source material, have been forced to rely on sexology's critical interpreters. Of course we do not naively imagine that plunging first hand into these excerpts will magically banish scepticism or dissipate hostility. After all, sexology's systematic method of fixing labels and categories is anathema to postmodern sensibilities. What we *do* hope is that this preliminary overview of early sexological literature will encourage readers to take sexology seriously by seeking out more of the original works. Our language today is replete with sexological neologisms (transvestism, sadism, bestiality, and so on); for better or worse, without them our sexual vocabulary would be profoundly limited. If we are to understand modern sexual discourse in all its historical complexity, an examination of these fascinating texts is the crucial place to start.

Notes

1 Roy Porter and Lesley Hall, *The Facts of Life: The Creation of Sexual Knowledge in Britain, 1650–1950* (Yale University Press, New Haven, 1995), p. 259.
2 Edward Carpenter received a letter in 1912 from a man who complained that the British Museum had 'all the standard works on the subject [of sex] . . . in a receptacle called the Private Case', as well as items 'which may be described as filth'. Ibid.
3 See especially Jeffrey Weeks, *Coming Out: Homosexual Politics in Britain from the Nineteenth Century to the Present* (Quartet Books, London, 1977) and *Sex, Politics and Society: The Regulation of Sexuality since 1800* (Longman, London, 1981).
4 Sheila Jeffreys, *The Spinster and Her Enemies: Feminism and Sexuality 1880–1930* (Pandora, London, 1985), p. 112.
5 Lillian Faderman, *Odd Girls and Twilight Lovers: A History of Lesbian Life in Twentieth-Century America* (Columbia University Press, New York, 1991), p. 48.
6 Margaret Jackson, *The Real Facts of Life: Feminism and the Politics of Sexuality c. 1850–1940* (Taylor & Francis, London, 1994), p. 121.
7 Harry Oosterhuis, 'Richard von Krafft-Ebing's "Step-Children of Nature"': Psychiatry and the Making of Homosexual Identity', in Vernon A. Rosario (ed.), *Science and Homosexualities* (Routledge, London, 1997), p. 72.

Part I

Gender and Sexual Difference

Introduction

Lucy Bland

The rise of sexology in Europe in the mid to late nineteenth century co-existed with the rise of the women's movement. The challenge to the existing roles assigned to women instigated what became known as the 'Woman Question': the question of what constituted women's nature and destiny. Sexology's pronouncements contributed to this debate. Evolutionary theory, in broad circulation at this time, fed into both the 'Woman Question' more widely, and sexology more specifically. Charles Darwin held that sex differences were rooted in 'sexual selection', a concept discussed in his *The Descent of Man and Selection in Relation to Sex* of 1871. Competition, he asserted, was not just for food and space (the process of natural selection) but also for mates (sexual selection), and certain characteristics specific to one sex, such as peacocks' tail-feathers, had developed accordingly, to attract the opposite sex. To Darwin, the combination of natural and sexual selection had resulted in 'man attaining to a higher eminence, in whatever he takes up, than can woman – whether requiring deep thought, reason or imagination, or merely the use of senses and hands'.

Scottish biologists Patrick Geddes (1854–1932) and J. Arthur Thomson (1858–1935), although holding to many of Darwin's assumptions concerning sex differences, took issue with his concept of sexual selection. In contrast to Darwin, who saw most sex differences as functional and dynamic – existing for a specific purpose (to aid sexual selection) and changing over time – Geddes and Thomson presented a view of sex differences which was static, essentialist and ahistoric. In their book *The Evolution of Sex* of 1889 they pronounced that all such differences were simply reflections of the different metabolisms of the primary sex cells, the egg and the sperm. The sperm, they argued, was small and active and dissipated energy, and thus 'katabolic', while the egg was large, passive and energy-conserving, and thus 'anabolic'. Therefore, they claimed, males everywhere, including human males, were more active and variable, while females were more passive and conservative.

The sexologist Havelock Ellis (1859–1939) selected *The Evolution of Sex* as the first volume of his 'Contemporary Science Series', rendering the book cheap and easy to obtain. The volume became a best-seller, hugely popular among scientists and social commentators of the day. Geddes and Thomson had deduced a dichotomy between the sexes which neatly reflected conventional assumptions concerning male rationality, individuality and assertiveness, female intuition, altruism and passivity. Although the two biologists professed support for women's rights, and saw the two sexes as 'complementary and mutually dependent', the logic of their argument was deeply conservative, for sex differences were engrained in our evolutionary history: 'What was decided among the prehistoric Protozoa cannot be annulled by Act of Parliament.' *The Evolution of Sex* reinforced the limiting constructions of femininity against which feminists were rebelling.

The ideas of Geddes and Thomson influenced Ellis's own work, both his writings on sex and on criminology. In late nineteenth-century Europe, criminology and sexology were emerging side by side, both concerned with the classification of pathology and abnormality. Ellis wrote *The Criminal* in 1890 in order to introduce English readers to some of the ideas of the Italian criminal anthropologist Cesare Lombroso (1835–1909). In reflecting on the possible causes of low criminality among women, Ellis combined evolutionary and biologistic explanations (Geddes and Thomson's thesis as to the different 'energies' of the sexes, and Darwin's notion of sexual selection) with a more sociological perspective, namely women's 'domestic seclusion' and thus lesser criminal opportunity. Lombroso's *The Female Offender*, written in 1893 with his son-in-law Guglielmo Ferrero (1871–1943), and translated into English two years later, likewise drew both on Geddes and Thomson's idea of 'the immobility of the ovule compared with the zoosperm' and on Darwin's 'sexual selection'. But unlike Ellis, Lombroso and Ferrero presented no sociological element. Although acknowledging the rarity of female criminality, they announced that where it occurred it was generally of a greater severity than that of males, due to women's childlike, defective moral sense (another Darwinian assertion) and lesser sensitivity to pain. Such ideas fed into the 'Woman Question' as further ammunition against feminist demands.

Havelock Ellis may have been interested in criminology, but his central project was the study of sex; this included assertions about sex difference.

In Ellis's widely read and reprinted *Man and Woman* of 1894, Geddes and Thomson's central thesis resurfaced, along with many of the conventional assumptions about gender difference, including the 'naturalness' of 'separate spheres' and women's closeness to nature. In *Sex, Politics and Society* Jeffrey Weeks correctly points out that in Ellis's concern to describe the roots of sexual behaviour and document its enormous variations, he adopted two contradictory approaches: biological determinism and cultural relativism.[1] This in part explains the uneasy co-existence of conservatism and radicalism in Ellis's conclusions. In his *Man and Woman*, it was the more conservative side of Ellis which was to the fore. Indeed, he assumed that there existed a natural harmony between the sexes which amounted to 'cosmic conservatism', with each sex following 'the laws of its own nature' – 'laws' most favourable to reproduction.

To Ellis, one of these 'natural laws' was female modesty, which he regarded as the main psychic secondary sexual characteristic. He elaborated on this theme in *The Evolution of Modesty, The Phenomena of Sexual Periodicity, Auto-Erotism*, published in 1899. He argued that sexual modesty in the female was an inevitable by-product of the male's sexual aggressiveness and of her 'sexual periodicity', and was central to courtship, reflecting the 'primordial urge' of the female to be conquered. Such assumptions informed sex and marriage manuals throughout the interwar period, reinforcing both the supposed 'naturalness' of heterosexuality, as well as a rather narrow and oppressive view of heterosexual relations. What was radical about Ellis, however, was his stress on the erotic rights of women.

Another work which would become influential was *Sex and Character*, written by Otto Weininger (1880–1903) in 1903. Weininger was an Austrian Jew who committed suicide four months after the publication of his book. He saw his book as the answer to the 'Woman Question', arguing that woman was wholly sexual and content simply with sexual matters, including reproduction: 'to put it bluntly, man possesses sexual organs, but [woman's] sexual organs possess her'. Man could transcend sexuality, but woman was incapable of reason and self-knowledge. Although the book was explicitly misogynist and anti-semitic, it was taken seriously by a number of feminists, sexologists and sexual radicals, including Edward Carpenter, not least because Weininger was aware of femininity's destructiveness to women, and he attempted to analyse the roots of misogyny.

Ellis, August Forel and Iwan Bloch were cited at the 1929 Sex Reform Congress in London as the founding fathers of sexology. Both Forel (1848–1931), a Swiss psychiatrist, and Bloch (1872–1922), a German doctor, agreed with Ellis that women were as sexual as men, yet more passive. Bloch, however, suggested that women's sexual sensibility was possibly greater than man's. Although he listed a number of physical differences between the sexes, he was at pains to suggest that these differences, such as women's more childlike skulls, did not constitute inferiority.

One of the most explicitly feminist of male sex theorists of this period was a Polish naturalized Frenchman, Jean Finot (1856–1922). As a pacifist and anti-racist (drawing parallels between sexual and racial discrimination), Finot condemned science for providing backing to popular prejudices. He particularly mocked the claims of Geddes and Thomson, whose ideas, twenty-four years after the first publication of *The Evolution of Sex*, were still in circulation. Finot was an environmentalist who claimed that if one was to enlarge women's social, educational and occupational environments, women would change accordingly. But biological reductionism still dominated the 'Woman Question' debate, and the discovery of sex hormones in the early years of the twentieth century was taken by many as further 'scientific' proof of innate sex differences. Throughout the interwar years, assumptions about gender shifted little; even today, in reading these early sexologists, we hear echoes of many still current ideologies concerning men and women.

Note

1 Jeffrey Weeks, *Sex, Politics and Society: The Regulation of Sexuality since 1800* (Longman, London, 1981).

The Evolution of Sex (1889)
Patrick Geddes and J. Arthur Thomson

Intellectual and Emotional Differences between the Sexes. – We have seen that a deep difference in constitution expresses itself in the distinctions between male and female, whether these be physical or mental. The differences may be exaggerated or lessened, but to obliterate them it would be necessary to have all the evolution over again on a new basis. What was decided among the prehistoric Protozoa cannot be annulled by Act of Parliament. In this mere outline we cannot of course do more than indicate the relation of the biological differences between the sexes to the resulting psychological and social differentiations; for more than this neither space nor powers suffice. We must insist upon the biological considerations underlying the relation of the sexes, which have been too much discussed by contemporary writers of all schools, as if the known facts of sex did not exist at all, or almost if these were a mere matter of muscular strength or weight of brain. [...]

All disputants have tolerably agreed in neglecting the historic, and still more the biological factors; while, so far as the past evolution of the present state of things is taken into account at all, the position of women is regarded as having simply been that in which the stronger muscle and brain of man was able to place her. The past of the race is thus depicted in the most sinister colours, and the whole view is supposed to be confirmed by appeal to the practice of the most degenerate races, and this again as described with the scanty sympathy or impartiality of the average white traveller, missionary, or settler.

As we have already said, we cannot attempt a full discussion of the question, but our book would be left, as biological books for the most part are, without point, and its essential thesis useless, if we did not, in conclusion, seek to call attention to the fundamental facts of organic difference, say rather divergent lines of differentiation, underlying the whole problem of the sexes. We shall only suggest, as the best argument for the adoption of our standpoint, the way in which it becomes possible relatively to affiliate the most varied standpoints. We shall not so readily abuse the poor savage, who lies idle in the sun for days after his return from the hunting, while his heavy-laden wife toils and moils without complaint or cease; but bearing in view the extreme bursts of exertion which such a life of incessant struggle with nature and his fellows for food and for life involves upon him, and the consequent necessity of correspondingly utilising every opportunity of repose to recruit and eke out the short and precarious life so indispensable to wife and weans, we shall see that this crude domestic economy is the best, the most moral, and the most kindly attainable under the circumstances. Again, the traveller from town, who thinks the agricultural labourer a greedy brute for eating the morsel of bacon and leaving his wife and children only the bread, does not see that by acting otherwise the total ration would soon be still further lowered, by diminished earnings, loss of employment, or loss of health.

The actual relations of fisherman and fishwife, of the smallest farmer and his wife, seem to us to give a truer as well as a healthier picture of antique industrial society, than those we find in current literature; and if we admit that such life is deficient in refinement (although, on all deeper grounds, from religion to ballad poetry, we might even largely dispute this), it has still much to teach in respect of simplicity and health.

The old view of the subjection of women was not, in fact, so much of tyranny as it seemed, but roughly tended to express the average division of labour; of course hardships were frequent, but these have been exaggerated. The absolute ratification of this by law and religion was merely of a piece with the whole order of belief and practice, in which men crushed themselves still more than their mates. Being absolute, however, such theories had to be overthrown, and the application of the idea of equality, which had done such good service in demolishing the established castes, was a natural and serviceable one. We have above traced the development of this, however, and it is now full time to re-emphasise, this time of course with all scientific relativity instead of a dogmatic authority, the biological factors of the case, and to suggest their possible service in destroying the economic fallacies at present so prevalent, and still more towards reconstituting that complex and sympathetic co-operation between the differentiated sexes in and around which all progress past or future must depend. Instead of men and women merely labouring to produce things as the past economic theories insisted, or competing over the distribution of them, as we at present think so important, a further swing of economic theory will lead us round upon a higher spiral to the direct organic facts. So it is not for the sake of production or distribution, of self-interest or mechanism, or any other idol of the economists, that the male organism organises the climax of his life's struggle and labour, but for his mate; as she, and then he, also for their little ones. Production is for consumption; the species is its own highest, its sole essential product. The social order will clear itself, as it comes more in touch with biology.

It is equally certain that the two sexes are complementary and mutually dependent. Virtually asexual organisms, like Bacteria, occupy no high place in Nature's roll of honour; virtually unisexual organisms, like many rotifers, are great rarities. Parthenogenesis may be an organic ideal, but it is one which has failed to realise itself. Males and females, like the sex-elements, are mutually dependent, and that not merely because they are males and females, but also in functions not directly associated with those of sex. But to dispute whether males or females are the higher, is like disputing the relative superiority of animals or plants. Each is higher in its own way, and the two are complementary.

While there are broad general distinctions between the intellectual, and especially the emotional, characteristics of males and females among the higher animals, these not unfrequently tend to become mingled. There is, however, no evidence that they might be gradually obliterated. The sea-horse, the obstetric frog, many male birds, are certainly maternal; while a few females fight for the males, and are stronger, or more passionate than their mates. But these are rarities. It is generally true that the males are more active, energetic, eager, passionate, and variable; the females more passive, conservative, sluggish, and stable. The males, or, to return to the terms of our thesis, the more katabolic organisms, are more variable, and therefore [...] are very frequently the leaders in evolutionary progress, while the more anabolic females tend rather to preserve the constancy and integrity of the species; thus, in a word, the general heredity is perpetuated primarily by the female, while variations are introduced by the male. Yet along paths where the reproductive sacrifice was one of the determinants of progress, we shall see later that they must have the credit of leading the way. The more active males, with a consequently wider range of experience, may have bigger brains and more intelligence; but the females, especially as mothers, have indubitably a larger and more habitual share of the altruistic emotions. The males being usually stronger, have greater independence and courage; the females excel in constancy of affection and in sympathy. The spasmodic bursts of activity characteristic of males contrast with the continuous patience of the females, which we take to be an expression of constitutional contrast, and by no means, as some would have us believe, a mere product of masculine bullying. The stronger lust and passion of males is likewise the obverse of predominant katabolism.

That men should have greater cerebral variability and therefore more originality, while women have greater stability and therefore more 'common sense', are facts both consistent with the general theory of sex and verifiable in common experience. The woman, conserving the effects of past variations, has what may be called the greater integrating intelligence; the man, introducing new variations, is stronger in differentiation. The feminine passivity is expressed in greater patience, more openmindedness, greater appreciation of subtle details, and consequently what we call more rapid intuition. The masculine activity lends a greater power of maximum effort, of scientific insight, or cerebral experiment with impressions, and is associated with an unobservant or impatient disregard of minute details, but with a stronger grasp of generalities. Man thinks more, women [*sic*] feels more. He discovers more, but remembers less; she is more receptive, and less forgetful.

The Criminal (1890)
Havelock Ellis

It is worth while to enumerate briefly the probable causes of the sexual variation in criminality. There are perhaps five special causes acting on women: (1) physical weakness, (2) sexual selection, (3) domestic seclusion, (4) prostitution, (5) maternity.

There are firstly the physical and psychical traditions of the race embodied in the organisation of men and women. The extreme but rather spasmodic energy of men favours outbursts of violence, while the activities of women are at a lower but more even level, and their avocations have tended to develop the conservative rather than the destructive instincts. Apart from this, even if women were trained in violence, the superior strength of men would still make crimes of violence in women very hazardous and dangerous. Under existing circumstances, when a woman wants a crime committed, she can usually find a man to do it for her.

I have already frequently had occasion to note the approximation of criminal women in physical character to ordinary men. This has always been more or less carefully recorded, both in popular proverbs and in the records of criminal trials. Thus Sarah Chesham, a notorious wholesale poisoner, who killed several children, including her own, as well as her husband, was described as 'a woman of masculine proportions'; and a girl called Bouhours, who was executed at Paris at the age of twenty-two, for murdering and robbing several men who had been her lovers, is described as of agreeable appearance, and of sweet and feminine manners, but of remarkable muscular strength; she dressed as a man; her chief pleasure was to wrestle with men, and her favourite weapon was the hammer.

Marro has recently suggested that sexual selection has exerted a marked influence in diminishing the criminality of women. Masculine, unsexed, ugly, abnormal women – the women, that is, most strongly marked with the signs of degeneration, and therefore the tendency to criminality – would be to a large extent passed by in the choice of a mate, and would tend to be eliminated. It seems likely that this selection may have, at all events to some extent, existed, and exerted influence; it is, however, not universally accepted.

The domestic seclusion of women is an undoubted factor in the determination of the amount of women's criminality. In the Baltic provinces of Russia, where the women share the occupations of the men, the level of feminine criminality is very high. In Spain, the most backward of the large countries of Europe, where the education of women is at a very low level, and the women lead a very domesticated life, the level of feminine criminality is extremely low; the same is true, to a less extent, of Italy. In England, on the other hand, which has taken the lead in enlarging the sphere of women's work, the level of feminine criminality has for half a century been rising. Reference may perhaps also here be made to the fact that there is much more criminality among Irishwomen in England than among Irishwomen at home who lead a more domestic life. It is a very significant fact that Marro found among his women criminals, in marked contrast to the men, a very large proportion (35 out of 41) who possessed some more or less honourable occupation; a large proportion of the women who were possessed of some property. It may not be out of place to observe that the growing criminality of women is but the inevitable accident of a beneficial transition. Criminality, we must remember, is a natural element of life, regulated by natural laws, and as women come to touch life at more various points and to feel more of its stress, they will naturally develop the same tendency to criminality as exists among men, just as they are developing the same diseases, such as general paralysis. Our efforts must be directed, not to the vain attempt to repress the energies of women, but to the larger task of improving the conditions of life, and so diminishing the tendency to criminality among both sexes alike.

Prostitution exerts an undoubted influence in diminishing the criminality of women, in spite of the fact that the prostitute generally lives on the borderland of crime. If, however, it were not for prostitution there would be no alternative but crime for the large numbers of women who are always falling out of the social ranks. As it is, in those families in which the brothers become criminals, the sisters with considerable regularity join the less outcast class of prostitutes; sometimes in league with their criminal brothers, but yet possessing a more recognised means of livelihood. [. . .]

The strongest barrier of all against criminality in women is maternity. The proportion of criminals among young women with children is very small. Among men criminals the celibates are in a very large majority, but among women maternity acts as a still greater deterrent. Not only are young married women comparatively free from crime, but among married women, as Bertillon pointed out, those with children are distinctly less criminal than those without children. Of Marro's 41 criminal women, although all but one (who was undeveloped and ugly) confessed to having had sexual relationships, 12 had never been married, 10 were widows, 14 were married, but of these 7 (50 per cent.) were separated from their husbands. There is some significance, doubtless, also in the fact that while in men the maximum of criminality falls at about the age of 25, in women this is not so. That is the age of maximum child-bearing; the age of maximum criminality in women is delayed until nearly the age of 35. In the 130 women condemned for premeditated murder, and studied by Salsotto, the average age was 34. Marro found that for nearly every class of criminals the average age of the women was much higher than that of the men. It is clear that the woman without children is heavily handicapped in the race of life; the stress that is upon her is written largely in these facts concerning criminality. One might suspect this beforehand. Crime is simply a word to signify the extreme anti-social instincts of human beings; the life led most closely in harmony with the social ends of existence must be the most free from crime.

It may be said – to sum up our brief discussion of this large question of women's criminality – that certain great barriers, partly artificial, partly natural, have everywhere served to protect women from crime. It is not possible absolutely to prove this conclusion, because women cannot be put strictly under the same conditions as men; a woman who lived under the same conditions as men, it need scarcely be said, would no longer be a woman.

The Female Offender (1893)
Cesare Lombroso and Guglielmo Ferrero

2. *Social and atavistic reasons for the rarity of the type.* – The remarkable rarity of anomalies (already revealed by their crania) is not a new phenomenon in the female, nor is it in contradiction to the undoubted fact that atavistically she is nearer to her origin than the male, and ought consequently to abound more in anomalies. [. . .]

Compilers of public statutes have also noted the conservative tendency of women in all questions of social order; a conservatism of which the primary cause is to be sought in the immobility of the ovule compared with the zoosperm.

To this add that the female, on whom falls the larger share of the duty of bringing up the family, necessarily leads a more sedentary life, and is less exposed than the male to the varying conditions of time and space in her environment. More especially is this the case among the greater number of vertebrates, and still more of savages, where the struggle for life, both for parents and progeny, devolves primarily upon the male, and is the incessant cause of variations and peculiar adaptations in functions and organs.

Now, once we admit that the primitive type of a species is more clearly represented in the female, we must proceed to argue thence that the typical forms of our race, being better organised and fixed in the woman through the action of time and long heredity, joined to fewer ancestral variations, are less subject to transformation and deformation by the influences which determine special and retrogressive variations in the male.

Another very potent factor has been sexual selection. Man not only refused to *marry* a deformed female, but ate her, while, on the other hand, preserving for his enjoyment the handsome woman who gratified his peculiar instincts. In those days he was the stronger, and choice rested with him. [. . .]

Yet another reason for the comparative rarity of the criminal type in women is that congenitally they are less inclined to crime than men. Atavism must be held to account for this fact, savage females, and still more, civilised females, being by nature less ferocious than males. It is the *occasional* offender whom we meet with most frequently among women; and as occasional criminals have no special physiognomy, they can offer no examples of the type. And woman's inability in this respect is all the greater that even when a *born* offender she is, in the majority of cases, an adulteress, a calumniator, a swindler, or a mere accomplice – offences, every one of them, which require an attractive appearance, and prohibit the development of repulsive facial characteristics. [. . .]

[W]e may assert that if female born criminals are fewer in number than the males, they are often much more ferocious.

What is the explanation? We have seen that the normal woman is naturally less sensitive to pain than a man, and compassion is the offspring of sensitiveness. If the one be wanting, so will the other be.

We also saw that women have many traits in common with children; that their moral sense is deficient; that they are revengeful, jealous, inclined to vengeances of a refined cruelty.

In ordinary cases these defects are neutralised by piety, maternity, want of passion, sexual coldness, by weakness and an undeveloped intelligence. But when a morbid activity of the psychical centres intensifies the bad qualities of women, and induces them to seek relief in evil deeds; when piety and maternal sentiments are wanting, and in their place are strong passions and intensely erotic tendencies, much muscular strength and a superior intelligence for the conception and execution of evil, it is clear that the innocuous semi-criminal present in the normal woman must be transformed into a born criminal more terrible than any man.

What terrific criminals would children be if they had strong passions, muscular strength, and sufficient intelligence; and if, moreover, their evil tendencies were exasperated by a morbid psychical activity! And women are big children; their evil tendencies are more numerous and more varied than men's, but generally remain latent. When they are awakened and excited they produce results proportionately greater.

Moreover, the born female criminal is, so to speak, doubly exceptional, as a woman and as a criminal. For criminals are an exception among civilised people, and women are an exception among criminals, the natural form of retrogression in women being prostitution and not crime. The primitive woman was impure rather than criminal.

As a double exception, the criminal woman is consequently a monster. Her normal sister is kept in the paths of virtue by many causes, such as maternity, piety, weakness, and when these counter influences fail, and a woman commits a crime, we may conclude that her wickedness must have been enormous before it could triumph over so many obstacles.

Man and Woman (1894)
Havelock Ellis

Abstract thought in women seems usually, on the whole, to be marked by a certain docility and receptiveness. Even in trivial matters the average woman more easily accepts statements and opinions than a man, and in more serious matters she is prepared to die for a statement or an opinion, provided it is uttered with such authority and unction that her emotional nature is sufficiently thrilled. This is allied with woman's suggestibility, and it seems to have to some extent an organic basis, so that while the culture of the more abstract powers of thought may make it impossible to obey this instinct, there is still a struggle; or else the more purely rational method is attained – and often distorted in the attaining – by the complete suppression of the other elements. [. . .] The latter method leads further, if only further into error. It is not simply that women are more ready than men to accept what is already accepted and what is most in accordance with appearances – and that it is inconceivable, for instance, that a woman should have devised the Copernican system – but they are less able than men to stand alone. It is difficult to recall examples of women who have patiently and slowly fought their way at once to perfection and to fame in the face of complete indifference, like, for instance, Balzac, – apart from the fact that a woman of talent is usually in more command of her means and able to reach a certain degree of success at an early period. It is still more difficult to recall a woman who for any abstract and intellectual end has fought her way to success through obloquy and contempt, or without reaching success, like a Roger Bacon or a Galileo, a Wagner or an Ibsen. Not only does the woman crave more for sympathy, but she has not the same sturdy independence. The hero of Ibsen's *Enemy of the People*, who had realised that the strongest man in the world is the man who stands most alone, could scarcely have been a woman. When a man is attacked by general paralysis he usually displays an extravagant degree of egoism and self-reliance; when a woman is the victim of the same disease it is not self-reliant egoism but extreme vanity which she displays. The disease liberates the tendencies that are latent in each – the man's to independence, the woman's to dependence, on the opinion of others. [. . .]

A woman instinctively responds more easily than a man to influences from without, even in spite of herself. A young woman, especially if her nervous control is at all defective, involuntarily changes when an individual of the opposite sex approaches; however indifferent he may be to her personally, she cannot prevent the instinctive response of her vasomotor and muscular system, and becomes at once shyer and more alive. Again, a man's rigid facial expression does not respond as a woman's does to the faces it encounters. [. . .] A large portion of the 'tact' of women has the same basis. This affectability has often been brought as a reproach against women, even by their own sex, but we must remember that to a large extent it is physiological. [. . .]

The comparatively larger extent of the sexual sphere in women and of the visceral regions generally, – for in women at puberty [. . .] a new keyboard and a fresh series of pipes are added to the instrument, – the physiological tendency to anaemia, and the existence of inevitable periodicity of function in women, conspire to furnish a broader basis for the play of emotion which no change in environment or habit could remove. [. . .] [A]ll the most characteristic features of women's nature are correlated with emotionality, and the half of women's psychic nature would remain unexplained if we struck out this factor. [. . .]

The affectability of women exposes them, as I have had occasion to point out, to very diabolical manifestations. It is also the source of very much of what is most angelic in women – their impulses of tenderness, their compassion, their moods of divine childhood. Poets have racked their brains to express and to account for this mixture of heaven and hell. We see that the key is really a very simple one; both the heaven and hell of women are but aspects of the same physiological affectability. [. . .]

On the whole, there can be no doubt whatever that if we leave out of consideration the interpretative arts, the artistic impulse is vastly more spontaneous, more pronounced, and more widely spread among men than among women. There is thus a certain justification for Schopenhauer's description of women as the unaesthetic sex. Even in the matter of cooking we may see how emphatic is the tendency for an art to fall into the hands of men. All over the world cooking, as an industry, is women's business, yet wherever cooking rises from an industry to become something of an art it is nearly always in the hands of a man.

When we consider the proportion of women, as compared to men, who obtain even moderate fame, we find that it is even at the present day extremely small. [. . .]

[G.] Ferrero[1] has sought the explanation of the small part played by women in art, and their defective sense for purely aesthetic beauty, in their less keen sexual emotions. This is doubtless an important factor. The sexual sphere in women is more massive and extended than in men, but it is less energetic in its manifestations. In men the sexual instinct is a restless source of energy which overflows into all sorts of channels. At the same time, the rarity of women artists of the first rank is largely due to another cause which we shall be concerned with later on – the greater variational tendency of men. [. . .]

We must regard genius as an organic congenital abnormality (although the evidence in proof of this cannot be entered into here), and in nearly every department it is, undeniably, of more frequent occurrence among men than among women. The statement of this fact has sometimes been regarded by women as a slur upon their sex; they have sought to explain it by lack of opportunity, education, etc. It does not appear that women have been equally anxious to find fallacies in the statement that idiocy is more common among men. Yet the two statements must be taken together. Genius is more common among men by virtue of the same general tendency by which idiocy is more common among men. The two facts are but two aspects of a larger zoological fact – the greater variability of the male. [. . .]

We have, therefore, to recognise that in men, as in males generally, there is an organic variational tendency to diverge from the average, in women, as in females generally, an organic tendency, notwithstanding all their facility for minor oscillations, to stability and conservatism, involving a diminished individualism and variability. [. . .]

A large part of the joy that men and women take in each other is rooted in this sexual difference in variability. The progressive and divergent energies of men call out and satisfy the twin instincts of women to accept and follow a leader, and to expend tenderness on a reckless and erring child, instincts often intermingled in delicious confusion. And in women men find beings who have not wandered so far as they have from the typical life of earth's creatures; women are for men the human embodiments of the restful responsiveness of Nature. [. . .]

While women have been largely absorbed in that sphere of sexuality which is Nature's, men have roamed the earth, sharpening their aptitudes and energies in perpetual conflict with Nature. It has thus come about that the subjugation of Nature by Man has often practically involved the subjugation, physical and mental, of women by men. [. . .] The lust of power and knowledge, the research for artistic perfection, are usually masculine characters; and so most certainly are the suppression of natural emotion and the degradation of sexuality and maternity. [. . .] The hope of our future civilisation lies in the development in equal freedom of both the masculine and feminine elements in life.

Note

1 G. Ferrero, 'Woman's Sphere in Art', *New Review*, November 1893.

Sex and Character (1903)
Otto Weininger

The condition of sexual excitement is the supreme moment of a woman's life. The woman is devoted wholly to sexual matters, that is to say, to the spheres of begetting and of reproduction. Her relations to her husband and children complete her life, whereas the male is something more than sexual. In this respect, rather than in the relative strength of the sexual impulses, there is a real difference between the sexes. It is important to distinguish between the intensity with which sexual matters are pursued and the proportion of the total activities of life that are devoted to them and to their accessory cares. The greater absorption of the human female by the sphere of sexual activities is the most significant difference between the sexes.

The female, moreover, is completely occupied and content with sexual matters, whilst the male is interested in much else, in war and sport, in social affairs and feasting, in philosophy and science, in business and politics, in religion and art. I do not mean to imply that this difference has always existed, as I do not think that important. As in the case of the Jewish question, it may be said that the Jews have their present character because it has been forced upon them, and that at one time they were different. It is now impossible to prove this, and we may leave it to those who believe in the modification by the environment to accept it. The historical evidence is equivocal on the point. In the question of women, we have to take people as they exist to-day. If, however, we happen to come on attributes that could not possibly have been grafted on them from without, we may believe that such have always been with them. [. . .]

The female principle is, then, nothing more than sexuality; the male principle is sexual and something more. This difference is notable in the different way in which men and women enter the period of puberty. In the case of the male the onset of puberty is a crisis; he feels that something new and strange has come into his being, that something has been added to his powers and feelings independently of his will. The physiological stimulus to sexual activity appears to come from outside his being, to be independent of his will, and many men remember the disturbing event throughout their after lives. The woman, on the other hand, not only is not disturbed by the onset of puberty, but feels that her importance has been increased by it. The male, as a youth, has no longing for the onset of sexual maturity; the female, from the time when she is still quite a young girl, looks forward to that time as one from which everything is to be expected. Man's arrival at maturity is frequently accompanied by feelings of repulsion and disgust; the young female watches the development of her body at the approach of puberty with excitement and impatient delight. It seems as if the onset of puberty were a side path in the normal development of man, whereas in the case of woman it is the direct conclusion. There are few boys approaching puberty to whom the idea that they would marry (in the general sense, not a particular girl) would not appear ridiculous, whilst the smallest girl is almost invariably excited and interested in the question of her future marriage. For such reasons a woman assigns positive value only to her period of maturity in her own case and in that of other women; in childhood, as in old age, she has no real relation to the world. The thought of her childhood is for her, later on, only the remembrance of her stupidity; she faces the approach of old age with dislike and abhorrence. The only real memories of her childhood are connected with sex, and these fade away in the intensely greater significance of her maturity. The passage of a woman from virginity is the great dividing point of her life, whilst the corresponding event in the case of a male has very little relation to the course of his life. [. . .]

And so sexual union, considered ethically, psychologically, and biologically, is allied to murder; it is the negation of the woman and the man; in its extreme case it robs them of their consciousness to give life to the child. The highest form of eroticism, as much as the lowest form of sexuality, uses the woman not for herself but as means to an end – to preserve the individuality of the artist. The artist has used the woman merely as the screen on which to project his own idea.

The real psychology of the loved woman is always a matter of indifference. In the moment when a man loves a woman, he neither understands her nor wishes to understand her, although understanding is the only moral basis of association in mankind. A human being cannot love another that he fully understands, because he would then necessarily see the imperfections which are an inevitable part of the human individual, and love can attach itself only to perfection. Love of a woman is possible only when it does not consider her real qualities, and so is able to replace the actual psychical reality by a different and quite imaginary reality. The attempt to realise one's ideal in a woman, instead of the woman herself, is a necessary destruction of the empirical personality of the woman. And so the attempt is cruel to the woman; it is the egoism of love that disregards the woman, and cares nothing for her real inner life.

Thus the parallel between sexuality and love is complete. Love is murder. The sexual impulse destroys the body and mind of the woman, and the psychical eroticism destroys her psychical existence. Ordinary sexuality regards the woman only as a means of gratifying passion or of begetting children. The higher eroticism is merciless to the woman, requiring her to be merely the vehicle of a projected personality, or the mother of psychical children. Love is not only anti-logical, as it denies the objective truth of the woman and requires only an illusory image of her, but it is anti-ethical with regard to her. [. . .]

The last form in which the immorality reveals itself is that love prevents the worthlessness of woman from being realised, inasmuch as it always replaced her by an imaginary projection. Madonna worship itself is fundamentally immoral, inasmuch as it is a shutting of the eyes to truth. The Madonna worship of the great artists is a destruction of woman, and is possible only by a complete neglect of the women as they exist in experience, a replacement of actuality by a symbol, a re-creation of woman to serve the purposes of man, and a murder of woman as she exists. [. . .]

The ideas 'man' and 'woman' cannot be investigated separately; their significance can be found out only by placing them side by side and contrasting them. The key to their natures must be found in their relations to each other. In attempting to discover the nature of erotics I went a little way into this subject. The relation of man to woman is simply that of subject to object. Woman seeks her consummation as the object. She is the plaything of husband or child, and, however we may try to hide it, she is anxious to be nothing but such a chattel.

No one misunderstands so thoroughly what a woman wants as he who tries to find out what is passing within her, endeavouring to share her feelings and hopes, her experiences and her real nature.

Woman does not wish to be treated as an active agent; she wants to remain always and throughout – this is just her womanhood – purely passive, to feel herself under another's will. She demands only to be desired physically, to be taken possession of, like a new property.

Just as mere sensation only attains reality when it is apprehended, *i.e.*, when it becomes objective, so a woman is brought to a sense of her existence only by her husband or children – by these as subjects to whom she is the object – so obtaining the gift of an existence.

The contrast between the subject and the object in the theory of knowledge corresponds ontologically to the contrast between form and matter. It is no more than a translation of this distinction from the theory of experience to metaphysics. Matter, which in itself is absolutely unindividualised and so can assume any form, of itself has no definite and lasting qualities, and has as little essence as mere perception, the matter of experience, has in itself any existence. If the Platonic conception is followed out, it will be apparent that that great thinker asserted to be nothing what the ordinary Philistine regards as the highest form of reality. According to Plato, the negation of existence is no other than matter. Form is the only real existence. Aristotle carried the Platonic conception into the regions of biology. For Plato form is the parent and creator of all reality. For Aristotle, in the sexual process the male principle is the active, formative agent, the female principle the passive matter on which the form is impressed. In my view, the

significance of woman in humanity is explained by the Platonic and Aristotelian conception. Woman is the material on which man acts. Man as the
microcosm is compounded of the lower and higher life. Woman is matter, is
nothing. This knowledge gives us the keystone to our structure, and it makes
everything clear that was indistinct, it gives things a coherent form. Woman's sexual part depends on contact; it is the absorbing and not the liberating impulse. It coincides with this, that the keenest sense woman has, and
the only one she has more highly developed than man, is the sense of touch.
The eye and the ear lead to the unlimited and give glimpses of infinity; the
sense of touch necessitates physical limitations to our own actions: one is
affected by what one feels; it is the eminently sordid sense, and suited to the
physical requirements of an earth-bound being.

Man is form, woman is matter: if that is so it must find expression in
the relations between their respective psychic experiences. [. . .]

Woman is nothing but man's expression and projection of his own sexuality. Every man creates himself a woman, in which he embodies himself
and his own guilt.

But woman is not herself guilty; she is made so by the guilt of others,
and everything for which woman is blamed should be laid at man's door.

Love strives to cover guilt, instead of conquering it; it elevates woman
instead of nullifying her. The 'something' folds the 'nothing' in its arms,
and thinks thus to free the universe of negation and drown all objections;
whereas the nothing would only disappear if the something put it away.

Since man's hatred for woman is not conscious hatred of his own sexuality, his love is his most intense effort to save woman as woman, instead of
desiring to nullify her in himself. And the consciousness of guilt comes
from the fact that the object of guilt is coveted instead of being annihilated.

Woman alone, then, is guilt; and is so through man's fault. And if female-
ness signifies pairing, it is only because all guilt endeavours to increase its
circle. What woman, always unconsciously, accomplishes, she does because
she cannot help it; it is her reason for being, her whole nature. She is only a
part of man, his other, ineradicable, his lower part. So matter appears to be
as inexplicable a riddle as form; woman as unending as man, negation as
eternal as existence; but this eternity is only the eternity of guilt.

The Sexual Question (1906)
August Forel

The Sexual Appetite in Woman. – In the sexual act the role of the woman
differs from that of the man not only by being passive, but also by the

absence of seminal ejaculations. In spite of this the analogies are considerable. The erection of the clitoris and its voluptuous sensations, the secretion from the glands of *Bartholin* which resembles ejaculation in the male, the venereal orgasm itself which often exceeds in intensity that of man, are phenomena which establish harmony in sexual connection. [. . .]

Frequency of the Sexual Appetite in Woman. – As regards pure sexual appetite, extremes are much more common and more considerable in woman than in man. In her this appetite is developed much less often spontaneously than in him, and where it is so, it is generally later. Voluptuous sensations are usually only awakened by coitus. [. . .]

Nature of the Sexual Appetite in Woman. – The zone of sexual excitation is less specially limited to the sexual organs in woman than in man. The nipples constitute in her an entire zone and their friction excites voluptuousness. If we consider the importance in the life of woman, of pregnancy, suckling, and all the maternal functions, we can understand why the mixture of her sentiments and sensations is so different from that of man. Her smaller stature and strength, together with her passive role in coitus, explain why she aspires to a strong male support. This is simply a question of natural phylogenetic adaptation. This is why a young girl sighs for a courageous, strong and enterprising man, who is superior to her, whom she is obliged to respect, and in whose arms she feels secure. Strength and skill in man are the ideal of the young savage and uncultured girl, his intellectual and moral superiority that of the young cultivated girl.

As a rule women are much more the slaves of their instincts and habits than men. In primitive peoples, hardiness and boldness in men were qualities which made for success. This explains why, even at the present day, the boldest and most audacious Don Juans excite most strongly the sexual desires of women, and succeed in turning the heads of most young girls, in spite of their worst faults in other respects. Nothing is more repugnant to the feminine instinct than timidity and awkwardness in man. In our time women become more and more enthusiastic over the intellectual superiority of man, which excites their desire. Without being indifferent to it, simple bodily beauty in man excites the appetite of women to a less extent. [. . .] While the normal man is generally attracted to coitus by nearly every more-or-less young and healthy woman, this is by no means the case in the normal woman with regard to man. She is also much more constant than man from the sexual point of view. It is rarely possible for her to experience sexual desire for several men at once; her senses are nearly always attracted to one lover only.

The instinct of procreation is much stronger in woman than in man, and is combined with the desire to give herself passively, to play the part of one who devotes herself, who is conquered, mastered and subjugated.

These negative aspirations form part of the normal sexual appetite of woman.

The Sexual Life of Our Time (1907)
Iwan Bloch

The difference between the sexes is the *original cause* of the human sexual life, the primeval preliminary of all human civilization. The existence of this difference can be proved, alike in physical and psychical relations, already in the fundamental phenomenon of human love, in which, because here the relations are simple and uncomplicated, it is most easily visible.

Waldeyer, in his notable address on the somatic differences between the sexes, delivered in 1895 at the Anthropological Congress in Kassel, drew attention to the fact that the higher development of any particular species is notably characterized by the increasing differentiation of the sexes. The further we advance in the animal and vegetable world from the lower to the higher forms, the more markedly are the male and the female individuals distinguished one from another. In the human species also, in the course of phylogenetic development, this sexual differentiation increases in extent.

In the development of these sexual differences, the antagonism first shown by Herbert Spencer to exist between reproduction and the higher evolutionary tendency plays an important part. Among the higher species of animals the males exhibit a stronger evolutionary tendency than the females, owing to the fact that their share in the work of reproduction has become less important. The more extensive organic expenditure demanded by the reproductive functions limits the feminine development to a notably greater extent than the masculine. In the human species this retardation of growth in the female is especially increased in consequence of menstruation, and this affords a striking example of the truth of Spencer's law. [. . .]

We have already noted the fact that under the influence of the continually increasing predominance of the brain in the male, certain retrogressive processes have also made themselves manifest (as, for example, the increasing loss of hair); and these processes in woman have gone farther than in man, because in her case the progressive development is *in its very nature* less extensive. Hence recent investigators, such as Havelock Ellis, have actually come to the conclusion that the ideal type, towards which the bodily development of mankind is striving, is represented by the feminine – that is, by a youthful type.

It is, however, very doubtful if this evolution will go so far that the *primitive* difference between man and woman, founded as it is in the very nature of the sexual, will ever pass away. On the contrary, notwithstanding the retrogressive changes associated with the excessive development of the brain, we find that there is *an increasing differentiation of the sexes induced by civilization*. [. . .]

The contrast between the sexes becomes with advancing civilization continually sharper and more individualized, whereas in primitive conditions, and even at the present day among agricultural labourers and the proletariat, it is less sharp and to some extent even obliterated. [. . .]

Certain phenomena and aberrations of the movement for the emancipation of women, such as the adoption of a masculine style of dress and the use of tobacco, are no more than *relapses* into a primitive condition, which among the common people has persisted unaltered to the present day. We need merely allude to the man's hat, the short coat, and the high-laced boot of the Tyrolese women, and to the tobacco-smoking of the women at the wedding festivals among the German peasantry. A false 'emancipation' of this kind is frequently encountered among peasants, vagabonds, and gipsies, to which, moreover, the neuter designation of the women of this class as *das Mensch* and 'woman-fellow', etc., bears witness. [. . .]

Sexual differences comprise for the most part the diverse development of the so-called 'secondary sexual characters' – that is to say, all the differential characteristics which distinguish man from woman, over and above those strictly related to the work of sex – for instance, stature, skeleton, muscles, skin, voice, etc.

The masculine body has evolved to a greater extent than the feminine body as a force-producing machine, for in man the bones and the muscles have a larger development, whereas in woman we observe a greater development of fat, whereby the plasticity of the body is enhanced, but its mechanical utility and energy are impaired. [. . .]

The supporting framework of the body, the osseous skeleton, exhibits important differences in man and woman. The bones of women are on the whole smaller and weaker. Especially extensive sexual differences are noticeable in the pelvis. Wiedersheim regards these sexual differences of the woman's pelvis as a specific characteristic of the human species. In all the anthropoid apes they are far less strongly marked than in man. Moreover, these differences exhibit a progressive development, which is to an important extent dependent upon advancing civilization. For this reason, [. . .] among the majority of savage races the differences between the male and the female pelvis are far less extensive than among civilized nations. The characteristic peculiarities of the pelvis of the European woman, which can be distinguished from the male pelvis at a glance – namely, its greater

extent in transverse diameter, the greater depression and the wider opening of the anterior osseous arch – are far less marked among women of the
South African races and among the South Sea Islanders.

The enlargement of the female pelvis in the course of human evolution
is dependent upon the most important of all the factors of civilization, the
brain. Even in the human foetus the great size of the brain gives rise to a
far greater proportionate development of the skull than we find in the
foetus of any other mammal. This influences the pelvic inlet and the sacrum,
but also the large pelvis, since, in consequence of the adoption by man of
the upright posture, the pregnant uterus expands more laterally, and thus
opens out the iliac fossae. In the lower races of man, it is precisely this
plate-like expansion of the iliac fossae which is so much less developed
than in the case of civilized races. [. . .]

Corresponding with the slighter development of the skeleton, the *muscular system* in woman is also less strongly developed; the muscles contain a larger percentage of water than those of man, and in this point also
we find a resemblance to the juvenile state.

On the other hand, *the development of fat* in woman is much greater
than in man. [. . .] In the female two regions of the body are distinguished
by a specially abundant deposit of fat, the breast and the buttocks, whereby
both parts receive the stamp of extremely prominent secondary sexual
characters. Upon this greater deposit of fat depends the softer, more
rounded form of the feminine body; whilst the muscular system is less
developed than in man. Man, on the other hand, is especially powerful in
the head, neck, breast, and upper extremities. The contrast between the
typical beauty of man and woman, respectively, is mainly explicable by
the differences just enumerated. [. . .]

Larynx and *voice* remain infantile in woman. Woman's larynx is notably smaller than man's. After puberty woman's voice is, on the average,
in the deep tones an octave, in the high tones two octaves, higher than
man's. [. . .]

Woman's skull remains, in respect of numerous peculiarities of structure, strikingly like the skull of the child. This infantile quality of a woman's skull, we must again point out, justifies *no* conclusion regarding the
inferiority of woman. [. . .]

If we wish to sum up in a word the *nature* of the physical sexual differences, we must say: *Woman remains more akin to the child than man*.

This, however, in no way constitutes an inferiority, as Havelock Ellis
and Oskar Schultze have convincingly shown. It is only the expression of
a primitive difference in nature, brought about by the adaptation of the
female body to the purposes of reproduction. [. . .]

In respect of *artistic endowment* the male sex is unquestionably superior to the female. The long series of male poets, musicians, painters, sculp-

tors, of the highest genius cannot be matched by any notable number of striking female personalities in the same sphere of artistic activity. Even the art of cooking has been further developed by men. Without doubt the differences in sexuality are the principal causes of this deficiency. The impetuous, aggressive character of the male sexual impulse also favours poietic endeavours, the transformation of sexual energy into higher plastic activity, as it fulfils itself in the moments of most exalted artistic conception. The greater variability of the male also serves to explain the greater frequency of male artists of the first rank. [. . .]

An old and still unsettled subject of dispute is the strength and nature of sexual sensibility in woman. Whilst the manifestation of sexual appetite and sexual enjoyment in the male are fairly simple – and in man [. . .] the copulatory impulse is much more powerful than the reproductive impulse – the sexual sensibility of woman is still involved in obscurity. [. . .]

I have myself asked a great many cultured women about this matter. *Without exception*, they declared the theory of the lesser sexual sensibility of women to be erroneous; many were even of opinion that sexual sensibility was greater and more enduring in woman than in man.

When we actually consider the physical bases of feminine sexuality, we must admit that women's sexual sphere is a much *more widely extended* one than that of men. [. . .]

It is possible, however, that the greater extension of the sexual sphere in woman gives rise, if one may use the expression, to a greater dispersal of sexual sensations, which are not, as they are in man, closely concentrated to a particular point, and for this reason the spontaneous resolution of the libido (in the form of the sexual orgasm) is rendered more difficult. [. . .]

How much more woman is sexuality than man is can be observed in asylums, where the conventional inhibitions are withdrawn. Here [. . .] the women greatly exceed the men in fluency, malignity, and *obscenity*; and in this relation there is no difference between the shameless virago from the most depraved classes of London and the elegant lady of the upper circles. Noise, uncleanliness, and sexual depravity in speech and demeanour, are much commoner in the women's wards of asylums than on the male side. In all forms of acute mental disorder [. . .] the sexual element plays a much more prominent part in woman than in man. [. . .]

In the majority of cases the sexual fridigity of woman is, in fact, apparent merely – either because behind the veil prescribed by conventional morality, behind the apparent coldness, there is concealed an ardent sexuality, or else because the particular man with whom she has had intercourse has not succeeded rightly in awakening her erotic sensibility, so complicated and so difficult to arouse. When he has succeeded in doing so, the sexual insensibility will in the majority of cases disappear. [. . .]

Speaking generally, the sexual sensibility of woman is, as we have seen, of quite a different nature from that of man; but in intensity it is at least as great as that of man.

Studies in the Psychology of Sex, vol. I: *The Evolution of Modesty,* The Phenomena of Sexual Periodicity Auto-Erotism [1899] (1900)
Havelock Ellis

Modesty, which may be provisionally defined as an almost instinctive fear prompting to concealment and usually centering around the sexual processes, while common to both sexes is more peculiarly feminine, so that it may almost be regarded as the chief secondary sexual character of women on the psychical side. The woman who is lacking in this kind of fear is lacking, also, in sexual attractiveness to the normal and average man. [. . .]

The sexual modesty of the female animal is rooted in the sexual periodicity of the female, and is an involuntary expression of the organic fact that the time for love is not now. Inasmuch as this fact is true of the greater part of the lives of all female animals below man, the expression itself becomes so habitual that it even intrudes at those moments when it has ceased to be in place. We may see this again illustrated in the bitch, who, when in heat, herself runs after the male, and again turns to flee, perhaps only submitting with much persuasion to his embrace. Thus, modesty becomes something more than a mere refusal of the male; it becomes an invitation to the male, and is mixed up with his ideas of what is sexually desirable in the female. This would alone serve to account for the existence of modesty as a psychical secondary sexual character. [. . .] The sexual modesty of the female is thus an inevitable by-product of the naturally aggressive attitude of the male in sexual relationships, and the naturally defensive attitude of the female, this again being founded on the fact that, while – in man and the species allied to him – the sexual function in the female is periodic, and during most of life a function to be guarded from the opposite sex, in the male it rarely or never needs to be so guarded. [. . .]

It is impossible to contemplate this series of phenomena, so radically persistent whatever its changes of form, and so constant throughout every stage of civilization, without feeling that, although modesty cannot properly be called an instinct, there must be some physiological basis to support it. Undoubtedly such a basis is formed by that vasomotor mechanism of which the most obvious outward sign is, in human beings, the blush. All the allied emotional forms of fear – shame, bashfulness, timidity – are to some extent upheld by this mechanism, but such is especially the case with the emotion we are now concerned with. The blush is the sanction of modesty.

Problems of the Sexes (1913)
Jean Finot

The qualities which thus separate the two sexes are merely the expression of a constitutional contrast, assert authoritative biologists, such as Geddes and Thomson, and not, as people would have us believe, the product of masculine oppression.

The organic difference which separates the cells will become the basis of the whole problem of the sexes. The males, having more catabolic organisms, that is, organisms which are more active, more prodigal, will march at the head of evolution and progress, while the women, who are more passive (anabolic), whose constructive processes dominate life, will be more patient and more stable, and will especially tend toward preserving the steadfastness and integrity of the species.

Men, by virtue of the same principle, will have more originality and will show more cerebral variety, but women will have more common sense (P. Geddes and Thomson). [. . .]

Eminent scientists thus contest the essential basis of all these biological speculations. Weismann, for instance, states that the spermatozoön and the egg-cell show no physiological distinction. [. . .] And the differences in their external appearance? These merely serve to facilitate the union of the nuclei of the two cells, but their contents are always the same. Then what becomes of the larger body of the egg? What is its meaning? This larger body performs the part of nutritive aliment for the use of both the cells.

In short, the cells, male and female, have each a nucleus. Both are alike. It is upon their conjugation that fecundation depends. As to the external form which separates the spermatozoön from the egg, it possesses no importance. The larger body of the egg serves as nutrition for both cells. [. . .]

Let us take the opposite side of the adopted interpretation, and while admitting the authenticity of the facts, we shall arrive at conclusions which, although diametrically opposed, will have the same chances of being truthful. [. . .]

Does not the spermatozoön of man, smaller, more variable, already indicate the versatility, the fickleness and the weakness of man? The passive ovule incarnates seriousness and weight.

The government of men and affairs should belong to woman; for since she is more balanced, more reflective, more stable, she will be able to perform her duties with continuity in her ideas and proceedings. Distrust arises concerning the spermatozoön. His instability, permitting him to be unduly influenced by circumstances, his vagabondage which is directed by his very nature, make him a dangerous element in social and political life.

He must be regarded with suspicion and kept away from commanding positions. Nature herself has indicated our path. Woman must rule, and man has only to submit to her laws and inspiration.

Thus, for whole pages, we could continue to demonstrate the superiority of woman and the necessity for the slavery of man. And we should doubtless have as many reasons for arguing the veracity of our conclusions as our adversaries have for maintaining the contrary. It is evident that these two antiphrases are equally false and inadmissible. Science permits us only to prove the differentiated appearance of the two germs, but she does not authorise us to draw from this fact inferences either favourable or adverse to woman. [. . .]

This is the whole question: are there psychological qualities peculiar to woman, and if so, what are these qualities? What distinguishes, and will distinguish, woman from man, in spite of the conditions of her life? Inseparable from her sex, these qualities must accompany her everywhere and remain independent of her economic or social position.

The biologists have already told us that they are proved by the essential differences which separate the two cells whose union creates the living being. The psychologists will easily derive from these distinctions the support necessary to bolster up their preconceived dogmas. Woman through her entire physiological structure, as well as in her psychological qualities, will manifest especially this need of conservation; a predominance of nutrition without, a peace of mind within. She will long for the calmness and repose to which the special development of her tissues destines her. The roundness of her body, her abundantly developed adipose system, the form of her pelvis and of her hips, in short, the 'dead weight' which her organism shows, render her sedentary and domestic. The contrary qualities will characterise man. He will be more agile and ready to act. Stalwart and enterprising by nature, his body, unencumbered by the things which weigh down woman, will permit him to be more active and energetic. Everything will tend to drive him away from his fireside, everything will urge upon him the necessity of war and of conquest. Woman, thanks to her special structure, will incarnate organic saving; man will expend the forces that woman by the channel of heredity will bequeath to him. By standing guard over his home, she will also make it easier for him to run off and devote himself to all sorts of pranks.

The reasoning of the biologists and of the psychologists is, we observe, analogous. From their observation of the differences of the two cells that produce life these investigators not only derive all the qualities of woman but seek justification for the part she has played through history. It is man's nature to be pugnacious and warlike, and to have an energetic, explosive, impatient temper; it is woman's inclination to be gentle, patient, domestic. While he will engage in all sorts of physical and mental adventures to which his disposition prompts him, and will have an obvious tendency toward novelty and change, she, the guardian of the home, will be conservative both through taste and temperament. She will follow the natural tendencies of her body, which will impel her toward the safe-keeping of the acquired qualities and ideas. Shut up within her dwelling, she will spend her days in arranging all the petty details of life. Her pusillanimous mind will become more concrete than that of man. She will lose herself in details and he will be captivated by abstractions. And, as she is strongly attached to the past, she will not like the criticism which tends toward its destruction. Man will create revolutions; woman will strive to calm them and to lessen their violent effects. As religion seeks especially to secure peace of mind, and preaches a passive reconciliation with fate, woman will be devout. She will be the more inclined to religion because the patience necessary to await salvation in an indeterminate future is dictated to her by her mode of thought and life. She will be guilty also of fewer penal offences than man, for crime requires a larger expenditure of energy and an emancipation from routine. Lacking ideas, woman will become the prey of her feelings. War, science, and the higher forms of art will be to her an unknown realm. Genius and originality will shun her abode. Condemned to mediocrity of ideas and of life, she will drag out her existence, limiting herself to the enjoyment of the intellectual treasures which man will create and rendering obedience to the laws which he will establish in his own favour. [. . .]

Woman, they tell us, is condemned by imperious and immutable biological laws to be and to remain in the future what she is at the present day. But are all the psychological qualities of woman really in the ovule? Is this really the resting-place of the virtues which will become the joy or the horror of man?

The interpretation given to the appearance of the ovule is erroneous, as we have seen, from the biological standpoint, and this interpretation is no less so when the point in question is to establish sexual psychology. Here also we find premises wholly arbitrary, whose falsity and unreliable character are revealed when the supreme proof is applied, the proof of life. [. . .]

Woman, morally, is only the result of the conditions imposed upon her by life. She will be sublime in goodness or odious in cruelty, according to the surrounding environment which makes her think and act. [. . .]

Races called inferior, which lie sunk in the baseness of numberless vices, as soon as they emerge from their unhealthy environment become equal to the best peoples. [. . .] The negroes of the United States, whose forefathers were recruited a century ago from the most degraded African tribes, are distinguished, at the present day, by marvellous progress in the economic and social domain. [. . .]

With the change in her education and in her social position, she will regain veracity, that virtue of the masters, and abandon falsehood, the heritage of centuries of servitude. Thus the eternal feminine, that assemblage of qualities termed exclusively womanly, is being altered under our eyes. For, during this oscillation of the changing conditions of our life, our souls do not cease to vary and develop. Neither man nor woman, the one no more than the other, is created for falsehood or for truth. And if falsehood so penetrates our life, it is because it has been introduced into it by the abnormal and erroneous relations which unite the two sexes. For duplicity engenders falsehood, as the plague causes fatal illnesses. [. . .]

Woman is equal to man. This is the essential principle evolved from our study. From the intellectual, moral, or physiological standpoint nothing authorises their gradation. The 'stronger sex' is no stronger than the other. The differences proved are merely the results of the special conditions in which they develop. There are no implacable organic conditions which could impose upon the woman a weaker mentality, or give to the man a more robust constitution.

The great physiological function, maternity, which separates the two sexes, renders them to a certain extent unlike, but not inferior to each other. *Unlikeness in equality,* this is the foundation of the entire sexual policy. Woman has the right to require, and man has the duty to grant her, the same social or political rights. Harmony between the members of the entire human race, and their progress toward greater happiness, will be the first result.

Part II

Homosexualities

Introduction

Laura Doan and Chris Waters

In the late nineteenth century a series of distinct 'scientific', clinical and discursive practices established a new taxonomy of 'deviant' sexual behaviour predicated upon the presumed existence of a normative heterosexuality. 'Sexual inversion' was initially the umbrella term for any activity that deviated from this norm; however, by the early twentieth century, the phrase became synonymous with homosexuality, denoting a sexuality where sexual desire was directed towards a member of the same sex. Historians are sharply divided over the question of whether the labelling of the unique identity and character of the 'homosexual' was a positive or negative development for those who experienced same-sex desires. Some welcome the sexological creation of the homosexual for its powerful explanatory models of self-identity and its facilitation of a modern gay and lesbian subculture. Others, however, disparage sexology for the role it is thought to have played in the stigmatizing and pathologizing of homosexuals and homosexual desire. The documents in this part, which include several case histories where individuals narrate their own life experiences, allow the reader to negotiate these two critiques in order to understand how sexology contributed to twentieth-century ways of thinking about same-sex desire.

The early work of sexologists gradually began to familiarize the European and North American public with the existence of a new species of being variously labelled the Urning, Uranian, intermediate type, invert or homosexual. Sexologists concentrated far more on men than women, who were more invisible and marginalized in the public sphere. In Britain, the Criminal Law Amendment Act of 1885 included the notorious Labouchère

Amendment, which criminalized so-called acts of 'gross indecency' between men, though no law was ever passed against lesbianism. By the time the sensational trials of Oscar Wilde took place in 1895, male homosexuality was extensively debated, and its various manifestations and etiology subject to intensive scrutiny. The popular press viewed Wilde's predatory sexual relationships with younger men of lower social standing as pathological and claimed that his sexual vices were wilfully chosen, representative of a widespread breakdown of moral standards and of the increasing prevalence of degenerative influences in society at large. When the British medical journal, *The Lancet* reviewed the earliest edition of the British sexologist Havelock Ellis's *Sexual Inversion* (written originally in collaboration with John Addington Symonds and first published in German in 1896), it echoed many popular sentiments and strenuously resisted Ellis's claim that homosexuality was a mere anomaly, a part of nature. Instead, the journal reiterated the prevailing belief that it was always an 'acquired and depraved manifestation of the sexual passion'. It is against this backdrop that we must assess some of the first interventions made by sexologists, for their work attempted to counter such claims by deeming homosexual behaviour to be less the result of misguided choice than the outcome of an innate, congenital condition over which the individual had little control.

If, in popular thought, behaviour like Wilde's was viewed as a sin and a crime, in some sexological writing, especially in the early work of Richard von Krafft-Ebing (1840–1902), homosexuality was seen as a sickness, a manifestation of 'functional degeneration'. By the turn of the century, two approaches to homosexuality, which overlapped at many points, had become increasingly ascendant, both of which were eager to distance themselves from the notion that same-sex sexual activity was an illness. On the one hand, there was the 'third sex' model of homosexuality, put forward by Karl Heinrich Ulrichs in Germany and circulated widely in Britain by Edward Carpenter (1844–1929). On the other, there was the work of Ellis, the British sexologist who both documented what he termed 'sexual inversion' and provided a language of homosexual selfhood through which many individuals came to understand their desires in the first third of the twentieth century. In the work of these writers homosexuality was viewed neither as an illness that needed to be 'cured', nor as a vice that was freely chosen; as Otto Weininger put it, inversion was not pathological, it was not a hideous anomaly or an acquired vice, and it was not the result of an 'execrable seduction'.

Writing in Britain at a time when the advent of the 'new woman' seemed to be breaking down what had been viewed as the natural, biological roles of men and women, Carpenter noted the existence of a growing rapprochement between the sexes, of men who were more feminine and women who were more masculine, as he put it. It was within this context that we must understand his notion of the 'third sex', of the homosexual as a type of person who belonged to one sex as far as his or her body was concerned, but who belonged mentally and emotionally to the opposite sex. For Carpenter the male homosexual possessed a feminine soul encased in a male body, while the female homosexual, underneath her female body, could be characterized by her masculine soul and temperament; both were what he termed 'intermediate types'. While using a slightly different terminology, Ellis shared quite similar beliefs. His notion of 'sexual inversion' (embraced by Stella Browne (1882–1955) in her subsequent writing on female inversion) often, but not always, entailed some form of gender inversion whereby masculine attributes were common in female inverts and feminine attributes could be noted in male inverts. While Ellis sometimes challenged the equation of effeminacy and male homosexuality, he was by and large committed to the belief that lesbianism was accompanied by a recognizable mannishness.

For Carpenter, 'nature' was responsible for the existence of the 'intermediate types', just as for Ellis the invert was a naturally occurring phenomenon. Ellis was convinced that sexual inversion was what he termed a 'congenital anomaly', and by 1910 the new science of endocrinology began to offer him a way of explaining this anomaly in hormonal terms, or what he referred to as an uncoordination of the 'internal secretions'. While he admitted that certain environmental factors external to an individual's unique biological make-up might excite this 'latent condition', Ellis insisted that such factors required 'a favourable organic predisposition' upon which to act. It followed that Ellis had little sympathy for those who claimed to be able to 'cure' what for him was always an inborn condition. Stella Browne believed likewise, holding that the homosexual impulse should have the same right to existence and expression as the heterosexual. Nevertheless, she also viewed sexual inversion as in part the result of society's repression of the 'normal erotic impulse', and believed that if society were to adopt a less prudish attitude towards sex in general, and if women's right to sexual pleasure were to be affirmed, then inversion might diminish. This somewhat ambivalent attitude to inversion led her to refute claims made by Carpenter and others that inverts were 'superior' to heterosexuals. Moreover, like Ellis, Browne also embraced the division of female sexual inverts into two groups: the 'pseudo' and the true or congenital invert. The former was seen as vulnerable to the sexual and corrupting advances of the latter, a belief that would culminate in the myth of the predatory lesbian.

By the 1920s, the mapping of homosexual identities in terms of sexual inversion, or of the third sex, was being challenged by the advent of new, psychoanalytic understandings of sexual development. By studying the psychic mechanisms that determined sexual object choice, Sigmund Freud opposed the work of those sexologists who believed that homosexuals needed to be studied as a special category of person. For Freud, both homosexual and heterosexual object choices were simply two outcomes of each person's unique development, a process that began in a shared, polymorphous, infant bisexuality. Freud rarely judged same-sex object choice to be inferior, inadequate or abnormal, despite his tendency to cast homosexuality as an inhibition of 'normal' psychosexual progress. Many of his followers, however, did not always share their mentor's sentiments. One early advocate of psychoanalytic theories of homosexuality in Britain, C. Stanford Read (b. 1871), viewed homosexuality as a form of arrested development, a regression to an earlier mode of sexual gratification that was both abnormal and yet treatable by therapeutic means. Likewise, Thomas Ross (1875–1941) argued that psychoanalysis could enlighten patients about the forces that had disrupted their 'normal' development into a mature form of heterosexual adulthood and, consequently, help them overcome their homosexual impulses.

The shift in thinking from earlier sexological models of congenital inversion to newer models of psychosexual development was no mere academic matter. It affected how many individuals conceived of their sexual desires, it impinged on the kinds of strategy developed by sexual reformers, and it influenced many policy-makers in the drafting of social legislation. The patient in Ross's study, for example, was reluctant to break with the model of congenital inversion through which he understood his desires, and hesitant to reconceptualize himself in psychoanalytic terms of regression, or of 'thwarted heterosexuality'. Likewise, many reformers often felt they were better served in their work by Ellis than by Freud. For them, the congenital invert could be imagined as incurable, an object of pity against whom penal sanctions should be removed. But the person whose homosexual condition resulted from 'arrested development' – whose status appeared to be acquired, rather than innate – was often viewed as suitable for treatment. By the 1930s, many criminologists (as seen here in the writing of William Norwood East (1872–1953) and William de Bargue Hubert (1904–47)) were beginning to argue for at least a limited application of psychoanalytic ideas in attempting to understand the causes of homosexual behaviour and, in some instances, to attempt to redirect such behaviour in more 'acceptable' directions.

Exodus

Sometimes in a different form, and often expressed in a very different language, these debates are still with us today. Whether homosexuality is deemed to be the result of 'nature' or 'nurture', whether it is 'congenital' or freely chosen, whether it is a vice, a crime, a sickness, or a mere anomaly – or even whether the heterosexual/homosexual binary distinction is still a useful one to make – there is no doubt that many of the terms of these debates were set for us by a number of thinkers who made their mark between the 1890s and 1930s. We are still struggling with their various legacies today.

Psychopathia Sexualis [1886] (12th edn, 1903)
Richard von Krafft-Ebing

Congenital sexual inversion in women

Science in its present stage has but few data to fall back on, so far as the occurrence of homosexual instinct in woman is concerned as compared with man.

It would not be fair to draw from this the conclusion that sexual inversion in women is rare, for if this anomaly is really a manifestation of functional degeneration, then degenerative influences will prevail alike in the female as well as in the male.

The causes of apparent infrequency in woman may be found in the following facts: (1) It is more difficult to gain the confidence of the sexually perverse woman; (2) this anomaly, in so far as it leads to sexual intercourse, among women, does not fall (in Germany at any rate) under the criminal code, and therefore remains hidden from public knowledge; (3) sexual inversion does not affect woman in the same manner as it does man, for it does not render woman impotent; (4) because woman (whether sexually inverted or not) is by nature not as sensual and certainly not as aggressive in the pursuit of sexual needs as man, for which reason the inverted sexual intercourse among women is less noticeable, and by outsiders is considered mere friendship. Indeed, there are cases on record (psychical hermaphroditism, even homosexuality) in which the causes of *frigidas uxoris* [female frigidity] remain unknown even to the husband.

Certain passages in the Bible, the history of Greece ('Sapphic Love'), the moral history of Ancient Rome and of the Middle Ages, offer proofs that *congressus intersexualis feminarum* [sexual meeting of women] took place at all times, the same as it is practiced now-a-days in the harem, in female prisons, brothels and young ladies' seminaries. [. . .]

The chief reason why inverted sexuality in woman is still covered with the veil of mystery is that the homosexual act so far as woman is concerned, does not fall under the law. [. . .]

I have through long experience gained the impression that inverted sexuality occurs in woman as frequently as in man. But the chaster education of the girl deprives the sexual instinct of its predominant character; seduction to mutual masturbation is less frequent; the sexual instinct in the girl begins to develop only when she is, with the advent of puberty, introduced to the society of the other sex, and is thus naturally led primarily into hetero-sexual channels. All these circumstances work in her favour, often serve to correct abnormal inclinations and tastes, and force her into the ways of normal sexual intercourse. We may, however, safely assume that many cases of frigidity or anaphrodisia in married women are rooted in undeveloped or suppressed antipathic sexual instinct.

The situation changes when the predisposed female is also tainted with other anomalies of an hypersexual character and is led through it or seduced by other females to masturbation or homosexual acts.

In these cases we find situations analogous to those which have been described as existing in men afflicted with 'acquired' antipathic sexual instinct.

As possible sources from which homosexual love in woman may spring, the following may be mentioned:

1   Constitutional hypersexuality impelling to automasturbation. This leads to neurasthenia and its evil consequences, to anaphrodisia in the normal sexual intercourse so long as *libido* remains active.

2   Hypersexuality also leads *faute de mieux* [for want of something better] to homosexual intercourse (inmates of prisons, daughters of the high classes of society who are guarded so very carefully in their relations with men, or are afraid of impregnation, – this latter group is very numerous). Frequently female servants are the seducers, or lady friends with perverse sexual inclinations, and lady teachers in seminaries.

3   Wives of impotent husbands who can only sexually excite, but not satisfy, woman, thus producing in her *libido insatiata* [unsatisfied desire], recourse to masturbation, *pollutiones feminae* [pollutions of a woman], neurasthenia, nausea for coitus and ultimately disgust with the male sex in general.

4   Prostitutes of gross sensuality who, disgusted with the intercourse with perverse and impotent men by whom they are used for the performance of the most revolting sexual acts, seek compensation in the sympathetic embrace of persons of their own sex. These cases are of very frequent occurrence.

Careful observation of the ladies of large cities soon convinces one that homosexuality is by no means a rarity. Uranism may nearly always be suspected in females wearing their hair short, or who dress in the fashion of men, or pursue the sports and pastimes of their male acquaintances; also in opera singers and actresses, who appear in male attire on the stage by preference. [. . .] *or profession?*

[M]any homosexual women do not betray their anomaly by external appearances nor by mental (masculine) sexual characteristics. [. . .]

The female urning may chiefly be found in the haunts of boys. She is the rival in their play, preferring the rocking-horse, playing at soldiers, etc., to dolls and other girlish occupations. The toilet is neglected, and rough boyish manners are affected. Love for art finds a substitute in the pursuits of the sciences. At times smoking and drinking are cultivated even with passion.

Perfumes and sweetmeats are disdained. The consciousness of being a woman and thus to be deprived of the gay college life, or to be barred out from the military career, produces painful reflections.

The masculine soul, heaving in the female bosom, finds pleasure in the pursuit of manly sports, and in manifestations of courage and bravado. There is a strong desire to imitate the male fashion in dressing the hair and in general attire, under favourable circumstances even to don male attire and impose in it. Arrests of women in men's clothing are by no means of rare occurrence. [. . .]

Gynandry represents the extreme grade of degenerate homosexuality. The woman of this type possesses of the feminine qualities only the genital organs; thought, sentiment, action, even external appearance are those of the man. [. . .]

Mutatis mutandis [with due alteration of details], the situation is the same as with the man-loving man. These creatures seek, find, recognize, love one another, often live together as 'father' and 'mother' in pseudo marriage. Suspicion may always be turned towards homosexuality when one reads in the advertisement columns of the daily papers: 'Wanted, by a lady, a lady friend and companion.' [. . .]

When viraginity prevails marriage is impossible, for the very thought of *coitus cum viro* [coitus with a man] arouses disgust and horror.

The intersexual gratification among these women seems to be reduced to kissing and embraces, which seems to satisfy those of weak sexual instinct, but produces in sexually neurasthenic females ejaculation.

Automasturbation, for want of something better, seems to occur in all grades of the anomaly the same as in men.

Strongly sensual individuals may resort to cunnilingus or mutual masturbation.

In grades 3 and 4 the desire to adopt the active *role* towards the beloved person of the same sex seems to invite the use of the priapus.

The Intermediate Sex (1896)
Edward Carpenter

In late years (and since the arrival of the New Woman amongst us) many things in the relation of men and women to each other have altered, or at any rate become clearer. The growing sense of equality in habits and customs – university studies, art, music, politics, the bicycle, etc. – all these things have brought about a *rapprochement* between the sexes. If the modern woman is a little more masculine in some ways than her predecessor, the modern man (it is to be hoped), while by no means effeminate, is a little more sensitive in temperament and artistic in feeling than the original John Bull. It is beginning to be recognised that the sexes do not or should not normally form two groups hopelessly isolated in habit and feeling from each other, but that they rather represent the two poles of *one* group – which is the human race; so that while certainly the extreme specimens at either pole are vastly divergent, there are great numbers in the middle region who (though differing corporeally as men and women) are by emotion and temperament very near to each other. We all know women with a strong dash of the masculine temperament, and we all know men whose almost feminine sensibility and intuition seem to belie their bodily form. Nature, it might appear, in mixing the elements which go to compose each individual, does not always keep her two groups of ingredients – which represent the two sexes – properly apart, but often throws them crosswise in a somewhat baffling manner, now this way and now that; yet wisely, we must think – for if a severe distinction of elements were always maintained the two sexes would soon drift into far latitudes and absolutely cease to understand each other. As it is, there are some remarkable and (we think) indispensable types of character in whom there is such a union or balance of the feminine and masculine qualities that these people become to a great extent the interpreters of men and women to each other. [. . .]

  K.H. Ulrichs [. . .] pointed out that there were people born in such a position – as it were on the dividing line between the sexes – that while belonging distinctly to one sex as far as their bodies are concerned they may be said to belong *mentally* and *emotionally* to the other; that there were men, for instance, who might be described as of feminine soul enclosed in a male body (*anima muliebris in corpore virili inclusa*), or in other cases, women whose definition would be just the reverse. And he maintained that this doubleness of nature was to a great extent proved by the special direction of their love-sentiment. For in such cases, as indeed might be expected, the (apparently) masculine person instead of forming a love-union with a female tended to contract romantic friendships with one of his own sex; while the apparently feminine would, instead of marrying in the usual way, devote herself to the love of another feminine.

People of this kind (*i.e.*, having this special variation of the love-sentiment) he called Urnings; and though we are not obliged to accept his theory about the crosswise connexion between 'soul' and 'body', since at best these words are somewhat vague and indefinite; yet his work was important because it was one of the first attempts, in modern times, to recognise the existence of what might be called an Intermediate sex, and to give at any rate *some* explanation of it. [. . .]

Contrary to the general impression, one of the first points that emerges from this study is that 'Urnings', or Uranians, are by no means so very rare; but that they form, beneath the surface of society, a large class. It remains difficult, however, to get an exact statement of their numbers; and this for more than one reason: partly because, owing to the want of any general understanding of their case, these folk tend to conceal their true feelings from all but their own kind, and indeed often deliberately act in such a manner as to lead the world astray [. . .] and partly because it is indubitable that the numbers do vary very greatly, not only in different countries but even in different classes in the same country. [. . .]

In the second place it emerges (also contrary to the general impression) that men and women of the exclusively Uranian type are by no means necessarily morbid in any way – unless, indeed, their peculiar temperament be pronounced in itself morbid. Formerly it was assumed as a matter of course, that the type was merely a result of disease and degeneration; but now with the examination of the actual facts it appears that, on the contrary, many are fine, healthy specimens of their sex, muscular and well-developed in body, of powerful brain, high standard of conduct, and with nothing abnormal or morbid of any kind observable in their physical structure or constitution. This is of course not true of all, and there still remain a certain number of cases of weakly type to support the neuro-pathic view. Yet it is very noticeable that this view is much less insisted on by the later writers than by the earlier. It is also worth noticing that it is now acknowledged that even in the most healthy cases the special affectional temperament of the 'Intermediate' is, as a rule, ineradicable; so much so that when (as in not a few instances) such men and women, from social or other considerations, have forced themselves to marry and even have children, they have still not been able to overcome their own bias, or the leaning after all of their life-attachment to some friend of their own sex. [. . .]

It would be a great mistake to suppose that their attachments are necessarily sexual, or connected with sexual acts. On the contrary (as abundant evidence shows), they are often purely emotional in their character;

and to confuse Uranians (as is so often done) with libertines having no law but curiosity in self-indulgence is to do them a great wrong. At the same time, it is evident that their special temperament may sometimes cause them difficulty in regard to their sexual relations. Into this subject we need not just now enter. But we may point out how hard it is, especially for the young among them, that a veil of complete silence should be drawn over the subject, leading to the most painful misunderstandings, and perversions and confusions of mind; and that there should be no hint of guidance; nor any recognition of the solitary and really serious inner struggles they may have to face! [. . .]

As indicated then already, in bodily structure there is, as a rule, nothing to distinguish the subjects of our discussion from ordinary men and women; but if we take the general mental characteristics it appears from almost universal testimony that the male tends to be of a rather gentle, emotional disposition – with defects, if such exist, in the direction of subtlety, evasiveness, timidity, vanity, etc.; while the female is just the opposite, fiery, active, bold and truthful, with defects running to brusqueness and coarseness. Moreover, the mind of the former is generally intuitive and instinctive in its perceptions, with more or less of artistic feeling; while the mind of the latter is more logical, scientific, and precise than usual with the normal woman. [. . .]

We have so far limited ourselves to some very general characteristics of the Intermediate race. It may help to clear and fix our ideas if we now describe more in detail, first, what may be called the extreme and exaggerated types of the race, and then the more normal and perfect types. By doing so we shall get a more definite and concrete view of our subject.

In the first place, then, the extreme specimens – as in most cases of extremes – are not particularly attractive, sometimes quite the reverse. In the male of this kind we have a distinctly effeminate type, sentimental, lackadaisical, mincing in gait and manners, something of a chatterbox, skilful at the needle and in woman's work, sometimes taking pleasure in dressing in woman's clothes; his figure not unfrequently betraying a tendency towards the feminine, large at the hips, supple, not muscular, the face wanting in hair, the voice inclining to be high-pitched, etc.; while his dwelling-room is orderly in the extreme, even natty, and choice of decoration and perfume. His affection, too, is often feminine in character, clinging, dependent and jealous, as of one desiring to be loved almost more than to love.

On the other hand, as the extreme type of the homogenic female, we have a rather markedly aggressive person, of strong passions, masculine manners and movements, practical in the conduct of life, sensuous rather than sentimental in love, often untidy, and *outré* in attire; her figure muscular, her voice rather low in pitch; her dwelling-room decorated with sporting-scenes, pistols, etc., and not without a suspicion of the fragrant weed in the atmosphere; while her love (generally to rather soft and feminine specimens of her own sex) is often a sort of furor, similar to the ordinary masculine love, and at times almost uncontrollable.

These are types which, on account of their salience, everyone will recognise more or less. Naturally, when they occur they excite a good deal of attention, and it is not an uncommon impression that most persons of the homogenic nature belong to either one or other of these classes. But in reality, of course, these extreme developments are rare, and for the most part the temperament in question is embodied in men and women of quite normal and unsensational exterior. [. . .] And it may be supposed that we may draw the same conclusion with regard to women of this class – namely, that the majority of them do not exhibit pronounced masculine habits. In fact, while these extreme cases are of the greatest value from a scientific point of view as marking tendencies and limits of development in certain directions, it would be a serious mistake to look upon them as representative cases of the whole phases of human evolution concerned. [. . .]

The instinctive artistic nature of the male of this class, his sensitive spirit, his wavelike emotional temperament, combined with hardihood of intellect and body; and the frank, free nature of the female, her masculine independence and strength wedded to thoroughly feminine grace of form and manner; may be said to give them both, through their double nature, command of life in all its phases, and a certain freemasonry of the secrets of the two sexes which may well favour their function as reconcilers and interpreters.

'Editorial on the publication of Havelock Ellis's *Sexual Inversion*' (1896)
The Lancet

[Havelock Ellis's] book is the first of a series of studies in the psychology of sex and deals with a phase of the question which we must all admit to exist – namely, sexual inversion. It is allowed that this subject touches the very lowest depths to which humanity has fallen. But for all that it is a subject which cannot be ignored and one which is not made any less powerful for ill by the pretence that there is no such thing. But while we admit that the subject of sexual inversion has its proper claims for discussion we are very clear as to the propriety of limiting that discussion to persons of particular attainments. When Mr. Havelock Ellis's book was sent to us for review we did not review it, and our reason for this neglect of the work of the Editor of the 'Contemporary Science Series' was not connected with its theme or wholly with the manner of its presentment. Mr. Havelock Ellis's book is written in a purely dispassionate and scientific style and the only exception we take to the treatment is that we consider some of his quotations unnecessary because a scientific public is already familiar with the originals, and some of them useless, being drawn from tainted sources. [. . .] What decided us not to notice the book was its method of publication. Why was it not published through a house able to take proper measures for introducing it as a scientific book to a scientific audience? And for other reasons, which it would serve no purpose to particularise, we considered the circumstances attendant upon its issue suspicious. We believed that the book would fall into the hands of readers totally unable to derive benefit from it as a work of science and very ready to draw evil lessons from its necessarily disgusting passages. It must be pointed out, too, that a more than ordinary danger is attached to Mr. Havelock Ellis's work as a book for laymen in that the author's views happen to be that sexual inversion is far more prevalent than we believe it to be and that the legislature does injustice to many by regarding as crimes the practices with which it is bound up. He has failed to convince us on these points; and his historical references and the 'human documents' with which he has been furnished will, we think, fail equally to convince medical men that homo-sexuality is anything else than an acquired and depraved manifestation of the sexual passion; but, be that as it may, it is especially important that such matters should not be discussed by the man in the street, not to mention the boy and girl in the street.

again the children

Studies in the Psychology of Sex, vol. II: Sexual Inversion [1897] (3rd edn, 1915)
Havelock Ellis

The histories which follow have been obtained in various ways, and are of varying degrees of value. Some are of persons whom I have known very well for very long periods, and concerning whom I can speak very positively. A few are from complete strangers whose good faith, however, I judge from internal evidence that I am able to accept. Two or three were written by persons who – though educated, in one case a journalist – had never heard of inversion, and imagined that their own homosexual feelings were absolutely unique in the world. A fair number were written by persons whom I do not myself know, but who are well known to others in whose judgment I feel confidence. Perhaps the largest number are concerned with individuals who wrote to me spontaneously in the first place, and whom I have at intervals seen or heard from since, in some cases during a very long period, so that I have slowly been able to fill in their histories, although the narratives, as finally completed, may have the air of being written down at a single sitting. [. . .]

History VII. – "My parentage is very sound and healthy. Both my parents (who belong to the professional middle class) have good general health; nor can I trace any marked abnormal or diseased tendency, of mind or body, in any records of the family. [. . .]

"At the age of 8 or 9, and long before distinct sexual feelings declared themselves, I felt a friendly attraction toward my own sex, and this developed after the age of puberty into a passionate sense of love, which, however, never found any expression for itself till I was fully 20 years of age. I was a day-boarder at school and heard little of schooltalk on sex subjects, was very reserved and modest besides; no elder person or parent ever spoke to me on such matters; and the passion for my own sex developed gradually, utterly uninfluenced from the outside. I never even, during all this period, and till a good deal later, learned the practice of masturbation. My own sexual nature was a mystery to me. I found myself cut off from the understanding of others, felt myself an outcast, and, with a highly loving and clinging temperament, was intensely miserable. I thought about my male friends – sometimes boys of my own age, sometimes elder boys, and once even a master – during the day and dreamed about them at night, but was too convinced that I was a hopeless monstrosity ever to make any effectual advances. Later on it was much the same, but gradually, though slowly, I came to find that there were others like myself. I made a few special friends, and at last it came to me occasionally to sleep with them and to satisfy my imperious need by mutual embraces and emissions. Before this happened, however, I was once or twice on the brink of despair and madness with repressed passion and torment. [. . .]

"As a boy I was attracted in general by boys rather older than myself; after leaving school I still fell in love, in a romantic vein, with comrades of my own standing. Now, – at the age of 37, – my ideal of love is a powerful, strongly built man, of my own age or rather younger – preferably of the working class. Though having solid sense and character, he need not be specially intellectual. If endowed in the latter way, he must not be too glib or refined. Anything effeminate in a man, or anything of the cheap intellectual style, repels me very decisively.

"I have never had to do with actual pederasty, so called. My chief desire in love is bodily nearness or contact, as to sleep naked with a naked friend;

the specially sexual, though urgent enough, seems a secondary matter. Pederasty, either active or passive, might seem in place to me with one I loved very devotedly and who also loved me to that degree; but I think not otherwise. I am an artist by temperament and choice, fond of all beautiful things, especially the male human form; of active, slight, muscular build; and sympathetic, but somewhat indecisive character, though possessing self-control.

"I cannot regard my sexual feelings as unnatural or abnormal, since they have disclosed themselves so perfectly naturally and spontaneously within me. All that I have read in books or heard spoken about the ordinary sexual love, its intensity and passion, lifelong devotion, love at first sight, etc., seems to me to be easily matched by my own experiences in the homosexual form; and, with regard to the morality of this complex subject, my feeling is that it is the same as should prevail in love between man and woman, namely: that no bodily satisfaction should be sought at the cost of another person's distress or degradation. I am sure that this kind of love is, notwithstanding the physical difficulties that attend it, as deeply stirring and ennobling as the other kind, if not more so; and I think that for a perfect relationship the actual sex gratifications (whatever they may be) probably hold a less important place in this love than in the other." [. . .]

The actively inverted woman [has] one fairly essential character: a more or less distinct trace of masculinity. She may not be, and frequently is not, what would be called a "mannish" woman, for the latter may imitate men on grounds of taste and habit unconnected with sexual perversion, while in the inverted woman the masculine traits are part of an organic instinct which she by no means always wishes to accentuate. The inverted woman's masculine element may, in the least degree, consist only in the fact that she makes advances to the woman to whom she is attracted and treats all men in a cool, direct manner, which may not exclude comradeship, but which excludes every sexual relationship. [. . .]

History XXXVII. – Miss M., the daughter of English parents (both musicians), who were both of what is described as "intense" temperament, and there is a neurotic element in the family, though no history of insanity or alcoholism, and she is herself free from nervous disease. At birth she was very small. In a portrait taken at the age of 4 the nose, mouth, and ears are abnormally large, and she wears a little boy's hat. As a child she did not care for dolls or for pretty clothes, and often wondered why other children found so much pleasure in them. "As far back as my memory goes," she writes, "I cannot recall a time when I was not different from other children. I felt bored when other little girls came to play with me, though I was never rough or boisterous in my sports." Sewing was distasteful to her. Still she cared little more for the pastimes of boys, and found her favorite amusement in reading, especially adventures and fairy-tales. She was always quiet, timid, and self-conscious. The instinct first made its appearance in the latter part of her eighth or the first part of her ninth year. She was strongly attracted by the face of a teacher who used to appear at a side-window on the second floor of the school-building and ring a bell to summon the children to their classes. The teacher's face seemed very beautiful, but sad, and she thought about her continually, though not coming in personal contact with her. A year later this teacher was married and left the school, and the impression gradually faded away. "There was no consciousness of sex at this time," she wrote; "no knowledge of sexual matters or practices, and the feelings evoked were feelings of pity and compassion and tenderness for a person who seemed to be very sad and very much depressed. It is this quality or combination of qualities which has always made the appeal in my own case." [. . .] Later on, at the age of 16, she loved another friend very dearly and devoted herself to her care. There was a tinge of masculinity among the women of this friend's family, but it is not clear if she can be termed inverted. This was the happiest period of Miss M.'s life. Upon the death of this friend, who had long been in ill health, eight years afterward, she resolved never to let her heart go out to anyone again.

Specific physical gratification plays no part in these relationships. The physical sexual feelings began to assert themselves at puberty, but not in association with her ideal emotions. "In that connection," she writes, "I would have considered such things a sacrilege. I fought them and in a measure successfully. The practice of self-indulgence which might have become a daily habit was only occasional. Her image evoked at such times drove away such feelings, for which I felt a repugnance, much preferring the romantic ideal feelings. In this way, quite unconscious of the fact that I was at all different from any other person, I contrived to train myself to suppress or at least to dominate my physical sensations when they arose. That is the reason why friendship and love have always seemed such holy and beautiful things to me. I have never connected the two sets of feelings. I think I am as strongly sexed as anyone, but I am able to hold a friend in my arms and experience deep comfort and peace without having even a hint of physical sexual feeling. Sexual expression may be quite necessary at certain times and right under certain conditions, but I am convinced that free expression of affection along sentimental channels will do much to minimize the necessity for it along specifically sexual channels." [. . .]

She is a musician, and herself attributes her nature in part to artistic temperament. She is of good intelligence, and shows remarkable talent for various branches of physical science. She is about 5 feet 4 inches in height, and her features are rather large. The pelvic measurements are normal, and the external sexual organs are fairly normal in most respects, though somewhat small. At a period ten years subsequent to the date of this history, further examination, under anesthetics, by a gynecologist, showed no traces of ovary on one side. The general conformation of the body is feminine. But with arms, palms up, extended in front of her with inner sides of hands touching, she cannot bring the inner sides of fore-arms together, as nearly every woman can, showing that the feminine angle of arm is lost. [. . .]

Miss M. can see nothing wrong in her feelings; and, until, at the age of 28, she came across the translation of Krafft-Ebing's book, she had no idea "that feelings like mine were 'under the ban of society' as he puts it, or were considered unnatural and depraved." She would like to help to bring light on the subject and to lift the shadow from other lives. "I em-phatically protest," she says, "against the uselessness and the inhumanity of attempts to 'cure' inverts. I am quite sure they have perfect right to live in freedom and happiness as long as they live unselfish lives. One must bear in mind that it is the soul that needs to be satisfied, and not merely the senses." [. . .]

The analysis of these cases leads directly up to a question of the first importance: What is sexual inversion? Is it, as many would have us be-lieve, an abominably acquired vice, to be stamped out by the prison? or is it, as a few assert, a beneficial variety of human emotion which should be tolerated or even fostered? Is it a diseased condition which qualifies its subject for the lunatic asylum? or is it a natural monstrosity, a human "sport," the manifestations of which must be regulated when they be-come antisocial? There is probably an element of truth in more than one of these views. [. . .]

The Freudians – alike of the orthodox and the heterodox schools – have sometimes contributed, unintentionally or not, to revive the now antiquated conception of homosexuality as an acquired phenomenon, and that by insisting that its mechanism is a purely psychic though uncon-scious process which may be readjusted to the normal order by psycho-analytic methods. Freud first put forth a comprehensive statement of his view of homosexuality in the original and pregnant little book, *Drei Abhandlungen zur Sexualtheorie* (1905). [. . .] When inverts are psycho-analytically studied, Freud believes, it is found that in early childhood they go through a phase of intense but brief fixation on a woman, usually the mother, or perhaps sister. Then, an internal censure inhibiting this incestuous impulse, they overcome it by identifying themselves with women and taking refuge in Narcissism, the self becoming the sexual object. Fi-nally they look for youthful males resembling themselves, whom they love as their mothers loved them. Their pursuit of men is thus determined by their flight from women. [. . .] Freud himself, however, is careful to state that this process only represents one type of stunted sexual activity, and that the problem of inversion is complex and diversified. [. . .]

Sexual inversion, therefore, remains a congenital anomaly, to be classed with other congenital abnormalities which have psychic concomitants. At the very least such congenital abnormality usually exists as a predisposition to inversion. It is probable that many persons go through the world with a congenital predisposition to inversion which always remains latent and unroused; in others the instinct is so strong that it forces its own way in spite of all obstacles; in others, again, the predisposition is weaker, and a powerful exciting cause plays the predominant part. [. . .]

The question of the treatment of homosexuality must be approached with discrimination, caution, and skepticism. Nowadays we can have but little sympathy with those who, at all costs, are prepared to "cure" the invert. There is no sound method of cure in radical cases. [. . .]

There can be no doubt that in slight and superficial cases of homosexuality, suggestion may really exert an influence. We can scarcely expect it to exert such influence when the homosexual tendency is deeply rooted in an organic inborn temperament.

Sex and Character (1903)
Otto Weininger

[I]t is not generally recognised that sexual inverts may be otherwise perfectly healthy, and with regard to other social matters quite normal. When they have been asked if they would have wished matters to be different with them in this respect, almost invariably they answer in the negative.

It is due to the erroneous conceptions that I have mentioned that homo-sexuality has not been considered in relation with other facts. Let those who regard sexual inversion as pathological, as a hideous anomaly of mental development (the view accepted by the populace), or believe it to be an acquired vice, the result of an execrable seduction, remember that there exist all transitional stages reaching from the most masculine male to the most effeminate male and so on to the sexual invert, the false and true hermaphrodite; and then, on the other side, successively through the sapphist to the virago and so on until the most feminine virgin is reached. [. . .]

Moreover, and this not only supports my view but can be explained only by it, there are no inverts who are completely sexually inverted. In all of them there is from the beginning an inclination to both sexes; they are, in fact, bisexual. It may be that later on they may actively encourage a slight leaning towards one sex or the other, and so become practically unisexual either in the normal or in the inverted sense, or surrounding influence may bring about this result for them. But in such processes the fundamental bisexuality is never obliterated and may at any time give evidence of its suppressed presence.

Reference has often been made, and in recent years has increasingly been made, to the relation between homo-sexuality and the presence of bisexual rudiments in the embryonic stages of animals and plants. What is new in my view is that according to it, homo-sexuality cannot be regarded as an atavism or as due to arrested embryonic development, or incomplete differentiation of sex; it cannot be regarded as an anomaly of rare occurrence interpolating itself in customary complete separation of the sexes. Homo-sexuality is merely the sexual condition of these intermediate sexual forms that stretch from one ideally sexual condition to the other sexual condition. In my view all actual organisms have both homo-sexuality and hetero-sexuality.

That the rudiment of homo-sexuality, in however weak a form, exists in every human being, corresponding to the greater or smaller development of the characters of the opposite sex, is proved conclusively from the fact that in the adolescent stage, while there is still a considerable amount of undifferentiated sexuality, and before the internal secretions have exerted their stimulating force, passionate attachments with a sensual side are the rule amongst boys as well as amongst girls.

A person who retains from that age onwards a marked tendency to 'friendship' with a person of his own sex must have a strong taint of the other sex in him. Those, however, are still more obviously intermediate sexual forms, who, after association with both sexes, fail to have aroused in them the normal passion for the opposite sex, but still endeavour to maintain confidential, devoted affection with those of their own sex.

There is no friendship between men that has not an element of sexuality in it, however little accentuated it may be in the nature of the friendship, and however painful the idea of the sexual element would be. But it is enough to remember that there can be no friendship unless there has been some attraction to draw the men together. Much of the affection, protection, and nepotism between men is due to the presence of unsuspected sexual compatibility. [. . .]

Inverted sexual attraction, then, is no exception to my law of sexual attraction, but is merely a special case of it. An individual who is half-man, half-woman, requires as sexual complement a being similarly equipped with a share of both sexes in order to fulfil the requirements of the law. This explains the fact that sexual inverts usually associate only with persons of similar character, and rarely admit to intimacy those who are normal. The sexual attraction is mutual, and this explains why sexual inverts so readily recognise each other. This being so, the normal element in human society has very little idea of the extent to which homo-sexuality is practised [sic], and when a case becomes public property, every normal young profligate thinks that he has a right to condemn such 'atrocities.' So recently as the year 1900 a professor of psychiatry in a German university urged that those who practiced homo-sexuality should be castrated.

The therapeutical remedies which have been used to combat homo-sexuality, in cases where such treatment has been attempted, are certainly less radical than the advice of the professor; but they serve to show only how little the nature of homo-sexuality was understood. The method used at present is hypnotism, and this can rest only on the theory that homo-sexuality is an acquired character. By suggesting the idea of the female form and of normal congress, it is sought to accustom those under treatment to normal relations. But the acknowledged results are very few. [. . .]

In spite of all the present-day clamour about the existence of different rights for different individualities, there is only one law that governs mankind, just as there is only one logic and not several logics. It is in opposition to that law, as well as to the theory of punishment according to which the legal offence, not the moral offence, is punished, th[at] we forbid the homo-sexualist to carry on his practices whilst we allow the hetero-sexualist full play, so long as both avoid open scandal. Speaking from the standpoint of a purer state of humanity and of a criminal law untainted by the pedagogic idea of punishment as a deterrent, the only logical and rational method of treatment for sexual inverts would be to allow them to seek and obtain what they require where they can, that is to say, amongst other inverts.

'Homosexuality' (1921)
C. Stanford Read

By the majority of individuals, and even of medical men, homosexuality has simply been regarded as a disgusting perversion which merits no further interest or investigation. This disgust and revolt of the moral sense is explained by Freud as due in great part to the existence in the ordinary mind of a homosexual component of the sex instinct, which finds indirect expression in condemnation of homosexuality in others, in the same way as the repression of the sexual instinct in the prude expresses itself in the condemnation of normal sexual activity. This idea seems to be confirmed by the great tolerance of homosexuality we see in some countries where sex repression is also much lessened. We must bear in mind that man is not the purely reasoning individual he deludes himself he is, and it is certain that he is largely swayed by unconscious emotional forces which warp his thought and action. The student of science is by no means an exception, and we should do well when new theories come before us, and controversy is apt to be rife, to dip thoughtfully into the chapters on the psychology of belief. [. . .]

The present discussion on those psycho-analytical principles which specially come within the domain of mental medicine is evidently a sign that an increased interest is being taken in Freudian doctrines; and those of us who cannot help but feel that some glimmer of human understanding of the essential meaning of psycho-pathological reactions has come about through their study trust that it will stimulate many to be dissatisfied with the old, more or less purely descriptive psychiatry, to look upon mental disease from a more psycho-biological point of view, and see if some, at any rate, of the psycho-analytical theories are not confirmed.

Homosexuality has been found through psycho-analysis to be the main factor in the causation of certain mental abnormalities, which for the first time have been thereby placed on a more satisfactory and scientific pathological basis. In its conscious form, where it is often carried into overt action, it is far more prevalent than is usually supposed, and I have a vivid recollection of how my eyes were opened in this respect when I started psycho-therapeutic practice, and had personal confidences given me of an intimate nature. At the outset one must differentiate the passive homosexual from the active type. The former is somehow developmentally abnormal and often has distinct feminine characteristics, while the latter, who is greatly in the majority, has acquired in the process of mental growth the condition which may therefore be regarded as a form of neurosis. [. . .]

Freud holds that the sexual instinct is not a new motive force which appears in a fully-fledged form at puberty, but a synthetic product formed from the combination of a number of partial impulses which were present throughout childhood. During the first period the child's sexuality is believed to centre in certain areas of its own body, and later it is its whole unified body which is the source of its regard. This latter is the stage of narcissism or self-love, which plays a very important part in the development of our later life. The tendency at this period, then, is for the child to take itself as its object-love, and to love itself in others who have similar genitals. Subsequently the love passes over to the opposite sex. Be it understood, however, that the sexuality here is only infantile in type, and must not be taken in an adult sense. The psycho-analytic theory is that homosexuals are only more strongly fixed than other people in this narcissistic stage, genital organs like their own being always the essential element for their love. [. . .]

The homosexual component has therefore its germ in all mankind, and finds its outlet normally in a sublimated form in friendships and companionship. Those, however, who are too prematurely fixed or arrested in the evolution of their sexual dispositions are exposed to the danger that a flood of libido which finds no outlet may, through failure in social life, strong outbursts of sexual needs, or through disappointment in the opposite sex, regress to this earlier form of gratification.

'Studies in Feminine Inversion' (1923)
F. W. Stella Browne

[W]hat I have to put before you to-day are only very fragmentary data, and suggestions on a peculiarly obscure subject. They have, however, this validity; that they are the result of close and careful observation, conducted so far as I am consciously aware, without any prejudice, though they would probably be much more illuminating had they been recorded by an observer who was herself entirely or predominantly homo-sexual. [. . .]

The cases which I will now briefly describe to you are all well-known to me; they are all innate, and very pronounced and deeply rooted – not episodical. At the same time – though I am sure there has been, in some of them at least, no definite and conscious physical expression – they are absolutely distinguishable from affectionate friendship. They have all of them, in varying degrees, the element of passion. [. . .]

Case A. Member of a small family, but numerous cousins on both sides. The mother's family is nervous, with a decided streak of eccentricity of varying kinds, and some of its members much above the average in intelligence. The father's family much more commonplace, but robust. She is of small-boned frame, but childish rather than feminine in appearance, certainly not in the least masculine. (Throughout this paper, I use the adjectives masculine and feminine, only as referring to the pitch of the voice and outline of the body as modified by greater or less development of the secondary sexual characteristics; *not* to mental or emotional qualities.) Quick and deft in movement, neat and rather dainty about her appearance. Much manual dexterity and indefatigable motor energy and activity. Never happy unless occupied in some fairly strenuous way, though she will not, of course, admit this, and derives great moral satisfaction from the consciousness of her own industry. Unfortunately many of these activities seem, to an unprejudiced observer, to be petty and irrelevant, and a subconscious way of finding a vent for frustrated emotional force.

A good organizer, but with too little sense of proportion or breadth of view for a position of supreme control. Strong sense of responsibility and capacity for detail. Methodical. Mentally very positive, emotionally shy, reserved, proud and extremely jealous. Some musical talent and keen appreciation of music. Can be extremely generous and devoted where her affections are stirred. Is virtually an agnostic, without having at all thought out the implications of that position. An absorbing devotion to a woman relative; a devotion of an unmistakably, though I believe unconsciously, passionate kind completely dominates her life; it has almost all the manifestations of a really great love; intense interest, idealisation, unremitting care, joy in service, and unsparing sacrifice of her own comfort and of the happiness of third parties. Has had some very long and close friendships with other women, into which the same element entered, to a much slighter extent; notably one with a cousin, a smart, shrewd, worldly little person, who did not lose by it. She is fond of children and has a gift for dealing with them, and very sympathetic and tender to animals. [. . .] Has an instinctive horror of men [. . .] and also quite a definite antagonism to them socially. [. . .] [A]s a rule, criticises even the most harmless or upright and well-intentioned men, unsparingly.

I consider that this woman's unconsciousness of the real nature of the mainspring of her life, and the deprivation of the liberating and illuminating effect of some definite and direct physical sex-expression, have had, and still have, a disastrous effect on a nature which has much inherent force and many fine qualities. Her whole outlook on life is subtly distorted and dislocated, moral values are confused and a false standard of values is set up. The hardening and narrowing effect of her way of life is shown in a tremendous array of prejudices on every conceivable topic: caste-prejudices, race-prejudices, down to prejudices founded on the slightest eccentricity of dress or unconventionality of behaviour; also in an immense intolerance of normal passion, even in its most legally sanctioned and certificated forms. As to unlegalised sex-relationships, they are of course considered the very depth alike of depravity and of crass folly. And all the while, her life revolves round a deep and ardent sex-passion, frustrated and exasperated through functional repression, but entirely justified in her own opinion as pure family affection and duty! Though the orthodox and conventional point of view she takes on sex-questions, generally, would logically condemn just *that* form of sex-passion, as peculiarly reprehensible.

Case B. Also the member of a small family though with numerous cousins, paternal and maternal. Family of marked ability – on both sides, especially the mother's. Of very graceful and attractive appearance, entirely feminine, beautiful eyes and classical features, but indifferent to her looks and abnormally lacking in vanity, self-confidence and animal vitality generally, though no one is quicker to appreciate any beauty or charm in other women. I think she is a pronounced psychic invert whose intuitive faculties and bent towards mysticism have never been cultivated. Keen instinctive delicacy and emotional depth, enthusiastically devoted and generous to friends; much personal pride (though no vanity) and reserve. Too amenable to group suggestions and the influences of tradition. Artistic and musical tastes and a faculty for literary criticism which has lain fallow for want of systematic exercise. Rather fond of animals and devoted to children, especially to young relatives and the children of friends. Has done good philanthropic work for children, but is essentially interested in *persons* rather than in theories, or institutions. Is a devout Christian and I think gets much support and comfort from her religious beliefs. A distaste, even positive disgust, for the physical side of sex, which is tending more and more to manifest itself in conventional moral attitudes and judgments. General social attitude towards men less definitely *hostile* than that of Case A. but absolutely aloof. Devoted to women friends and relatives, yet has had no full and satisfying expression of this devotion. This inhibition of a whole infinitely important set of feelings and activities has weakened her naturally very sound judgment, and also had a bad permanent effect on her bodily health.

Case C. The sixth, and second youngest of a large and very able and vigorous family. Tall, and of the typical Diana build; long limbs, broad shoulders, slight bust, narrow hips. Decidedly athletic. Voice agreeable in tone and quite deep, can whistle well. Extremely energetic and capable, any amount of initiative and enthusiasm, never afraid to assume responsibility; very dominating and managing, something of a tyrant in practise, though an extreme democrat in theory, and most intolerant towards different emotional temperaments. Scientific training; interested in politics and public affairs; logical and rationalistic bent of mind. Emotionally reserved, intense, jealous and monopolistic. Will always try to express all emotion in terms of reason and moral theory, and is thus capable of much mental dishonesty, while making a fetich of complete and meticulous truthfulness. An agnostic and quite militant and aggressive. The episode in her life which I observed fairly closely was a long and intimate friendship with a young girl – ten years her junior – of a very attractive and vivacious type, who roused the interest of both men and women keenly. Cleverness and physical charm in girls appealed to her, but she instinctively resented any independent divergent views or standard of values. For years she practically formed this girl's mental life, and they spent their holidays together. When the girl fell in love with and impulsively married a very masculine and brilliantly gifted man, who has since won great distinction in his special profession, C's agony of rage and desolation was terrible and pitiable, though here again, she tried to hide the real nature of her loss by misgivings as to the young man's 'type of ethical theory' – her own phrase! I cannot for a moment believe that she was ignorant of her own sex-nature. [...] She is a very strong personality, and a born ruler. Her attitude towards men was one of perfectly unembarrassed and equal comradeship.

Case D. Is on a less evolved plane than the three aforementioned, being conspicuously lacking in refinement of feeling and, to some extent, of habit. But is well above the average in vigor, energy and efficiency. A decided turn for carpentry, mechanics and executive manual work. Not tall; slim, boyish figure; very hard, strong muscles, singularly impassive face, with big magnetic eyes. The dominating tendency is very strong here, and is not held in leash by a high standard of either delicacy or principle. Is professionally associated with children and young girls, and shows her innate homosexual tendency by excess of petting and spoiling, and intense jealousy of any other person's contact with, or interest in the children. I do not definitely know if there is any physical expression of her feelings, beyond the kissing and embracing which is normal, and even, in some cases conventional, between women or between women and children. But the *emotional tone* is quite unmistakable; will rave for hours over some 'lovely kiddy', and injure the children's own best interests, as well as the working of the establishment, by unreasonable and unfair indulgence. [...]

Case E [...] Two assistant mistresses at a girls' boarding-school were completely inseparable. They took all their walks together, and spent all their time when they were 'off duty' and not walking, in one another's rooms – they occupied adjoining rooms.

One of them was a slim, graceful, restless, neurotic girl with a distinct consumptive tendency; quick in perception and easy in manner, but it seemed to me then, and it seems still, decidedly superficial and shallow. The other partner was an invert of the most pronounced physical type. Her tall, stiff, rather heavily muscular figure, her voice, and her chubby, fresh-coloured face, which was curiously eighteenth-century in outline and expression, were so like those of a very young and very well-groomed youth, that all the staff of the school nick-named her 'Boy', though I do not believe any of them clearly realised what this epithet – and her intimacy with a woman of such strongly contrasted type, implied. 'Boy' was extremely self-conscious and curiously inarticulate; she had musical tastes and played rather well – not in the colourless and amateurish style of the musical hack. I think music was an outlet for her. She was also fond of taking long walks, and of driving, and of dogs and horses. Beyond these matters I don't think I ever heard her express an opinion about anything. [...] There was some idealism in the relationship, at least on 'Boy's' side. [...]

I know of two modern English novels in which the subject is touched on with a good deal of subtlety, and in both cases in association with school life. *Regiment of Women* by Clemence Dane – a brilliant piece of psychology, and a novel by an Australian writer, cruder and shorter, but unmistakably powerful, *The Getting of Wisdom* by Henry Handel Richardson. [. . .]

I would draw your attention to one quality which two of my cases have in common, and to a very marked degree: the maternal instinct. Two of the most intensely maternal women I know are cases A and B, both congenital inverts. [. . .]

This problem of feminine inversion is very pressing and immediate, taking into consideration the fact that in the near future, for at least a generation, the circumstances of women's lives and work will tend, even more than at present, to favour the frigid, and next to the frigid, the inverted types. Even at present, the social and affectional side of the invert's nature has often fuller opportunity of satisfaction than the heterosexual woman's, but often at the cost of adequate and definite physical expression. And how decisive for vigor, sanity and serenity of body and mind, for efficiency, for happiness, for the mastery of life, and the understanding of one's fellow-creatures – just this definite physical expression is! The lack of it, 'normal' and 'abnormal', is at the root of most of what is most trivial and unsatisfactory in women's intellectual output, as well as of their besetting vice of cruelty. How can anyone be finely or greatly creative, if one's supreme moral law is a negation! Not to *live*, not to *do*, not even to try to understand. [. . .]

I think it is perhaps not wholly uncalled-for, to underline very strongly my opinion that the homo-sexual impulse *is not in any way superior to* the normal; it has a fully equal right to existence and expression, it is no worse, no lower; *but no better.*

By all means let the invert – let all of us – have as many and varied 'channels of sublimation' as possible; and far more than are at present available. But, to be honest, are we not too much inclined to make 'sublimation' an excuse for refusing to tackle fundamentals? The tragedy of the repressed invert is apt to be not only one of emotional frustration, but complete dislocation of mental values.

Moreover, our present social arrangements, founded as they are on the repression and degradation of the normal erotic impulse, artificially stimulate inversion and have thus forfeited all right to condemn it. There is a huge, persistent, indirect pressure on women of strong passions and fine brains to find an emotional outlet with other women. A woman who is unwilling to accept either marriage – under present laws – or prostitution, and at the same time refuses to limit her sexual life to auto-erotic manifestations, will find she has to struggle against the whole social order for what is nevertheless her most precious personal right. The right sort of woman faces the struggle and counts the cost well worth while; but it is impossible to avoid seeing that she risks the most painful experiences, and spends an incalculable amount of time and energy on things that should be matters of course. Under these conditions, some women who *are not innately or predominantly homosexual* do form more or less explicitly erotic relations with other women, yet these are makeshifts and essentially substitutes, which cannot replace the vital contact, mental and bodily, with congenial men.

'A Case of Homosexual Inversion' (1927)
T.A. Ross

The patient, who was seen first in January 1925, was a man of wide culture and possessed a great energy in his business, in which he had been highly successful. He was 47 years of age, and of spare habit of body; on physical examination he presented no features indicative of any departure from the masculine norm. His dress was on the whole careless; there was nothing neat about it. His physical health was good. [. . .]

So far as he could remember he had never taken any interest in women, save that he liked to talk to them in company. As a young man in the twenties he used to walk home from church in the company of two young ladies, and he enjoyed doing so. After some time their mother withdrew one of them, and he was thrown against his will exclusively into the company of the other. This was a source of worry to him. He felt that he was being regarded as an eligible suitor, and he soon gave up the friendship. Further exposures to the talk of marriage made him shun society; thereafter he occupied much of his spare time in philanthropic work. It did not strike him then that this betokened anything anomalous in his sexual attitude. He was simply not interested in the question, and disliked being pursued. His new interest lay chiefly among boys in the east of London. Among them he made many friends; certainly no trace of conscious sex feeling was aroused by them, not at any rate for many years.

A few years before he came under observation, however, he began to realize that there were some constituents among his ideas concerning the male sex besides those of normal philanthropy. He began to imagine a man taking him and 'doing something to him', what he did not clearly visualize, though he recognized it as something wrong. He became full of doubts and fears. In July 1922, two-and-a-half years before he came under observation, he had a miserable undefined interest in the 'behind' of a golf caddie, which made him so ashamed that he could not bear to mention it even to the doctor whom he was consulting at that time, on account of his doubts and fears. Later that summer he was bathing with a boy, who stood in front of him on the shore, naked, presenting his back and complaining of a pain in a vein just above the knee. The patient touched the vein and had a curious sensation of thrill. [. . .]

Some months later he was having a holiday with two brothers, whose ages were seventeen and twelve-and-a-half. He was reading to them. The younger was sprawling on the sofa, face down. He looked up from his book to see the elder gazing fondly, as he thought, at the arch of the buttocks of the younger. He dismissed the idea as crude. A little later the interest in the 'behind' increased, and about this time he dreamt of a valley between two hills. During a subsequent attack of influenza he realized without the aid of a psychoanalyst that this must mean the buttocks. It would not, however, be justifiable to cite this as an interpretation arrived at by the patient independently, without the help of the Freudian school. As was said at the beginning, the patient was a man of wide culture. When he came under observation he had considerable knowledge of psychoanalytic doctrine though he professed to have read little of the literature. Of late years general literature has been so full of this doctrine that no widely read person can hope to be in a state of virginity regarding it. All that is meant is that no analyst was in attendance.

About 18 months before he came under care he had a frank dream of a boy's buttocks, which recalled the memory of a homosexual act which he had witnessed at preparatory school. He recollected that at the sight of this occurrence no emotional feelings had been aroused, neither desire nor disgust. He had merely looked at it and forgotten about it. But after this dream he had no peace. Formerly he had been fond of boys and men; he used to go to his boys' clubs and boys' schools and been 'hail-fellow-well-met' with everybody. He had also got on splendidly with men. Now in his association with them there was nothing but degradation. Whenever he saw a boy, especially if he were wearing a short jacket, he could not avoid visualizing his bare buttocks. [. . .]

As time went on the anal interest with all its psychical disturbances began to assume the major role. The patient could not see a boy without the appearance of the anal image: he could not think of a woman without the word 'shit' coming to his mind. His misery became so intense that he could see no escape save by suicide, and in September 1924 he made an abortive attempt in this direction. After this he became more and more unfit to do his work, and on January 20, 1925, he came under care.

The patient then regarded himself as a pure homosexual of passive or feminine type. He regarded the matter as chemicophysical, hereditary, inevitable. What he desired was that somehow he should learn to reconcile himself to his terrible misfortune.

This view of the essentially hereditary physical nature of homosexuality is that which probably receives the greatest amount of support from sympathetic opinion. Uninformed opinion is usually that the homosexual is a vicious person who has chosen to do the wrong thing, when he could equally have chosen the right. The earlier scientific observers naturally reacted strongly against this view. They found among homosexuals many high-minded persons, valued public servants, courageous soldiers. [. . .] Havelock Ellis considers that the hereditary element is the most important factor in the genesis of the condition, though he points out that there is often some event which determines its manifestation. As might be expected, Freud and his school have explored the possibility of the condition being one which is acquired, and their conclusions differ considerably from those of the earlier writers. They may be summed up thus: passive homosexuality in the male and active homosexuality in the female are probably physically determined; active in the male and passive in the female stand a good chance of having been acquired. There is really not much difference between these views except that more emphasis is laid by one school on heredity and by the other on environment. For practical physicians the special doctrines insisted on by each are almost equally important. As the sequel of the case we are now studying shows, we shall be wise if we neither sit down with folded hands and say that nothing can be done, nor make promises that we can transform a sufferer from this anomaly into a perfectly normal heterosexual person. Anyone who has departed so far from ordinary development will probably always be a person for whom marriage should be regarded with considerable misgiving.

As stated above, the patient had regarded himself as a pure feminine, and no attempt was made at an early stage of his treatment to alter this belief. He had what seemed to him good reasons for his view. All his ideas of exalted love were associated with males; his dreams were of males, and of very masculine males indeed. [. . .] The patient also felt at home with women if he was in the company of several of them; he felt that he liked gossiping with them, 'with his sisters', as he put it. He had felt also that when he went to business meetings with men he would have liked to go gaily dressed and be the lady of the party. There was also the fact that in his phantasies of sexual union the penis of the partner was important; his own was not. Against this view there was the anal interest, which was certainly not an interest in his own anus, but in that of someone else, male or female. This seemed to negative pure passive homosexuality. [. . .]

Seeing [. . .] that what he was aiming at was reconciliation with his position, nothing at first was attempted beyond trying to achieve that end.

He was assured that one need not loathe oneself for that for which one is not responsible, that it could not at one and the same time be true that he was suffering from a physical anomaly and that he was blameworthy. [. . .]

When the patient came under care in January he had very little recollection of the facts of his boyhood, but he always maintained that he was sure that he had had no interest in girls. Soon after the week-end [he visited a preparatory school] [. . .] he remembered much to his astonishment that he had been in the habit of going to young people's parties, and that he had danced with girls with pleasure, even that he had sat out with several. The pleasure which he remembered now was not sexual in the sense in which he understood that term in later years. It was not accompanied by any physical manifestation. Indeed no such manifestation had happened to him at all till a few years before he came under observation, when his homosexual consciousness was aroused. A few days later there came a memory which seemed to decide not only that he was not an obligatory homosexual but also to explain why he had been diverted so completely from the heterosexual path. Somewhere about the age of 15 he was sitting on a lawn with his legs wide apart, and a girl came and sat between them close up with her back to him. His recollection is that he had no genital sensation whatever, but he suddenly found himself undoing her dress which fastened up the back; when he had got some way with this her mother appeared and was furious. He was staying at the house. She forbade her daughter to see him alone again, and next day he went home. He never returned to that house; he met the girl subsequently but disliked her.

It was pointed out to the patient that he had been interrupted while committing a heterosexual act, even though this aspect of it had not been in consciousness; it was also suggested that the whole affair had been rapidly subjected to repression, that his already delayed sex-consciousness was by the unpleasantness of the sequel to the act delayed still further, and that when it did develop it was inhibited from doing so in a heterosexual form. After the event an interview with a lady alone was avoided; the risk of unpleasantness was too great. The patient was told also that it is probably true that bisexuality is hardly abnormal in boys about the time of puberty, though the form of choice is the active masculine; the boy who acts the passive part often does so under duress. The patient, therefore, when puberty came to him at 40 years of age adopted the active role; he was male, homosexual, because up to the time of the awakening of sex-consciousness homosexuality had given him no trouble, while heterosexuality had. These considerations appeared to the patient to be reasonable. Thereafter his normal heterosexuality unfolded itself with inconvenient rapidity.

Report on the Psychological Treatment of Crime (1939)
W. Norwood East and W.H. de B. Hubert

108. *Etiology.* – Homosexuality has been practised [*sic*] apparently in all civilizations, and amongst all people of whom there is record. On the other hand, the social attitude that has been adopted towards it has varied very considerably. At times it has been approved of and encouraged, at others it has been severely condemned and punished. It is usual to speak of homosexuality as either acquired or of constitutional origin; such a classification is useful for descriptive purposes but a clearer view of the condition is obtained if it is regarded as the result of a combination of various causative factors. [. . .]

109. It was not found that a differentiation into the active or more masculine and the passive or more feminine type of homosexual was satisfactory or corresponded to the findings. A homosexual, usually, has as his sexual object a man or a boy of a type confined within quite narrow limits. Sometimes an effeminate type of homosexual had as his object a masculine type, but it was equally common to find that he was interested either in a man like himself or in a boy. [. . .]

As in the case of other sexual perverts, a constitutional factor showing itself as a tendency towards sexual perversion in general is often present. A specific inherited tendency towards homosexuality is also operative, in all probability, in certain cases; it is suggested strongly by the fact that in some families homosexuality recurs in circumstances in which propinquity or common environmental factors were unlikely to be the causative factor. It appeared fairly certain that a factor related to the physical type concerned also might play an important part. Attractive and good-looking boys and young men would be predisposed to the development of homosexuality because they would be more likely to be the focus of attention of homosexuals. Seduction in early youth or childhood was the commonest single environmental factor found in the series investigated. This sequence of events appeared most important in the causation of homosexuality, and is probably far more likely an explanation than one which depends upon the assumption that there is commonly some specific glandular influence acting in a feminine direction in these cases. [. . .]

117. *Treatment.* – It may be useful to mention first the indications that lead one to believe that any particular case will benefit by treatment. A suggestion that homosexuality has been encouraged considerably by the environment either directly (for example, by residence in a badly man-

aged school, etc.) or indirectly by events which have turned the individual away from women (early disappointment in love, venereal disease, etc.); the presence of modifiable personality or neurotic factors which have discouraged heterosexual interests; the presence of attitudes of mind or behaviour reactions which have sustained homosexual interest although not specifically related to it are all of good prognostic significance. [. . .]

Contra-indications to treatment are repeated homosexual practices over many years; friendly but quite uninterested relations with women (repulsion, dislike or disgust, often hide, neurotically, a positive sexual attraction); the presence of other well developed sexual perversions; and the presence of anti-social trends, whether in association with the practice of homosexuality or showing themselves in other ways. [. . .]

CASE XLVIII. – Aged 30 years. Gross indecency. Three years' penal servitude. *Family History.* – His father died when the prisoner was thirteen years of age. His mother and only sister were alive. There was no history of mental disease in the family. *Personal History.* – He was educated at a public school and at one of the older universities and obtained an arts degree. He then obtained a post as schoolmaster and three years later was ordained. He organised a Boys Brigade and also a Wolf Cub pack. At the age of sixteen years he was introduced to masturbation and had practised [*sic*] it since alone and with boys, many of whom he whipped and paid some to allow him to do so; actual sodomy was denied. Three years before the present offence he was sentenced to three terms of imprisonment for indecently assaulting boys. He was reconvicted for a similar offence and sentenced to twelve months' imprisonment three months after his release from prison on the first charges. He was not attracted to women and avoided them. He was carefully observed during his first sentence and was advised to place himself in the hands of a psychotherapist. He did not do so, however, until about to be arrested on the present charge. He then exploited a psychotherapist to report to the court that psychological treatment and not imprisonment was the only appropriate method of dealing with him. *Condition on Examination and Subsequent History.* – He was in good general health, and presented no evidence of disease of the central nervous system or of psychoneurosis. He was intelligent, plausible and insincere. He argued that his religious practices excused his moral offences; he projected his own faults on to others, and although he refused to co-operate in psychological treatment and had no desire to be divorced from his perversion, asserted that imprisonment would make him worse and that he should be released forthwith. He had no remorse for his conduct and no concern for his victims. He thought of no one's welfare and rights but his own. He endeavoured to avoid work in prison on the grounds that he had insufficient time for Biblical study. He protested that he was not a criminal. He illustrated the importance of early seduction. He showed, besides homosexuality, marked sadistic interests. In addition, a personality disorder was present which will, in all probability in later years show itself as a paranoiac reaction; it was enough to lead to a diagnosis of abnormality of the personality without taking into account his abnormal sexual practises [*sic*]. It was evident that psychotherapy was out of the question in a man showing this combination of features.

CASE L. – Aged 19 7/12ths years. Indecent assault on a male aged sixteen years. Six months' imprisonment. *Family History*. – He was taken care of by foster parents and no family history was available for consideration. *Personal History*. – This youth when two years old developed infantile paralysis, and was taken charge of by a charitable organisation. He left school in the highest class and was interested in games. He became a canvasser and was industrious, temperate and honest. At the age of eleven years he was seduced by a married man, and immoral practices took place between them over a rather prolonged period. He had been previously convicted of an indecent assault on a boy and had been placed on probation. He had interfered with other boys, taking them to a cinema for the purpose. He had had no heterosexual experience and was not attracted to girls. On the other hand, he was not averse to them. *Condition on Examination and Subsequent History*. – His general health was good, his physical development normal. He was alert, intelligent and possessed initiative and the capacity for sustained effort. He showed no undue emotional reaction, and no indication of any psychosis or psychoneurotic disorder. He was not essentially anti-social and was anxious to reinstate himself in the outer world. He was an excellent example of the importance of environmental influence. Early seduction, institutional life over many years away from feminine influence, a physical deformity which limited social and general activity, all strongly encouraged the development of homosexuality. Treatment in this case depended first of all in giving him an adequate understanding of the reasons for his difficulty and the directions in which he should strive to modify his environment in the future and, secondly, in developing, by therapeutic technique, his personality capabilities, by removing emotional obstructions. Provided his environment is not too heavily weighted against him, he should be successful.

Part III

Transsexuality and Bisexuality

Introduction

Jay Prosser and Merl Storr

For the transsexual, this period from the end of the nineteenth century to the middle of the twentieth was crucially formative. Although the transsexual would not be formally diagnosed until the late 1940s or early 1950s with the work of D.O. Cauldwell, MD, and endocrinologist Harry Benjamin in the USA, the work of earlier European sexologists on sexual inversion provided the necessary framework for these later diagnoses and, therefore, the conceptual vehicle (the transition we might say) essential for transsexual transitions themselves. First, the transgendered paradigm of sexual inversion – the profound degree to which sexual inversion was a cross-gendered category – set up the conditions under which transgender could emerge as identity. Second, the medicalization of transgender in sexual inversion, precisely its pathologization, enabled the recognition of unliveable cross-gender identity as a condition that could be diagnosed – and thus, as this logic would be extended, made liveable with a medical 'cure'. Third but by no means least pivotal, the sexological case history, the encounter between sexologists and inverts, enabled transgendered subjects to speak their stories and give transgendered shape to their lives. The transgendered self-identification reiterated poignantly here in these female case histories – 'I feel like a man' – would become *the* symptom of transsexuality, the sex changing of the body utterly dependent on such narrativization.

In addition to revealing the transgendering of the sexologists' frameworks then – exemplified here by Magnus Hirschfeld's (1868–1935) theory of sexual intermediaries where *all* subjects are to varying degrees transgendered and/or bisexual (there is a provocative intersection of our two axes here which reflects Hirschfeld's sense that sex in any absolute oppositional sense is impossible) – these excerpts demonstrate above all the profound transgendering of inverts in their self-conception. The commitment to cross-gender living and/or identification given in (or read through) their own words cannot be explained without recognizing transgender as identity, one irreducible to homosexuality. How could we explain, for instance, that Richard von Krafft-Ebing's Count Sandor was so convincing as a man that his wife thought she might become pregnant by him, without recourse to a transsexual trajectory: the narrative of the subject who (with that identifying tautology) already feels so differently sexed that she or he will do everything to configure the body to live out that sex? The clear-cut split between body and identity, between sex and gender, that characterizes transsexuality runs across the narratives of Havelock Ellis's D., of Krafft-Ebing's Sandor. There is a sense of wrong embodiment, of subjects caught in wrong bodies: indeed, of the body itself as something that can go wrong, 'a mysterious accident', sex as something that can slip and fail identity.

This period was also a crucial one for subjects who love more than one gender, although for different reasons. For sexology, the term 'bisexuality' continued to designate human (or animal) sexual dimorphism, and/or the co-existence of characteristics of both sexes in human (or animal) bodies. For example, male nipples and female facial hair were both regarded as evidence of the original bisexuality of the human species. This original bisexuality was regarded as ontogenetic (in the sexually undifferentiated and hence bisexual human foetus) and phylogenetic (in the sexually undifferentiated and hence bisexual primeval ancestors of the human species). Thus, for sexology during this period, 'bisexuality' was a sexual state rather than a subject position: subjects who love more than one gender were not 'bisexual', but were rather scattered through the various categories and grades of inversion, often (though not always) as 'psychical hermaphrodites' or as subjects whose inversion was 'acquired'. As such they were generally regarded by sexologists as more 'homosexual' than 'heterosexual', although a minority of subjects, such as Krafft-Ebing's eloquent Mrs M., did articulate a sense of themselves as equipoised between the two.

The change for conceptions of bisexuality came with the intervention into sexological fields of psychoanalysis, the influence of which increased through the 1920s and 1930s. By reimagining the relationship between the physical, the psychical and the sexual through the conception of a dynamic unconscious operating at the borders of mind and body, Freud and his followers reconfigured the term 'bisexual' to mean not just (physical) male and female, but (psychosexual) masculine and feminine. The meaning of these terms within psychoanalysis is vertiginously unstable, but their location in the psychosexual rather than the simply physical realm meant that 'bisexuality' began to signify something more like the sense of sexual preference or orientation in which the term is most commonly used today. Nevertheless, the term's psychoanalytic usage continued to bear the stamp of its sexological heritage in two ways: first, by continuing to mark bisexuality as an *original* predisposition (albeit now a psychical rather than a physical one, in the undifferentiated and hence bisexual sexuality of children); and second, by consequently marking bisexuality as *not* being a subject position – it is an infantile disposition *from which* subject positions will develop (along masculine/feminine and/ or heterosexual/homosexual axes).

This, then, is the meeting ground between transsexuality and bisexuality during this period: both are positioned, whether physically and psychically or both, as the site of a certain failure (as for Krafft-Ebing) or impossibility (as for Hirschfeld) of sexual differentiation, as intermediate or (physically or psychically) 'hermaphrodite' formations of a species whose sexual dimorphism appears to be both stable – essential, natural, dictated by the laws of evolution – and evanescent – the vanishing point for the very division between the sexes. For this reason, transsexuality and bisexuality are not only central to the stuff of sexology; we might say that no category in sexology takes its meaning without at least implicit reference to their layered and broad significance. Moreover, the conceptual centrality of transsexuality and bisexuality, sexology's inscription of them as sites in which the binaries of sex, gender and sexuality are both formed and dissolved, in which other identities both find and transcend their differences, continues to play out in important ways in cultural fantasies about transsexuality and bisexuality even today.

Psychopathia Sexualis [1886] (12th edn, 1903)
Richard von Krafft-Ebing

A Homosexual feeling as an acquired manifestation in both sexes

Antipathic sexuality

I Degree: Simple Reversal of Sexual Feeling This degree is attained when a person exercises an aphrodisiac effect over another person of the same sex who reciprocates the sexual feeling. Character and instinct, however, still correspond with the sex of the individual presenting the reversal of sexual feeling. He feels himself in the active *role*; he recognizes his impulse toward his own sex as an aberration and finally seeks aid.

With episodical improvement of the neurosis, at first even normal sexual feelings may reappear and assert themselves. [. . .]

CASE 126. Ilma S., aged twenty-nine; single, merchant's daughter; of a family having bad nervous taint. Father was a drinker and died by suicide, as also did the patient's brother and sister. A sister suffered with convulsive hysteria. Mother's father shot himself while insane. Mother was sickly, and paralyzed after apoplexy. The patient never had any severe illness. She was bright, enthusiastic and dreamy. Menses at the age of eighteen without difficulty; but thereafter they were very irregular. At fourteen, chlorosis and catalepsy from fright. Later, hysteria and an attack of hysterical insanity. At eighteen, relations with a young man which were not platonic. This man's love was passionately returned. From statements of the patient, it seemed that she was very sensual, and after separation from her lover practiced masturbation. After this she led a romantic life. In order to earn a living, she put on male clothing, and became a tutor; but she gave up her place because her mistress, not knowing her sex, fell in love with her and courted her. Then she became a railway employee. In the company of her companions, in order to conceal her sex, she was compelled to visit brothels with them, and hear the most vulgar stories. This became so distasteful to her that she gave up her place, resumed the garments of a female, and again sought to earn her living. She was arrested for theft, and on account of severe hystero-epilepsy was sent to the hospital. There inclination and impulse toward the same sex were discovered. The patient became troublesome on account of passionate love for female nurses and patients.

Her sexual inversion was considered congenital. With regard to this, the patient made some interesting statements: –

"I am judged incorrectly, if it is thought that I feel myself a man toward the female sex. In my whole thought and feeling I am much more a woman. Did I not love my cousin as only a woman can love a man?

"The change of my feelings originated in this, that in Pesth, dressed as a man, I had an opportunity to observe my cousin. I saw that I was wholly deceived in him. That gave me terrible heart-pangs. I knew that I could never love another man; that I belonged to those who love but once. Of similar effect was the fact that, in the society of my companions at the railway, I was compelled to hear the most offensive language and visit the most disreputable houses. As a result of the insight into men's motives, gained in this way, I took an unconquerable dislike to them. However, since I am of a very passionate nature and need to have some loving person on whom to depend, and to whom I can wholly surrender myself, I felt myself more and more powerfully drawn towards intelligent women and girls who were in sympathy with me."

The antipathic sexual instinct of this patient, which was clearly acquired, expressed itself in a stormy and decidedly sensual way, and was further augmented by masturbation; because constant control in hospitals made sexual satisfaction with the same sex impossible. Character and occupation remained feminine. There were no manifestations of viraginity. According to information lately received by the author, this patient, after two years of treatment in an asylum, was entirely freed of her neurosis and sexual inversion, and discharged cured. [. . .]

II Degree: Eviration and Defemination If, in cases of antipathic sexual instinct thus developed, no restoration occurs, then deep and lasting transformations of the *psychical* personality may occur. The process completing itself in this way may be briefly designated *eviration* (*defemination* in woman). The patient undergoes a deep change of character, particularly in his feelings and inclinations, which thus become those of a female. After this, he also feels himself to be a woman during the sexual act, has desire only for passive sexual indulgence, and, under certain circumstances, sinks to the level of a prostitute. In this condition of deep and more lasting psycho-sexual transformation, the individual is like unto the (congenital) urning of high grade. The possibility of a restoration of the previous mental and sexual personality seems in such a case precluded. [. . .]

III Degree: Stage of Transition to Change of Sex Delusion A further degree of development is represented by those cases in which *physical* sensation is also transformed in the sense of a *transmutatio sexus* [change of sex]. [. . .]

IV Degree: Metamorphosis Sexualis Paranoica [Delusion of Sexual Change] A final possible stage in this disease-process is the delusion of a transformation of sex. It arises from sexual neurasthenia that has developed into *neurasthenia universalis*, resulting in a mental disease, – *paranoia*. [. . .]

B   Homosexual feeling as an abnormal congenital manifestation

The essential feature of this strange manifestation of the sexual life is the want of sexual sensibility for the opposite sex, even to the extent of horror, while sexual inclination and impulse toward the same sex are present. At the same time, the genitals are normally developed, the sexual glands perform their functions properly, and the sexual type is completely differentiated.

Feeling, thought, will, and the whole character, in cases of complete development of the anomaly, correspond with the peculiar sexual instinct, but not with the sex which the individual represents anatomically and physiologically. This abnormal mode of feeling may not infrequently be recognized in the manner, dress and calling of the individuals, who may go so far as to yield to an impulse to put on the distinctive clothing corresponding with the sexual *role* in which they feel themselves to be.

Anthropologically and clinically, this abnormal manifestation presents various degrees of development: –

1   Traces of heterosexual, with predominating homosexual, instinct (psycho-sexual hermaphroditism).
2   There exists inclination only towards the same sex (homosexuality).
3   The entire mental existence is altered to correspond with the abnormal sexual instinct (effemination and viraginity).
4   The form of the body approaches that which corresponds to the abnormal sexual instinct. However actual transitions to hermaphrodites never occur, but, on the contrary, completely differentiated genitals; so that, just as in all pathological perversions of the sexual life, the cause must be sought in the brain (*androgyny* and *gynandry*). [. . .]

1   *Psychical hermaphroditism.* The characteristic mark of this degree of inversion of the sexual instinct is that, by the side of the pronounced sexual instinct and desire for the same sex, a desire toward the opposite sex is present; but the latter is much weaker and is manifested episodically only, while homosexuality is primary, and, in time and intensity, forms the most striking feature of the *vita sexualis* [sexual life].

The hetero-sexual instinct may be but rudimentary, manifesting itself simply in unconscious (dream) life; or (episodically, at least) it may be powerfully exhibited.

The sexual instinct toward the opposite sex may be strengthened by the exercise of will and self-control; by moral treatment, and possibly by hypnotic suggestion; by improvement of the constitution and the removal of *neuroses* (neurasthenia); but especially by abstinence from masturbation.

However, there is always the danger that homosexual feelings, in that they are the most powerful, may become permanent, and lead to enduring and exclusive antipathic sexual instinct. This is especially to be feared as a result of the influences of masturbation (just as in acquired inversion of the sexual instinct) and its neurasthenia and consequent exacerbations; and, further, it is to be found as a consequence of unfavourable experiences in sexual intercourse with persons of the opposite sex (defective feeling of pleasure in coitus, failure in coitus on account of weakness of erection and premature ejaculation, infection).

On the other hand, it is possible that aesthetic and ethical sympathy with persons of the opposite sex may favour the development of hetero-sexual desires. Thus it happens that the individual, according to the pre-dominance of favourable or unfavourable influences, experiences now hetero-sexual, now homosexual, feeling.

It seems to me probable that such hermaphrodites from constitutional taint are rather numerous. Since they attract very little attention socially, and since such secrets of married life are only exceptionally brought to the knowledge of the physician, it is at once apparent why this interesting and practically important transitional group to the group of absolute in-verted sexuality has thus far escaped scientific investigation.

Many cases of *frigiditas uxoris* and *mariti* [frigidity of wives and hus-bands] may possibly depend upon this anomaly. Sexual intercourse with the opposite sex is, in itself, possible. At any rate, in cases of this degree, no horror *sexus alterius* [of the other sex] exists. Here is a fertile field for the application of medical and moral therapeutics. [. . .]

The differential diagnosis from acquired antipathic sexual instinct may present difficulties; for, in such cases, so long as the vestiges of a normal sexual instinct are not absolutely lost, the actual symptoms are the same. [. . .]

In the first degree, the sexual satisfaction of homosexual impulses con-sists in passive and mutual onanism and coitus *inter femora* [between the thighs]. [. . .]

CASE 154. *Psychical hermaphroditism.* Mrs. M., forty-four years of age, claimed to be an instance illustrating the fact that in *one* and *the same* human being, be it man or woman, the inverted as well as the nor-mal direction of sexual life may be combined. The father of this lady was very musical, generally possessed considerable talents for art, was a great admirer of the gentle sex, and himself of exceptional beauty. He died, after repeated apoplectic attacks, with dementia in an asylum. His brother was neuropsychopathic, as a child was afflicted with somnambulism, and later on with *hyperasthesia sexualis* [excessive sexual desire]. Although married and father of several married sons, he fell desperately in love with Mrs. M., then eighteen years of age, and attempted to abduct her.

Her grandfather (on the paternal side) was very eccentric and a well known artist, who had originally studied theology, but for love of the dramatic art became a mimic and singer. He was given to excess in *Baccho et Venere* [heavy drinking and sexual excess], extravagant and fond of splendour, and died at the age of forty-nine from *apoplexia cerebri* [apoplexy]. Her moth-er's father and her mother both died of pulmonary *phthisis* [tuberculosis].

She had eleven brothers and sisters, but only six survived. Two brothers died at the age of sixteen and twenty of tuberculosis. One brother was suffering from laryngeal *phthisis* [tuberculosis]. Four living sisters the same as Mrs. M. were physically like unto the father, very nervous and shy. Two younger sisters were married and in good health, and both had healthy children. Another one, a maiden, was suffering from nervous affection.

Mrs. M. was the mother of four children, mostly delicate and neuropathic.

There was nothing of importance in the history of the patient's childhood. She learned easily, had gifts for poetry and aesthetics, was somewhat affected, loved to read novels and sentimental literature, was of neuropathic constitution and very sensitive to changes of temperature, the slightest draught would make her flesh creep. It is noteworthy, however, that one day when ten years of age she fancied her mother did not love her. There upon she put a lot of sulphur matches in her coffee and drank it to make herself ill, in order to draw her mother's love to herself.

Puberty began without difficulty at the age of eleven, with subsequent regular menses. Even previous to that period sexual life had awakened, which ever since was very potent. The first sentiments and emotions lay in the homosexual direction. She conceived a passionate, though platonic, affection for a young lady, wrote love-songs and sonnets to her, and never was happier than when, upon one occasion, she could admire the "charms of her beloved" in the bath, or when she could gaze upon the neck, shoulders and breasts of this lady whilst dressing. She could resist only with difficulty the desire to touch these physical charms. When a girl she was deeply in love with Raphael's and Guido Reni's Madonnas. She was irresistibly impelled to follow pretty girls and ladies by the hour, no matter how inclement the weather might be, admiring their air of refinement and watching for a chance of showing them a favour, giving them flowers, etc. The patient asserted that up to her nineteenth year she had not the slightest knowledge of the difference of sexes, since she had been brought up by a prudish old maiden aunt like a nun in a cloister. In consequence of this complete ignorance she fell a victim to a man who loved her passionately and insidiously betrayed her virtue. She became the wife of this man, gave birth to a child, and led an "eccentrically" sexual life with him, but felt satisfied with the sexual intercourse. A few years later she became a widow. Since then her affections again turned to persons of her own sex, the principal reason for which was, the patient averred, the fear of the results of sexual intercourse with man.

At the age of twenty-seven she entered upon a second marriage with a man of infirm constitution. It was not a love match. Thrice she became a mother, and fulfilled all the conditions of maternity; but her health ran down, and during the latter years her dislike for coitus ever increased, chiefly on account of her husband's infirmity, although her desire for sexual gratification remained strong.

Three years after her second husband's death, she discovered that her daughter by the first husband, now nine years of age, was given to masturbation and going into decline. She read an article about this vice in the *Enyclopaedia*, and now could not resist the temptation to try it herself and thus became an onanist. She hesitated to give a full account of this period of her life. She stated, however, that she became sexually so excited that she had to send her two daughters away from home in order to preserve them from something "terrible." The two boys could remain at home.

Patient became neurasthenic because of *ex masturbatione* [masturbation] (spinal irritation, pressure in the head, languor, mental constipation, etc.) at times even dysthymic, with worrying *tedium vitae* [boredom].

Her sexual inclinations turned now to woman, now to man. But she controlled herself, suffered much from her abstinence, especially since she resorted to masturbation on account of her neurasthenic afflictions only at the last instance. At the age of forty-four – still having regular periods – the patient suffered from a violent passion for a young man with whom, on account of her avocation, she was bound to be in constant contact.

The patient did not offer anything extraordinary in her external appearance; though graceful of build, she was slight of form. Pelvis decidedly feminine, but arms and legs large, and of pronounced masculine type. Female boots did not really fit her, and she had quite crippled and malformed her feet by forcing them into narrow shoes. Genitals quite normal. Excepting a *descensus uteri* [dropped womb] with hypertrophy of the vaginal portion, no changes were noticeable. She still claimed to be essentially homosexual, and declared that her inclination and desire for the opposite sex were only periodical and grossly sensual. Although she had strong sexual feelings towards the man aforementioned, yet her greatest and noblest pleasure she found in pressing a kiss upon the soft cheek of a sweet girl. This pleasure she enjoyed often, for she was the "favorite aunt" among these "dear creatures," to whom she rendered the services of the "cavalier" unstintingly, always feeling herself in the *role* of the man. [. . .]

CASE 166. *Gynandry*. History: On 4th November, 1889, the father-in-law of a certain Countess V, complained that the latter had swindled him out of 800F., under the pretense of requiring a bond as secretary of a stock company. It was ascertained that Sandor had entered into matrimonial contracts and escaped from the nuptials in the spring of 1889; and, more than this, that this ostensible Count Sandor was no man at all, but a woman in male attire – Sarolta (Charlotte), Countess V.

S. was arrested, and, on account of deception and forgery of public documents, brought to examination. At the first hearing S. confessed that she was born on the 6th Sept., 1866; that she was a female, Catholic, single, and worked as an authoress under the name of Count Sandor V.

From the autobiography of this man-woman I have gleaned the following remarkable facts that have been independently confirmed: –

S. came of an ancient, noble and highly respected family of Hungary, in which there had been eccentricity and family peculiarities. A sister of the maternal grandmother was hysterical, a somnambulist, and lay seventeen years in bed, on account of fancied paralysis. A second great-aunt spent seven years in bed, on account of a fancied fatal illness, and at the same time gave balls. A third had the whim that a certain table in her *salon* was bewitched. When anything was laid on this table, she would become greatly excited and cry, "Bewitched! bewitched!" and run with the object into a room which she called the "Black Chamber," and the key of which she never let out of her hands. After the death of this lady, there were found in this chamber a number of shawls, ornaments, bank-notes, etc. A fourth great-aunt during two years did not leave her room, and neither washed herself nor combed her hair; then she again made her appearance. All these ladies were, nonetheless, intellectual, finely educated and amiable.

S.'s mother was nervous, and could not bear the light of the moon.

She inherited many of the peculiarities of her father's family. One line in the family gave itself up almost entirely to spiritualism. Two blood relations on the father's side shot themselves. The majority of her male relatives were unusually talented; the females were decidedly narrow-minded and domesticated. S.'s father had a high position, which, however, on account of his eccentricity and extravagance (he wasted over a million and a half), he lost.

Among many foolish things that her father encouraged in her was the fact that he brought her up as a boy, called her Sandor, allowed her to ride, drive and hunt, admiring her muscular energy.

On the other hand, this foolish father allowed his second son to go about in female attire, and had him brought up as a girl. This farce ceased when the son was sent to a higher school at the age of fifteen.

Sarolta–Sandor remained under her father's influence till her twelfth year, and then came under the care of her eccentric maternal grandmother in Dresden, by whom, when the masculine play became too obvious, she was placed in an institute and made to wear female attire.

At thirteen she had a love-relation with an English girl, to whom she represented herself as a boy, and ran away with her.

Sarolta returned to her mother, who, however, could do nothing, and was compelled to allow her daughter to again become Sandor, wear male clothes, and, at least once a year, to fall in love with persons of her own sex.

At the same time S. received a careful education and made long journeys with her father, of course always as a young gentleman. She early became independent and visited *cafés*, even those of doubtful character, and, indeed, boasted one day that in a brothel she had had a girl sitting on each knee. S. was often intoxicated, had a passion for masculine sports and was a very skillful fencer.

She felt herself drawn particularly towards actresses, or others of similar position, and, if possible, towards those who were not very young. She asserted that she never had any inclination for a young man, and that she had felt, from year to year, an increasing dislike for young men.

"I preferred to go into the society of ladies with ugly, ill-favoured men, so that none of them could put me in the shade. If I noticed that any of the men awakened the sympathies of the ladies, I felt jealous. I preferred ladies who were bright and pretty; I could not endure them if they were fat or much inclined towards men. It delighted me if the passion of a lady was disclosed under a poetic veil. All immodesty in a woman was disgusting to me. I had an indescribable aversion for female attire – indeed, for everything feminine, but only in as far as it concerned me; for, on the other hand, I was all enthusiasm for the beautiful sex."

During the last ten years S. had lived almost constantly away from her relatives, in the guise of a man. She had had many *liaisons* with ladies, travelled much, spent much, and made debts.

At the same time she carried on literary work, and was a valued collaborator on two noted journals of the capital.

Her passion for ladies was very changeable; constancy in love was entirely wanting.

Only once did such a *liaison* last three years. It was years before that S., at Castle G., made the acquaintance of Emma E., who was ten years older than herself. She fell in love with her, made a marriage contract with her, and they lived together as man and wife for three years at the capital.

A new love, which proved fatal to S., caused her to sever her matrimonial relations with E. The latter would not have it so. Only with the greatest sacrifice was S. able to purchase her freedom from E., who still looked upon herself as a divorced wife, and regarded herself as the Countess V.! That S. also had the power to excite passion in other women was shown by the fact that when she (before her marriage with E.) had grown tired of a Miss D., after having spent thousands of guldens on her, she was threatened with shooting by D. if she should become untrue.

It was in the summer of 1887, while at a watering-place, that S. made the acquaintance of a distinguished official's family. Immediately she fell in love with the daughter, Marie, and her love was returned.

Her mother and cousin tried in vain to break up this affair. During the winter the lovers corresponded zealously. In April, 1888, Count S. paid her a visit, and in May, 1889, attained her wish; in that Marie – who, in the meantime, had given up a position as teacher – became her bride in the presence of a friend of her lover, the ceremony being performed in an arbor, by a pseudo-priest, in Hungary. S., with her friend, forged the marriage certificate. The pair lived happily, and, without the interference of the father-in-law, this false marriage, probably, would have lasted much longer. It is remarkable that, during the comparatively long existence of the relation, S. was able to deceive completely the family of her bride with regard to her true sex.

S. was a passionate smoker, and in all respects her tastes and passions were masculine. Her letters and even legal documents reached her under the address of 'Count S.' She often spoke of having to drill. From remarks of the father-in-law it seems that S. (and she afterwards confessed it) knew how to imitate a scrotum with handkerchiefs or gloves stuffed in the trousers. The father-in-law also, on one occasion, noticed something like an erected member on his future son-in-law (probably a priapus). She also occasionally remarked that she was obliged to wear a suspensory bandage while riding. The fact is, S. wore a bandage around the body possibly as a means of retaining a priapus.

Though S. often had herself *pro forma* shaved [like a man], the servants in the hotel where she lived were convinced that she was a woman, because the chambermaids found traces of menstrual blood on her linen (which S. explained, however, as haemorrhoidal); and, on the occasion of a bath which S. was accustomed to take, they claimed to have convinced themselves of her real sex by looking through the key-hole.

The family of Marie make it seem probable that she for a long time was deceived with regard to the true sex of her false bridegroom. The following passage in a letter from Marie to S., 26th August, 1889, speaks in favour of the incredible simplicity and innocence of this unfortunate girl: "I don't like children any more, but if I had a little Bezerl or Patscherl by my Sandi – ah, what happiness, Sandi mine!"

A large number of manuscripts allow conclusions to be drawn concerning S.'s mental individuality. The chirography possesses the character of firmness and certainty. The characters are genuinely masculine. The same peculiarities repeat themselves everywhere in their contents – wild, unbridled passion; hatred and resistance to all that opposes the heart thirsting for love; poetical love, which is not marred by one ignoble blot, enthusiasm for the beautiful and noble; appreciation of science and the arts.

Her writings betray a wonderfully wide range of reading in classics of all languages, in citations from poets and prose writers of all lands. The evidence of those qualified to judge literary work shows that S.'s poetical and literary ability was by no means small. The letters and writings concerning the relations with Marie are psychologically worthy of notice.

S. speaks of the happiness there was for her when by M.'s side, and expresses boundless longing to see her beloved, if only for a moment. After such a happiness she could have but one wish – to exchange her cell for the grave. The bitterest thing was the knowledge that now Marie, too, hated her. Hot tears, enough to drown herself in, she had shed over her lost happiness. Whole quires of paper are given up to the apotheosis of this love, and reminiscences of the time of the first love and acquaintance.

S. complained of her heart, that would allow no reason to direct it; she expressed emotions which were such as only could be felt – not simulated. Then, again, there were outbreaks of most silly passion, with the declaration that she would not live without Marie. "Thy dear, sweet voice; the voice whose tone perchance would raise me from the dead; that has been for me like the warm breath of Paradise! Thy presence alone were enough to alleviate my mental and moral anguish. It was a magnetic stream; it was a peculiar power your being exercised over mine, which I cannot quite define; and, therefore, I cling to that ever-true definition: I love you because I love you. In the night of sorrow I had but one star – the star of Marie's love. That star has lost its light; now there remains but its shimmer – the sweet, sad memory which even lights with its soft ray the deepening night of death, a ray of hope."

This writing ends with the apostrophe: "Gentlemen, you learned in the law, psychologists and pathologists, do me justice; Love led me to take the step I took; all my deeds were conditioned by it. God put it in my heart.

"If he created me so, and not otherwise, am I then guilty; or is it the eternal, incomprehensible way of fate? I relied on God, that one day my emancipation would come; for my thought was only love itself, which is the foundation, the guiding principle, of His teaching and His kingdom.

"O God, Thou All-pitying, Almighty One! Thou sees my distress; Thou knowest how I suffer. Incline Thyself to me; extend Thy helping hand to me, deserted by all the world. Only God is just. How beautifully does Victor Hugo describe this in his 'Légendes du Siècle'! How sad do Mendelssohn's words sound to me: 'Nightly in dreams I see thee'!"

Though S. knew that none of her writings reached her lover, she did not grow tired of writing of her pain and delight in love, in page after page of deification of Marie. And to induce one more pure flood of tears, on one still, clear summer evening, when the lake was aglow with the setting sun like molten gold, and the bells of St. Anna and Maria-Wörth, blending in harmonious melancholy, gave tidings of rest and peace, she wrote: "For that poor soul, for this poor heart that beats for thee till the last breath."

Personal examination: The first meeting which the experts had with S. was in a measure, a time of embarrassment to both sides; for them, because perhaps S.'s somewhat dazzling and forced masculine carriage impressed them; for her, because she thought she was to be marked with the stigma of moral insanity. She had a pleasant and intelligent face, which, in spite of a certain delicacy of features and diminutiveness of all its parts, gave a decidedly masculine impression, had it not been for the absence of a moustache. It was even difficult for the experts to realize that they were concerned with a woman, despite the fact of female attire and constant association; while, on the other hand, intercourse with the man Sandor was much more free, natural, and apparently correct. The accused also felt this. She immediately became more open, more communicative, more free, as soon as she was treated like a man.

In spite of her inclination for the female sex, which had been present from her earliest years, she asserted that in her thirteenth year she first felt a trace of sexual feeling, which expressed itself in kisses, embraces, and caresses, with sexual pleasure, and this on the occasion of her elopement with the red-haired English girl from the Dresden institute. At that time feminine forms exclusively appeared to her in dream-pictures, and ever since, in sensual dreams, she felt herself in the situation of a man, and occasionally, also, at such times, experienced ejaculation.

She knew nothing of solitary or mutual onanism. Such a thing seemed very disgusting to her, and not conducive to manliness. She had, also, never allowed herself to be touched *ad genitalia* [on the genitals] by others, because it would have revealed her great secret. The menses began at seventeen, but were always scanty and without pain. It was plain to be seen that S. had a horror of speaking of menstruation; that it was a thing repugnant to her masculine consciousness and feeling. She recognized the abnormality of her sexual inclinations, but had no desire to have them changed, since in this perverse feeling she felt both well and happy. The idea of sexual intercourse with men disgusted her, and she also thought it would be impossible.

Her modesty was so great that she would prefer to sleep among men rather than among women. Thus, when it was necessary for her to answer the calls of nature or to change her linen, it was necessary for her to ask her companion in the cell to turn her face to the window, that she might not see her.

When occasionally S. came in contact with this companion – a woman from the lower walks of life – she experienced a sexual excitement that made her blush. Indeed, without being asked, S. related that she was overcome with actual fear when, in her cell, she was compelled to force herself into the unusual female attire. Her only comfort was that she was at least allowed to keep a shirt. Remarkable, and what also speaks for the significance of olfactory sensations in her *vita sexualis* [sexual life], is her statement that, on the occasions of Marie's absence, she had sought those places on which Marie's head was accustomed to repose, and smelled them, in order to experience the delight of inhaling the odour of her hair. Among women, those who were beautiful, or voluptuous, or quite young, did not particularly interest her. The physical charms of women she made subordinate. As by magnetic attraction, she felt herself drawn to those between twenty-four and thirty. She found her sexual satisfaction exclusively *cor-*

pore feminae [in the body of a woman] (never in her own person), in the form of manustupration of the beloved woman, or cunnilingus. Occasionally she availed herself of a stocking stuffed with oakum as a priapus. These admissions were made only unwillingly by S., and with apparent shame; just as in her writings immodesty or cynicism are never found.

She was religious, had a lively interest in all that is noble and beautiful – men excepted – and was very sensitive to the opinion others entertained of her morality.

She deeply regretted that in her passion she made Marie unhappy, and regarded her sexual feelings as perverse, and such a love of one woman for another, among normal individuals, as morally reprehensible. She had great literary talent and an extraordinary memory. Her only weakness was her great frivolity and her incapability to manage money and property reasonably. But she was conscious of this weakness, and did not care to talk about it.

She was 153 centimetres tall, of delicate build, thin, but remarkably muscular on the breast and thighs. Her gait in female attire was awkward. Her movements were powerful, not unpleasing, though they were somewhat masculine and lacking in grace. She greeted one with a firm pressure of the hand. Her whole carriage was decided, firm and somewhat self-conscious. Her glance was intelligent; mien somewhat diffident. Feet and hands remarkably small, having remained in an infantile stage of development. Extensor surfaces of the extremities remarkably well covered with hair, while there was not the slightest trace of beard, in spite of all shaving experiments. The hips did not correspond in any way with those of a female. Waist wanting. Pelvis so slim and so little prominent, that a line drawn from the axilla to the corresponding knee was straight – not curved inward by a waist or outward by the pelvis. The skull slightly oxycephalic, and in all its measurements below the average of the female skull by at least one centimetre.

Circumference of the head 52 centimetres; occipital half circumference, 24 centimetres; line from ear to ear, over the vertex, 23 centimetres; anterior half-circumference, 28.5 centimetres; line from glabella to occiput, 30 centimetres; ear-chin line, 26.5 centimetres; long diameter, 17 centimetres; greatest lateral diameter, 13 centimetres; diameter at auditory meati, 12 centimetres; zygomatic diameter, 11.2 centimetres. Upper jaw strikingly projecting, its alveolar process projecting beyond the upper jaw about 0.5 centimetre. Position of the teeth not fully normal; right upper canine not developed. Mouth remarkably small; ears prominent; lobes not differentiated, passing over into the skin of the cheek. Hard palate, narrow and high; voice rough and deep; breasts fairly well developed, soft and without secretion. Mons veneris covered with thick, dark hair. Genitals completely feminine, without trace of hermaphroditic appearance, but at the stage of development of those of a ten-year-old girl. The labia majora touching each other almost completely; labia minora having a cock's-comb-like form, and projecting under the labia majora. Clitoris small and very sensitive. Frenulum delicate; perineum very narrow; introitus vaginae narrow; mucous membrane normal. Hymen wanting (probably congenitally); likewise the carunculae myrtiformes. Vagina so narrow that the insertion of an erect male member would be impossible; also very sensitive; certain coitus had not taken place. Uterus felt, through the rectum, to be about the size of a walnut, immovable and retroflected.

Pelvis generally narrowed (dwarf-pelvis), and of decidedly masculine type. Distance between anterior superior spines 22.5 centimetres (instead of 26.3 centimetres). Distance between the crests of the ilii, 26.5 centimetres (instead of 29.3 centimetres); between the trochanters, 27.7 centimetres (31); the external conjugate diameter, 17.2 centimetres (19 to 20); therefore, the internal conjugate, presumably, 7.7 centimetres (10.8). On account of narrowness of the pelvis, the direction of the thighs not convergent, as in a woman, but straight.

The opinion given showed that in S. there was a congenitally abnormal inversion of the sexual instinct, which, indeed, expressed itself, anthropologically, in anomalies of development of the body, depending upon great hereditary taint; further, that the criminal acts of S. had their foundation in her abnormal and irresistible sexuality.

S.'s characteristic expressions – "God put love in my heart. If He created me so, and not otherwise, am I, then, guilty; or is it the eternal, incomprehensible way of fate?" – are really justified.

The court granted pardon. The "countess in male attire," as she was called in the newspapers, returned to her home, and again gave herself out as Count Sandor. Her only distress was her lost happiness with her beloved Marie.

A married woman, in Brandon, Wisconsin, whose case is reported by Dr. Kiernan ("The Medical Standard," 1888, November and December), was more fortunate. She eloped, in 1883, with a young girl, married her, and lived with her as husband undisturbed.

An interesting "historical" example of androgyny is a case reported by *Spitzka* ("Chicago Medical Review," 20th August, 1881). The gentleman in question was Governor of New York and lived in the reign of Queen Anne. He was apparently affected with moral insanity; was terribly licentious, and, in spite of his high position, could not keep himself from going about in the streets in female attire, coquetting with all the allurements of a prostitute.

In a picture of him that has been preserved, his narrow brow, asymmetrical face, feminine features, and sensual mouth at once attract attention. It is certain that he never actually regarded himself as a woman.

huh?

Studies in the Psychology of Sex, vol. II: *Sexual Inversion* [1897] (3rd edn, 1915)
Havelock Ellis

History XXXIX. – Miss D., actively engaged in the practice of her profession, aged 40. Heredity good, nervous system sound, general health on the whole satisfactory. Development feminine but manner and movements somewhat boyish. Menstruation scanty and painless. Hips normal, nates small, sexual organs showing some approximation toward infantile type with large labia minora and probably small vagina. Tendency to development of hair on body and especially lower limbs. The narrative is given in her own words:

"Ever since I can remember anything at all I could never think of myself as a girl and I was in perpetual trouble, with this as the real reason. When I was 5 or 6 years old I began to say to myself that, whatever anyone said, if I was not a boy at any rate I was not a girl. This has been my unchanged conviction all through my life.

"When I was little, nothing ever made me doubt it, in spite of external appearance. I regarded the conformation of my body as a mysterious accident. I could not see why it should have anything to do with the matter. The things that really affected the question were my own likes and dislikes, and the fact that I was not allowed to follow them. I was to like the things which belonged to me as a girl, – frocks and toys and games which I did not like at all. I fancy I was more strongly 'boyish' than the ordinary little boy. When I could only crawl my absorbing interest was hammers and carpet-nails. Before I could walk I begged to be put on horses' backs, so that I seem to have been born with the love of tools and animals which has never left me.

"I did not play with dolls, though my little sister did. I was often reproached for not playing her games. I always chose boys' toys, – tops and guns and horses; I hated being kept indoors and was always longing to go out. By the time I was 7 it seemed to me that everything I liked was called wrong for a girl. I left off telling my elders what I did like. They confused and wearied me by their talk of boys and girls. I did not believe them and could hardly imagine that they believed themselves. By the time I was 8 or 9 I used to wonder whether they were dupes, or liars, or hypocrites, or all three. I never believed or trusted a grown person in consequence. I led my younger brothers in everything. I was not at all a happy little child and often cried and was made irritable; I was so confused by the talk about boys and girls. I was held up as an evil example to other little girls who virtuously despised me. [. . .]

"When I was about 11 my parents got more mortified at my behavior and perpetually threatened me with a boarding-school. I was told for months how it would take the nonsense out of me – 'shape me,' 'turn me into a young lady.' My going was finally announced to me as a punishment to me for being what I was. [. . .]

"Dreaming was forced upon me. I dreamed fairy-tales by night and social dreams by day. In the nightdreams, sometimes in the daydreams, I was always the prince or the pirate, rescuing beauty in distress, or killing the unworthy. I had one dream which I dreamed over and over again and enjoyed and still sometimes dream. In this I was always hunting and fighting, often in the dark; there was usually a woman or a princess, whom I admired, somewhere in the background, but I have never really seen her. Sometimes I was a stowaway on board ship or an Indian hunter or a backwoodsman making a log-cabin for my wife or rather some companion. My daythoughts were not about the women round about me, or even about the one who was so kind to me; they were almost impersonal. I went on, at any rate, from myself to what I thought the really ideal and built up a very beautiful vision of solid human friendship in which there was everything that was strong and wholesome on either side, but very little of sex. To imagine this in its fullness I had to imagine all social, family, and educational conditions vastly different from anything I had come across. From this my thoughts ran largely on social matters. In whatever direction my thoughts ran I always surveyed them from the point of view of a boy. I was trying to wait patiently till I could escape from slavery and starvation, and trying to keep the open mind I have spoken of, though I never opened a book of poetry, or a novel, or a history, but I slipped naturally back into my non-girl's attitude and read it through my own eyes. All my surface-life was a sham, and only through books, which were few, did I ever see the world naturally. A consideration of social matters led me to feel very sorry for women, whom I regarded as made by a deliberate process of manufacture into the fools I thought they were, and by the same process that I myself was being made one. I felt more and more that men were to be envied and women pitied. I lay stress on this for it started in me a deliberate interest in women as women. I began to feel protective and kindly toward women and children and to excuse women from their responsibility for calamities such as my school-career. I never imagined that men required, or would have thanked me for, any sort of sympathy. But it came about in these ways, and without the least help that I can trace, that by the time I was 19 years of age I was keenly interested in all kinds of questions: pity for downtrodden women, suffrage questions, marriage laws, questions of liberty, freedom of thought, care of the poor, views of Nature and Man and God. All these things filled my mind to the exclusion of individual men and women. As soon as I left school I made a headlong plunge into books where these things were treated; I had the answers to everything to find after a long period of enforced starvation. [. . .]

"The next period of my life which covered about six years was not less important to my development, and was a time of extreme misery to me. It found me, on leaving school, almost a child. This time between 18 and 24 should, I think, count as my proper period of puberty, which probably in most children occupies the end years of their school-life.

"It was at this time that I began to make a good many friends of my own and to become aware of psychical and sexual attractions. I had never come across any theories on the subject, but I decided that I must belong to a third sex of some kind. I used to wonder if I was like the neuter bees! I knew physical and psychical sex feeling and yet I seemed to know it quite otherwise from other men and women. I asked myself if I could endure living a woman's life, bearing children and doing my duty by them. I asked myself what hiatus there could be between my bodily structure and my feelings, and also what was the meaning of the strong physical feelings which had me in their grip without choice of my own. [Experience of physical sex sensations first began about 16 in sleep; masturbation was accidentally discovered at the age of 19, abandoned at 28, and then at 34 deliberately resumed as a method of purely physical relief.] These three things simply would not be reconciled and I said to myself that I must find a way of living in which there was as little sex of any kind as possible. There was something that I simply lacked; that I never doubted. Curiously enough, I thought that the ultimate explanation might be that there were men's minds in women's bodies, but I was more concerned in finding a way of life than in asking riddles without answers.

"I thought that one day when I had money and opportunity I would dress in men's clothes and go to another country, in order that I might be unhampered by sex considerations and conventions. I determined to live an honorable, upright, but simple life.

"I had no idea at first that homosexual attractions in women existed; afterward observations on the lower animals put the idea into my head. I made no preparation in my mind for any sexual life, though I thought it would be a dreary business repressing my body all my days.

"My relations with other women were entirely pure. My attitude toward my sexual physical feelings was one of reserve and repression, and I think the growing conviction of my radical deficiency somewhere, would have made intimate affection for anyone, with any demonstration in it, a kind of impropriety for which I had no taste.

"However, between 21 and 24 other things happened to me.

"During these few years I saw plenty of men and plenty of women. As regards the men I liked them very well, but I never thought the man would turn up with whom I should care to live. Several men were very friendly with me and three in particular used to write me letters and give me much of their confidence. I invited two of them to visit at my house. All these men talked to me with freedom and even told me about their sexual ideas and doings. One asked me to believe that he was leading a good life; the other two owned that they were not. One discussed the question of homosexuality with me; he has never married. I liked one of them a good deal, being attracted by his softness and gentleness and almost feminine voice. It was hoped that I would take to him and he very cautiously made love to me. I allowed him to kiss me a few times and wrote him a few responsive letters, wondering what I liked in him. Someone then commented on the acquaintance and said 'marriage,' and I woke up to the fact that I did not really want him at all. I think he found the friendship too insipid and was glad to be out of it. All these men were a trifle feminine in characteristics, and two played no games. I thought it odd that they should all express admiration for the very boyish qualities in me that other people disliked. A fourth man, something of the same type, told another friend that he always felt surprised at how freely he was able to talk to me, but that he never could feel that I was a woman. Two of these were brilliantly clever men; two were artists.

"At the same period, or earlier, I made a number of women friends, and of course saw more of them. I chose out some and some chose me; I think I attracted them as much as, or even more than, they attracted me. I do not quite remember if this was so, though I can say for certain that it was so at school. There were three or four bright, clever, young women whom I got to know then with whom I was great friends. We were interested in books, social theories, politics, art. Sometimes I visited them or we went on exploring expeditions to many country places or towns. They all in the end either had love affairs or married. I know that in spite of all our free conversations they never talked to me as they did to each other; we were always a little shy with each other. But I got very fond of at least four of them. I admired them and when I was tired and worried I often thought how easily, if I had been a man, I could have married and settled down with one or the other. I used to think it would be delightful to have a woman to work for and take care of. My attraction to these women was very strong, but I don't think they knew it. I seldom even kissed them, but I should often have cheerfully given them a good hugging and kissing if I had thought it a right or proper thing to do. I never wanted them to kiss me half so much as I wanted to kiss them. In these years I felt this with every woman I admired.

"Occasionally, I experienced slight erections when close to other women. I am sure that no deliberate thought of mine caused them, and as I had them at other times too, when I was not expecting them, I think it may have been accidental. What I felt with my mind and what I felt with my body always at this time seemed apart. I cannot accurately describe the interest and attraction that women then were to me. I only know I never felt anything like it for men. All my feelings of desire to do kindnesses, to give presents, to be liked and respected and all such natural small matters, referred to women, not to men, and at this time, both openly and to myself, I said quite unhesitatingly that I liked women best. It must be remembered that at this time a dislike for men was being fostered in me by those who wanted me to marry, and this must have counted for more than I now remember.

"As regards my physical sexual feelings, which were well established during these few years, I don't think I often indulged in any erotic imaginations worth estimating, but so far as I did at all, I always imagined myself as a man loving a woman. I cannot recall ever imagining the opposite, but I seldom imagined anything at all, and I suppose ultimate sex sensations know no sex.

"But as time went on and my physical and psychical feelings met, at any rate in my own mind, I became fully aware of the meaning of love and even of homosexual possibilities.

"I should probably have thought more of this side of things except that during this time I was so worried by the difficulty of living in my home under the perpetual friction of comparison with other people. My life was a sham; I was an actor never off the boards. I had to play at being a something I was not from morning till night, and I had no cessation of the long fatigue I had had at school; in addition I had sex to deal with actively and consciously.

"Looking back on these twenty-four years of my life I only look back on a round of misery. The nervous strain was enormous and so was the moral strain. Instead of a child I felt myself, whenever I desired to please anyone else, a performing monkey. My pleasures were stolen or I was snubbed for taking them. I was not taught and was called a fool. My hand was against everybody's. How it was that with my high spirits and vivid imagination I did not grow up a moral imbecile full of perverted instincts I do not know. I describe myself as a docile child, but I was full of temptations to be otherwise. There were times when I was silent before people, but if I had had a knife in my hand I could have stuck it into them. If it had been desired to make me a thoroughly perverted being I can imagine no better way than the attempt to mould me by force into a particular pattern of girl.

"Looking at my instincts in my first childhood and my mental confusion over myself, I do not believe the most sympathetic and scientific treatment would have turned me into an average girl, but I see no reason why proper physical conditions should not have induced a better physical development and that in its turn have led to tastes more approximate to those of the normal woman. That I do not even now desire to be a normal woman is not to the point.

"Instead of any such help, I suffered during the time that should have been puberty from a profound mental and physical shock which was extended over several years, and in addition I suffered from the outrage of every fine and wholesome feeling I had. These things by checking my physical development gave, I am perfectly convinced, a traumatic impetus to my general abnormality, and this was further kept up by demanding of me (at the dawn of my real sexual activity, and when still practically a child) an interest in men and marriage which I was no more capable of feeling than any ordinary boy or girl of 15. If you had taken a boy of 13 and given him all my conditions, bound him hand and foot, when you became afraid of him petted him into docility, and then placed him in the world and, while urging normal sexuality upon him on the one hand, made him disgusted with it on the other, what would have been the probable result?

"Looking back, I can only say I think the results in my own case were marvellously good, and that I was saved from worse by my own innocence and by the physical backwardness which nature, probably in mercy, bestowed upon me.

"I find it difficult also to sum up the way in which I affect other women and they me. I can only record my conviction that I do affect a large number, whether abnormally or not I don't know, but I attract them and it would be easy for some of them to become very fond of me if I gave them a chance. They are also, I am certain, more shy with me than they are with other women.

'I find it difficult also to sum up their effect on me. I only know that some women attract me and some tempt me physically, and have done ever since I was about 22 or 23. I know that psychically I have always been more interested in women than in men, but have not considered them the best companions or confidants. I feel protective towards them, never feel jealous of them, and hate having differences with them. And I feel always that I am not one of them. If there had been any period in my life when health and temptation and money and opportunity had made homosexual relations easy I cannot say how I should have resisted. I think that I have never had any such relations simply because I have in a way been safeguarded from them. For a long time I thought I must do without all actual sexual relations and acted up to that. If I had thought any relations right and possible I think I should have striven for heterosexual experiences because of the respect that I had cultivated, indeed I think always had, for the normal and natural. If I had thought it right to indulge any sort of gratification which was within my reach I think I might probably have chosen the homosexual as being perhaps more satisfying and more convenient. I always wanted love and friendship first; later I should have been glad of something to satisfy my sex hunger too, but by that time I could have done without it, or I thought so."

At a period rather later than that dealt with in this narrative, the subject of it became strongly attracted to a man who was of somewhat feminine and abnormal disposition. But on consideration she decided that it would not be wise to marry him.

Transvestites (1910)
Magnus Hirschfeld

[I]f we turn from the realm of the microscopic back to the macroscopic, from the many similar but in no way complete observations made by the cell researchers back to the considerations, as they must be concluded from facts available to everyone, then we, to make the rest simple, summarize what has preceded by separating the difference of the sexes into four clear groups that can be defined one from the other; they concern, as we see:

1   the sexual organs,
2   the other physical characteristics,
3   the sex drive,
4   the other emotional characteristics.

Accordingly, a complete womanly and "absolute" woman would be such a one who not only produces egg cells but also corresponds to the womanly type in every other respect; an "absolute" man would be such a one who forms semen cells yet also, at the same time, exhibits the manly average type in all other points. These kinds of absolute representatives of their sex are, however, first of all only abstractions, invented extremes; in reality they have not as yet been observed, but rather we have been able to prove that in every man, even if only to a small degree, there is his origin from the woman, in every woman the corresponding remains of manly origins.

However, if we ourselves assume that people existed who, to put a number on it, were 100 percent manly or possessed a likewise high womanly content, it still remains out of the question – and here too we find ourselves still in the area of simple facts of experience – that very many persons exist who, in spite of their carrying egg cells, exhibit characteristics that in general belong to the male sex, and that, on the other hand, there are people who secrete semen cells yet at the same time have observable womanly characteristics. Since in our use of language we usually describe the bearers of semen cells simply as men, the possessors of egg cells flatly as women, there are, therefore, women with manly, men with womanly characteristics, and these mixed forms are the ones that are understood under the expression "sexual intermediaries." We can order them most clearly as the sexual differences themselves, according to the four viewpoints we presented.

In the first group of the intermediaries, accordingly, belong such ones who lie in the area of the sexual organs, the hermaphrodites in a narrower sense, the so-called "pseudo-hermaphrodites," men who because of womanly split formations of the genitalia, women who because of an intensified growth of these organs, often give enough cause to be mistakenly identified regarding their sex at birth. [. . .]

The second heading of the sexual intermediaries concerns the physical characteristics outside of the sexual organs. In this case we find men with womanly mammary tissue (*gynecomastia*) and women without such (*andromastia*; also the word *A-mazon* means without breasts); women with manly hair, such as manly beard or manly pubes (*feminae barbatae, androtrichia*) and men with womanly hair type, such as womanly pubes, beardlessness, etc. Women with manly larynx and organ (*androglottia*) and men with womanly formed vocal chords and womanly voice production (*gynecoglottia*), men with womanly pelvis (*gynophysia*) and women with manly pelvis (*androphysia*). [. . .]

Under the second heading we also find men with womanly bone and muscular structure and women with manly skeleton and manly muscular systems, of manly size and figure, men with womanly, women with manly movements. [. . .]

Under the same heading we find men with the soft complexion of women, and women with the coarser skin of men; women who have to wear men's and men who have to wear women's glove and shoe sizes: in short, no matter what part of the body we were to treat, in almost every case we can always perceive manly profiles in women, womanly profiles in men.

Under the third heading of sexual intermediaries, persons divergent with regard to their sexual drive, we classify men who engage in sex with a woman as a woman, for example, having the tendency of being the succubus, who love aggressive women as well as participation in forms of masochism. [. . .]

Under the third heading, the corresponding condition for women, are ones who tend toward being the incubus, being sexually very aggressive (apart from prostitutes, whose actions naturally have other causes) as well as ones who exhibit sadistic impulses. With reference to the direction of the sex drive, in the case of men it indicates femininity when they feel attracted to women of manly appearance and character, to so-called "energetic women," sometimes even to homosexuals, also to manly clothed as well as to such ones who are considerably more mature, intellectual, and older than they themselves. On the other hand, women betray their manly mixture in a preference for the womanly kind of men, very dependent, very youthful, unusually gentle men, in general for such ones who in their traits of behavior and character correspond more to the feminine type. [. . .]

Finally, belonging also to this category of intermediaries are women who not only love womanly kind of men, but also manly kind of women (bisexuals) or also only the latter alone, or even totally in like manner as "true" men, women of the thoroughly womanly type (homosexuals). The opposite of this subdivision are men who, besides women of the manly kind, also love men of the feminine kind (bisexuals) or only these or even totally like women, more or less men who strongly express the manly type (homosexuals).

In Group Four, in which we understand the emotional particularities in indirect relation with the love life, ones to be counted as sexual intermediaries, are men whose feminine emotions and feelings are reflected in their manner of love, their direction of taste, their gestures and manners, their sensitivity, and many times in their particular way of writing, also men who more or less dress themselves as women or live totally as such; on the other side women of manly character, manly ways of thinking and writing, strong tendency toward manly passions, manly dress, naturally also such women who more or less lead the life of a man. Therefore, in this case also are our transvestites to be included. I would like to characterize this Group Four with a few sentences that I used more than ten years ago in introductory remarks in the *Yearbook for Sexual Intermediaries* (*Jahrbuch fuer sexuelle Zwischenstufen*):

> That the mental differences of the sexes contain very many exceptions is evident in history and everyday experiences. There are men with the gentle emotions of a Marie Baskiertschew, with feminine loyalty and modesty, with predominant reproductive gifts, with an almost unconquerable tendency to feminine preoccupations such as cleaning and cooking, also such ones who leave women behind in vanity, coquetry, love of gossip, and cowardice, and there are women who greatly outweigh the average man in energy and generosity, such as Christine of Sweden, in being abstract and having depth, such as Sonja Kowalewska, as many modern women in the women's movement in activity and ambition, who prefer men's games, such as gymnastics and hunting, and surpass the average man in toughness, crudeness, and rashness. There are women who are more suited to a public life; men more to a domestic life. There is not one specific characteristic of a woman that you would not also occasionally find in a man, no manly characteristic not also in a woman.

All of these other sexual characteristics can be present in very different degrees. This basically depends on one's age. Sexual characteristics appear most markedly between the ages of 20 and 50. As is known, after maturity, boys often exhibit feminine features as young men, girls boyish ones as young women. And later too, after the period of the fifth decade, matrons after change of life often assume superficial virile stigmata, while old men frequently take on many kinds of feminine features.

Above all, however, even at the prime of life itself, this mixing appears in varying degrees. It happens, to use an obvious example, that beard fluff appears on a woman's face, sometimes just a trace on the upper lip, sometimes so heavy that it needs to be shaved; indeed, it can even become a full beard in a woman's case. Of further importance is that these characteristics can appear isolated or combined. So, it often occurs, to use the same example, that a *femina barbata* ("bearded lady") possesses a full beard, yet in every other respect is thoroughly feminine. However, every combination imaginable can occur, every possible combination of manly and womanly characteristics. To account for the number of possible combinations for only the four main groups as a whole, let us imagine that the first group, the sexual parts, is "A," the second, the other physical characteristics, is "B," the third, the sex drive, is "C," the fourth, the other emotional characteristics, is "D," "m" as manly, "w" as womanly, "m+w" as mixed. We then get the following overview of the possible combinations. (The following account of the number of intermediary types was carried out by me with the aid of Prof. Dr K. F. Jordan.):

Table 1

$A_m B_m$	$C_m D_m$*	$A_w B_m$	$C_m D_m$	$A_{m+w} B_m$	$C_m D_m$
$A_m B_w$	$C_m D_m$	$A_w B_w$	$C_m D_m$	$A_{m+w} B_w$	$C_m D_m$
$A_m B_{m+w}$	$C_m D_m$	$A_w B_{m+w}$	$C_m D_m$	$A_{m+w} B_{m+w}$	$C_m D_m$
$A_m B_m$	$C_w D_m$	$A_w B_m$	$C_w D_m$	$A_{m+w} B_m$	$C_w D_m$
$A_m B_w$	$C_w D_m$	$A_w B_w$	$C_w D_m$	$A_{m+w} B_w$	$C_w D_m$
$A_m B_{m+w}$	$C_w D_m$	$A_w B_{m+w}$	$C_w D_m$	$A_{m+w} B_{m+w}$	$C_w D_m$
$A_m B_m$	$C_{m+w} D_m$	$A_w B_m$	$C_{m+w} D_m$	$A_{m+w} B_m$	$C_{m+w} D_m$
$A_m B_w$	$C_{m+w} D_m$	$A_w B_w$	$C_{m+w} D_m$	$A_{m+w} B_w$	$C_{m+w} D_m$
$A_m B_{m+w}$	$C_{m+w} D_m$	$A_w B_{m+w}$	$C_{m+w} D_m$	$A_{m+w} B_{m+w}$	$C_{m+w} D_m$

* An absolute man

The first horizontal row of table 1 contains three combinations of groups of sexual characteristics that are different in that while the secondary, tertiary, and fourth-order sexual features (B_m, C_m, D_m) agree, the primary group points to the three different possible cases A_m, A_w, and A_{m+w}.

The second and third horizontal rows of table 1 are repetitions of the first, with the difference, that the secondary sexual features are changed from B_m into B_w and B_m+_w.

In total that gives 3×3 or three squared or nine combinations.

The second and third horizontal columns of table1 are repetitions of the first column, with the difference that the tertiary sexual features are changed from Cm into Cw and Cm+w.

With that, all of table 1 contains: 3×9 or $3 \times 3 \times 3$ or three cubed or 27 combinations.

Then follow tables 2 and 3, which are different from table 1 in that the fourth-order sexual features are changed from D_m into D_w and D_m+_w, while everything else is combined as [in table 1].

Table 2

$A_m B_m$	$C_m D_w$	$A_w B_m$	$C_m D_w$	$A_m+_w B_m$	$C_m D_w$
$A_m B_w$	$C_m D_w$	$A_w B_w$	$C_m D_w$	$A_m+_w B_w$	$C_m D_w$
$A_m B_m+_w$	$C_m D_w$	$A_w B_m+_w$	$C_m D_w$	$A_m+_w B_m+_w$	$C_m D_w$
$A_m B_m$	$C_w D_w$	$A_w B_m$	$C_w D_w$	$A_m+_w B_m$	$C_w D_w$
$A_m B_w$	$C_w D_w$	$A_w B_w$	$C_w D_w$*	$A_m+_w B_w$	$C_w D_w$
$A_m B_m+_w$	$C_w D_w$	$A_w B_m+_w$	$C_w D_w$	$A_m+_w B_m+_w$	$C_w D_w$
$A_m B_m$	$C_m+_w D_w$	$A_w B_m$	$C_m+_w D_w$	$A_m+_w B_m$	$C_m+_w D_w$
$A_m B_w$	$C_m+_w D_w$	$A_w B_w$	$C_m+_w D_w$	$A_m+_w B_w$	$C_m+_w D_w$
$A_m B_m+_w$	$C_m+_w D_w$	$A_w B_m+_w$	$C_m+_w D_w$	$A_m+_w B_m+_w$	$C_m+_w D_w$

* An absolute woman

Table 3

$A_m B_m$	$C_m D_m+_w$	$A_w B_m$	$C_m D_m+_w$	$A_m+_w B_m$	$C_m D_m+_w$
$A_m B_w$	$C_m D_m+_w$	$A_w B_w$	$C_m D_m+_w$	$A_m+_w B_m$	$C_m D_m+_w$
$A_m B_m+_w$	$C_m D_m+_w$	$A_w B_m+_w$	$C_m D_m+_w$	$A_m+_w B_m+_w$	$C_m D_m+_w$
$A_m B_m$	$C_w D_m+_w$	$A_w B_m$	$C_m D_m+_w$	$A_m+_w B_m$	$C_w D_m+_w$
$A_m B_w$	$C_w D_m+_w$	$A_w B_w$	$C_w D_m+_w$	$A_m+_w B_w$	$C_w D_m+_w$
$A_m B_m+_w$	$C_w D_m+_w$	$A_w B_m+_w$	$C_w D_m+_w$	$A_m+_w B_m+_w$	$C_w D_m+_w$
$A_m B_m$	$C_m+_w D_m+_w$	$A_w B_m$	$C_m+_w D_m+_w$	$A_m+_w B_m$	$C_m+_w D_m+_w$
$A_m B_w$	$C_m+_w D_m+_w$	$A_w B_w$	$C_m+_w D_m+_w$	$A_m+_w B_w$	$C_m+_w D_m+_w$
$A_m B_m+_w$	$C_m+_w D_m+_w$	$A_w B_m+_w$	$C_m+_w D_m+_w$	$A_m+_w B_m+_w$	$C_m+_w D_m+_w$*

*Complete hermaphrodite

This gives the number of all possible combinations of the four main groups of characteristics, 3×27 or three to the fourth power or 81 combinations.

Then the groups of characteristics A, B, C, and D consist of a number of elements, individual features, therefore, that again can become evident as manly, womanly, or mixed characteristics.

Closer observation allows one – in favor of an agreement in the number – to divide each of the four groups of characteristics into four elements, although it is to be allowed that the analysis could without difficulty verify many, many more individual features.

Elements we observed were:

Group of characteristics A
(Primary sexual features)
1 Germ cell: A^1
2 Oviduct or spermatic duct: A^2
3 Sexual protuberance: A^3
4 Sexual groove: A^4

Group of characteristics B
(Secondary sexual features)
1 Hair: B^1
2 Larynx: B^2
3 Chest: B^3
4 Pelvis: B^4

Group of characteristics C
(Tertiary sexual features)
1 Orientation: C^1
2 Approach: C^2
3 Disposition: C^3
4 Manner of activity: C^4

Group of characteristics D
(Fourth-order sexual features)
1 Emotional life: D^1
2 Manner of thought: D^2
3 Occupation: D^3
4 Clothing: D^4

Each one of these 4×4 or 16 characteristics can, then, as stated, again, be of a manly, womanly, or mixed nature (m, w, and m+w), so that since all 16 characteristics are present somehow in each individual, there is a much greater possibility of combinations than in our previous account, where we did not reduce the groups of characteristics into their constituents but rather looked upon them as units.

As an example, let us take the first of such combinations: $A^1_m\ A^2_m\ A^3_m\ A^4_m\ B^1_m\ B^2_m\ B^3_m\ B^4_m\ C^1_m\ C^2_m\ C^3_m\ C^4_m\ D^1_m\ D^2_m\ D^3_m\ D^4_m$ would mean a complete man of the most pronounced kind, i.e., germ cell, spermatic duct, sexual protrusion, and sexual groove in his case would be of the manly type; the same for the hair, larynx, chest, and pelvis; his sexual drive and sexual behavior would manifest itself in the direction (whether young or old), in the kind of approach (whether aggressively courting or alluring), in the disposition (rooted partly in the emotional, partly in the sensual), in the kind of activity (whether active or passive, incubus or succubus), in the manly character, i.e., the object of his desire would be the normal (characteristically feminine) woman, and in relation to her he would step forth aggressively and actively emotionally and sensually; finally, he would also depict himself as a powerful and strong manly person in his emotional life and in his manner of thinking, in his activities and in the clothing he chose, as a master of logic, not preferring sewing and crocheting or cooking and such things, but rather using his muscles and mental powers, and would prefer men's over women's clothing.

From this aspect, how much has the number of combinations grown?

First of all, variations A^1 (as A^1_m, A^1_w, and A^1_{m+w}) produces three cases. Each of these cases, through variations of A^2 (as A^2_m, A^2_w, and A^2_{m+w}), yield three more cases, so that makes 3×3 or three squared or 9 combinations.

And again each of these cases falls under three more cases by variations of A^3, which produces 3×9 or three squared ($= 27$) combinations. And so forth: for each of the 16 elements of the four groups of characteristics A, B, C, and D there is a trebling of the number. As a total number of all possible combinations, this produces three to the power of 16 or

$$43,046,721 \text{ combinations.}$$

This enormous number could at first be surprising, since it equals approximately a third of the total number of the world population (estimated at 1,450 million); but with closer consideration it becomes not only understandable but also could be considered as too small, because we observed that there are hardly two humans who are exactly alike. In appearance as well as in essence there is such an extraordinary number of deviations and nuances that each individual appears as somewhat distinct. This is true, as is scientifically verified here, especially of the sexual particularities of humans. There would be a greater number if we were to separate the four groups of characteristics A, B, C, and D into the four elements for each one, which, as stated, would be acknowledged as thoroughly justified. For example, if each of the four elements were divided into only two subdivisions, let us say, hairiness into beard and hair on the head, or clothing into under and outer garments, and so forth, then the amount of possibilities of sexual varieties would overtake the number of the world population. [. . .]

After this general observation of the sexual mixed forms, if we return to the main subject of the work, the erotic drive to cross-dress, it will then become clearer to us in many respects and less of a rare phenomenon. The important conclusions put in order not only its place as a natural phenomenon, but also its etiology, prognosis, and therapy. We have indicated that it belongs to Group Four of the intermediaries; with respect to the three first groups of the sexual differences, the sex organs, the remaining physical characteristics, and the sex drive, these men exhibit no or only insignificant deviations from the norm, unessential in any case in comparison to the remaining psychosexual characteristics, the urge to dress as a woman and the desire to live as a woman as much as possible.

As we have seen, since in this case it is a matter of a form of the intermediaries, which clearly brings into relief what has thus far been described, it appears fitting, too, to give the new form a new name, a special scientific stamp. The term I use to characterize the most obvious internal and external images of the persons concerned, their feelings and thoughts, their drive to put on the clothing of the opposite sex, is taken from the Latin "trans" = across and "vestitus" = dressed, used also by the Roman classical writers as "transvestism." Both men and women are termed "transvestites." One disadvantage of the term is that it describes only the external side, while the internal is limitless. [. . .]

If one wanted to stress the condition that it is not simply a matter of cross-dressing, but rather more of a sexual drive to change, then the word "metamorphosis" would be better. One could call the persons sexual metamorphotics, the drive sexual-metamorphotic, and the phenomenon sexual metamorphism, the preference of cross-dressing as sexual metamorphosis. Apart from the ungainly expression, I would be against it because Krafft-Ebing already has designated the mania of sexual metamorphosis as metamorphosis sexualis paranoica, which, as discussed above, we had to differentiate sharply from the drive of sexual metamorphosis.

Sex researchers repeatedly used the practice, and in my opinion not a very happy one, of naming sexual anomalies after persons who have become famous by them because they had especially strong tendencies toward them. Some such words are sadism, masochism, narcissism, retifism, and onanism, after the biblical Onan. The corresponding "fame" is lacking among heterosexual transvestites. Perhaps the acumen of my readers will produce an expression that would better hit upon the core of the phenomenon than the provisional one, which, I imagine, will not be universally satisfactory.

Part IV

Heterosexuality, Marriage and Sex Manuals

Introduction

Lesley Hall

Early sexologists destabilized assumptions about the 'naturalness' of normal heterosexuality by emphasizing that 'normal' sexual intercourse was not a simple natural act to which instinct would provide a reliable guide, but a problematic area. These selections illustrate characteristic concern with female sexual pleasure and satisfaction, and an underlying assumption that male desire by comparison was far less complicated.

Havelock Ellis was the great pioneering figure in British sexology. Though best remembered for his work on sexual 'abnormalities', he saw all sexual phenomena as interrelated and made many statements on heterosexual relations. He was enormously influential on subsequent writers. In the selected passage Ellis characteristically relates heterosexual intercourse to a wide range of phenomena, zoological, anthropological, historical, biological, psychological and sociological, while critiquing contemporary social conditions, especially as they affect the relations of the sexes. He deconstructs the metaphor of courtship in order to reconstruct it as a 'complex and subtle game' which should precede all occasions of sexual intercourse.

By the 1920s Ellis's ideas, once confined to a radical margin, were even influencing religious discourses around sexuality. A. Herbert Gray (1868–1956) was a Presbyterian minister who wrote several books of sexual advice, of which *Men, Women and God* (1923) is perhaps the best known. He presents sexuality as a God-given pleasure, stressing the contribution of a good sex relationship to making a truly Christian marriage, deploying ideas initially advanced by sexologists to assist in bringing about this happy state of affairs.

While Gray's particular religious bias is obvious, few contemporary writers on heterosexuality dared to detach it from marriage. Usually it was argued that by purveying enlightenment on sexual matters, marriage would be improved and this central institution of society maintained in better order. Few went so far as Dora Russell (1894–1986) in claiming that sexual relations might be licit and beautiful even without matrimony. Dora Black was a feminist intellectual who married Bertrand Russell in 1921. She was active in the birth control and sex reform movements as well as in the Labour Party, and founded a progressive school with her husband, with whom she had an 'open marriage' which, however, ended acrimoniously in divorce in 1935. Russell writes from the standpoint of a modern woman of the 1920s who knew from her own experience and that of friends and colleagues that women were having affairs, which did not have the deleterious effects ascribed to them by tradition.

However, Russell writes largely of the theory rather than the practice of marriage. She may have felt that to write of the latter was supererogatory given that a few years previous to her own work *Hypatia*, Marie Stopes's epoch-making marriage manual *Married Love* (1918) had appeared and become an enormous best-seller. Stopes (1880–1958), a university lecturer in botany, had conducted a course of research in sexological literature which enabled her to undertake proceedings for annulment against her husband following a disastrous first marriage. 'Knowledge gained at such a cost' of personal suffering, she felt, should be made available for the public benefit. In *Married Love* Stopes moves from poetic evocations of women's nature and the potential of marriage ('love-tide', 'initiate of love's mysteries', 'flower-wreathed lovemaking'), which many of her readers found profoundly spiritually moving, to a careful, explicit and scientific account of the mechanics of sexual intercourse ('the stimulated penis, enlarged and stiffened', 'a secretion of mucus lubricates the opening of the vagina'). She presented points which Ellis had made a decade or so earlier – the scandal of female sexual ignorance, the dangers of wedding night trauma, the necessity of preliminary wooing – in a way which made them acceptable to a much larger and more popular audience. Unlike Ellis, who stressed the underlying connections between 'the normal basis' and the 'extreme aberrations', Stopes presented herself as the prophet of the normal and the natural, the saviour of 'happy, mating couples' and 'all those who are betrothed in love'.

Unlike Stopes, with her delineation of the unrecognized but powerful 'sexual tides' of women, Theodore Van de Velde (1873–1937) turned the spotlight back onto the men with his exhortations to males to be the 'educators and initiators of their wives'. Van de Velde, who, according to Edward Brecher, 'taught a generation how to copulate', was a Dutch gynaecologist who had (himself married) eloped with a married patient and had to leave the Netherlands. None the less, he positions himself as speaking for the 'delicate differentiations and modifications' within the realm of the normal, eschewing 'certain abnormal sexual practices' and keeping the 'Hell-gate of the realm of Sexual Perversions firmly closed'. This still allows him to give details of a wide variety of different sexual positions, and instructions as to the best mode of performing cunnilingus (on fellatio he is somewhat more reticent). It was perhaps because of Van de Velde's contribution to extending the average person's erotic repertoire that the British feminist sex radical Stella Browne translated this somewhat conservative and patriarchal text.

Helena Wright (1887–1982) was a qualified doctor, and it may be for that reason that her text is a good deal drier in style than Stopes's, although Wright reiterates many of the same points ('wife needs to be courted and wooed. [. . .]]atmosphere of peace and leisure'). She is far more explicit about the importance of clitoral stimulation for female sexual arousal and satisfaction. This may reflect the impact of Stopes's own work in creating a climate of opinion rendering a greater degree of candour possible, or Wright's status as a medical woman and the notion that some things could be said by a doctor but not by a lay person. Wright, though aware of the concept of vaginal orgasm, treats this as a theoretical ideal, while promoting the practically efficacious stimulation of the clitoris. She also makes the still rather unusual suggestion (though this had been mentioned by Ellis) that sometimes the woman might take the sexual initiative, though this is presented more as a way of gratifying a husband than as a spontaneous manifestation of her own desires.

Studies in the Psychology of Sex, vol. III: Analysis of the Sexual Impulse (1903)
Havelock Ellis

The conjunction of the sexes is seen to be an end only to be obtained with much struggle; the difficulty of achieving sexual erethism in both sexes, the difficulty of so stimulating such erethism in the female that her instinctive coyness is overcome, these difficulties the best and most vigorous males, those most adapted in other respects to carry on the race, may most easily overcome. [. . .]

Force is the foundation of virility, and its psychic manifestation is courage. In the struggle for life violence is the first virtue. The modesty of women – in its primordial form consisting in physical resistance, active or passive, to the assaults of the male – aided selection by putting to the test man's most important quality, force. Thus it is that when choosing among rivals for her favors a woman attributes value to violence. [. . .]

The relation of love to pain is one of the most difficult problems, and yet one of the most fundamental, in the whole range of sexual psychology. Why is it that love inflicts, and even seeks to inflict, pain? Why is it that love suffers pain, and even seeks to suffer it? In answering that question, it seems to me, we have to take an apparently circuitous route, sometimes going beyond the ostensible limits of sex altogether; but if we can succeed in answering it we shall have come very near one of the great mysteries of love. At the same time we shall have made clear the normal basis on which rest the extreme aberrations of love.

The chief key to the relationship of love to pain is to be found by returning to the consideration of the essential phenomena of courtship in the animal world generally. Courtship is a play, a game; even its combats are often, to a large extent, mock-combats; but the process behind it is one of terrible earnestness, and the play may at any moment become deadly. Courtship tends to involve a mock-combat between males for the possession of the female which may at any time become a real combat; it is a pursuit of the female by the male which may at any time become a kind of persecution; so that, as Colin Scott remarks, "Courting may be looked upon as a refined and delicate form of combat." The note of courtship, more especially among mammals, is very easily forced, and as soon as we force it we reach pain. The intimate and inevitable association in the animal world of combat – of the fighting and hunting impulses – with the process of courtship alone suffices to bring love into close connection with pain.

Among mammals the male wins the female very largely by the display of force. The infliction of pain must inevitably be a frequent indirect result of the exertion of power. It is even more than this; the infliction of pain by the male on the female may itself be a gratification of the impulse to exert force. This tendency has always to be held in check, for it is of the essence of courtship that the male should win the female, and she can only be won by the promise of pleasure. The tendency of the male to inflict pain must be restrained, so far as the female is concerned, by the consideration of what is pleasing to her. Yet, the more carefully we study the essential elements of courtship, the clearer it becomes that, playful as these manifestations may seem on the surface, in every direction they are verging on pain. It is so among animals generally; it is so in man among savages.

At the outset, then, the impulse to inflict pain is brought into courtship, and at the same time rendered a pleasurable idea to the female, because with primitive man, as well as among his immediate ancestors, the victor in love has been the bravest and strongest rather than the most beautiful or the most skillful. Until he can fight he is not reckoned a man and he cannot hope to win a woman. Among the African Masai a man is not supposed to marry until he has blooded his spear, and in a very different part of the world, among the Dyaks of Borneo, there can be little doubt that the chief incentive to head-hunting is the desire to please the woman, the possession of a head decapitated by himself being an excellent way of winning a maiden's favor. [. . .] Here, indeed, we have the source of that love of cruelty which some have found so marked in women. This is a phase of courtship which helps us to understand how it is that, as we shall see, the idea of pain, having become associated with sexual emotion, may be pleasurable to women.

Thus, in order to understand the connection between love and pain, we have once more to return to the consideration, under a somewhat new aspect, of the fundamental elements in the sexual impulse. In discussing the "Evolution of Modesty" we found that the primary part of the female in courtship is the playful, yet serious, assumption of the role of a hunted animal who lures on the pursuer, not with the object of escaping, but with the object of being finally caught. In considering the "Analysis of the Sexual Impulse" we found that the primary part of the male in courtship is by the display of his energy and skill to capture the female or to arouse in her an emotional condition which leads her to surrender herself to him, this process itself at the same time heightening his own excitement. In the playing of these two different parts is attained in both male and female that charging of nervous energy, that degree of vascular tumescence necessary for adequate discharge and detumescence in an explosion by which sperm-cells and germ-cells are brought together for the propagation of the race. We are now concerned with the necessary interplay of the differing male and female roles in courtship, and with the accidental emotional by-products. Both male and female are instinctively seeking the same end of sexual union at the moment of highest excitement. There cannot, therefore, be real conflict. But there is the semblance of a conflict, an apparent clash of aim, an appearance of cruelty. Moreover, – and this is a significant moment in the process from our present point of view, – when there are rivals for the possession of one female there is always a possibility of actual combat, so tending to introduce an element of real violence, of undisguised cruelty, which the male inflicts on his rival and which the female views with satisfaction and delight in the prowess of the successful claimant. Here we are brought close to the zoölogical root of the connection between love and pain. [. . .]

This association between love and pain still persists even among the most normal civilized men and women possessing well-developed sexual impulses. The masculine tendency to delight in domination, the feminine tendency to delight in submission, still maintain the ancient traditions when the male animal pursued the female. The phenomena of "marriage by capture," in its real and its simulated forms, have been traced to various causes. But it has to be remembered that these causes could only have been operative in the presence of a favorable emotional aptitude, constituted by the zoölogical history of our race and still traceable even to-day. To exert power, as psychologists well recognize, is one of our most primary impulses, and it always tends to be manifested in the attitude of a man toward the woman he loves.

It might be possible to maintain that the primitive element of more or less latent cruelty in courtship tends to be more rather than less marked in civilized man. In civilization the opportunity of dissipating the surplus energy of the courtship process by inflicting pain on rivals usually has to be inhibited; thus the woman to be wooed tends to become the recipient of the whole of this energy, both in its pleasure-giving and its pain-giving aspects. Moreover, the natural process of courtship, as it exists among animals and usually among the lower human races, tends to become disguised and distorted in civilization, as well by economic conditions as by conventional social conditions and even ethical prescription. It becomes forgotten that the woman's pleasure is an essential element in the process of courtship. A woman is often reduced to seek a man for the sake of maintenance; she is taught that pleasure is sinful or shameful, that sex-matters are disgusting, and that it is a woman's duty, and also her best policy, to be in subjection to her husband. Thus, various external checks which normally inhibit any passing over of masculine sexual energy into cruelty are liable to be removed.

We have to admit that a certain pleasure in manifesting his power over a woman by inflicting pain upon her is an outcome and survival of the primitive process of courtship, and an almost or quite normal constituent of the sexual impulse in man. But it must be at once added that in the normal well-balanced and well-conditioned man this constituent of the sexual impulse, when present, is always held in check. When the normal man inflicts, or feels the impulse to inflict, some degree of physical pain on the woman he loves he can scarcely be said to be moved by cruelty. He feels, more or less obscurely, that the pain he inflicts, or desires to inflict, is really a part of his love, and that, moreover, it is not really resented by the woman on whom it is exercised. His feeling is by no means always according to knowledge, but it has to be taken into account as an essential part of his emotional state. The physical force, the teasing and bullying, which he may be moved to exert under the stress of sexual excitement, are, he usually more or less unconsciously persuades himself, not really unwelcome to the object of his love. Moreover, we have to bear in mind the fact – a very significant fact from more than one point of view – that the normal manifestations of a woman's sexual pleasure are exceedingly like those of pain. "The outward expressions of pain," as a lady very truly writes, "– tears, cries, etc., – which are laid stress on to prove the cruelty of the person who inflicts it, are not so different from those of a woman in the ecstasy of passion, when she implores the man to desist, though that is really the last thing she desires." If a man is convinced that he is causing real and unmitigated pain, he becomes repentant at once. If this is not the case he must either be regarded as a radically abnormal person or as carried away by passion to a point of temporary insanity. [. . .]

We thus see that there are here two separate groups of feelings: one, in the masculine line, which delights in displaying force and often inflicts pain or the simulacrum of pain; the other, in the feminine line, which delights in submitting to that force, and even finds pleasure in a slight amount of pain, or the idea of pain, when associated with the experiences of love. We see, also, that these two groups of feelings are complementary. Within the limits consistent with normal and healthy life, what men are impelled to give women love to receive. So that we need not unduly deprecate the "cruelty" of men within these limits, nor unduly commiserate the women who are subjected to it. [. . .]

There is certainly one purely natural sexual difference of a fundamental character, which lies at the basis of whatever truth may be in the assertion that women are not susceptible of sexual emotion. As may be seen when considering the phenomena of modesty, the part played by the female in courtship throughout Nature is usually different from that played by the male, and is, in some respects, a more difficult and complex part. Except when the male fails to play his part properly, she is usually comparatively passive; in the proper playing of her part she has to appear to shun the male, to flee from his approaches – even actually to repel them.

Courtship resembles very closely, indeed, a drama or game; and the aggressiveness of the male, the coyness of the female, are alike unconsciously assumed in order to bring about in the most effectual manner the ultimate union of the sexes. The seeming reluctance of the female is not intended to inhibit sexual activity either in the male or in herself, but to increase it in both. The passivity of the female, therefore, is not a real, but only an apparent, passivity, and this holds true of our own species as much as of the lower animals. [. . .]

There is another characteristic of great significance by which the sexual impulse in women differs from that in men: the widely unlike character of the physical mechanism involved in the process of coitus. Considering how obvious this difference is, it is strange that its fundamental importance should so often be underrated. In man the process of tumescence and detumescence is simple. In women it is complex. In man we have the more or less spontaneously erectile penis, which needs but very simple conditions to secure the ejaculation which brings relief. In women we have in the clitoris a corresponding apparatus on a small scale, but behind this has developed a much more extensive mechanism, which also demands satisfaction, and requires for that satisfaction the presence of various conditions that are almost antagonistic. Naturally the more complex mechanism is the more easily disturbed. It is the difference, roughly speaking, between a lock and a key. This analogy is far from indicating all the difficulties involved. We have to imagine a lock that not only requires a key to fit it, but should only be entered at the right moment, and, under the best conditions, can only become adjusted to the key by considerable use. The fact that the man takes the more active part in coitus has increased these difficulties; the woman is too often taught to believe that the whole function is low and impure, only to be submitted to at her husband's will and for his sake, and the man has no proper knowledge of the mechanism involved and the best way of dealing with it. The grossest brutality thus may be, and not infrequently is, exercised in all innocence by an ignorant husband who simply believes that he is performing his "marital duties." For a woman to exercise this physical brutality on a man is with difficulty possible; a man's pleasurable excitement is usually the necessary condition of the woman's sexual gratification. But the reverse is not the case, and if the man is sufficiently ignorant or sufficiently coarse-grained to be satisfied with the woman's submission, he may easily become to her, in all innocence, a cause of torture.

To the man coitus must be in some slight degree pleasurable or it cannot take place at all. To the woman the same act which, under some circumstances, in the desire it arouses and the satisfaction it imparts, will cause the whole universe to shrivel into nothingness, under other circumstances will be a source of anguish, physical and mental. This is so to some extent even in the presence of the right and fit man. There can be no doubt whatever that the mucus which is so profusely poured out over the external sexual organs in woman during the excitement of sexual desire has for its end the lubrication of the parts and the facilitation of the passage of the intromittent organ. The most casual inspection of the cold, contracted, dry vulva in its usual aspect and the same when distended, hot, and moist, suffices to show which condition is and which is not that ready for intercourse, and until the proper condition is reached it is certain that coitus should not be attempted.

The varying sensitiveness of the female parts again offers difficulties. Sexual relations in women are, at the onset, almost inevitably painful; and to some extent the same experience may be repeated at every act of coitus. Ordinary tactile sensibility in the female genito-urinary region is notably obtuse, but at the beginning of the sexual act there is normally a hyperaesthesia which may be painful or pleasurable, as excitement culminates passing into a seeming anaesthesia, which even craves for rough contact; so that in sexual excitement a woman normally displays in quick succession that same quality of sensibility to superficial pressure and insensibility to deep pressure which the hysterical woman exhibits simultaneously.

Thus we see that a highly important practical result follows from the greater complexity of the sexual apparatus in women and the greater difficulty with which it is aroused. In coitus the orgasm tends to occur more slowly in women than in men. It may easily happen that the whole process of detumescence is completed in the man before it has begun in his partner, who is left either cold or unsatisfied.

It is thus a result of the complexity of the sexual mechanism in women that the whole attitude of a woman toward the sexual relationship is liable to be affected disastrously by the husband's lack of skill or consideration in initiating her into this intimate mystery. Normally the stage of apparent repulsion and passivity, often associated with great sensitiveness, physical and moral, passes into one of active participation and aid in the consummation of the sexual act. But if, from whatever cause, there is partial arrest on the woman's side of this evolution in the process of courtship, if her submission is merely a mental and deliberate act of will, and not an instinctive and impulsive participation, there is a necessary failure of sexual relief and gratification. When we find that a woman displays a certain degree of indifference in sexual relationships, and a failure of complete gratification, we have to recognize that the fault may possibly lie, not in her, but in the defective skill of a lover who has not known how to play successfully the complex and subtle game of courtship. Sexual coldness due to the shock and suffering of the wedding-night is a phenomenon that is far too frequent. Hence it is that many women may never experience sexual gratification and relief, through no defect on their part, but through the failure of the husband to understand the lover's part. We make a false analogy when we compare the courtship of animals exclusively with our own courtships before marriage. Courtship, properly understood, is the process whereby both the male and the female are brought into that state of sexual tumescence which is a more or less necessary condition for sexual intercourse. The play of courtship cannot, therefore, be considered to be definitely brought to an end by the ceremony of marriage; it may more properly be regarded as the natural preliminary to every act of coitus. [. . .]

There is a further important difference, though intimately related to some of these differences already mentioned, between the sexual impulse in women and in men. In women it is at once larger and more diffused. In men the sexual impulse is, as it were, focused to a single point. This is necessarily so, for the whole of the essentially necessary part of the male in the process of human procreation is confined to the ejaculation of semen into the vagina. But in women, mainly owing to the fact that women are the child-bearers, in place of one primary sexual center and one primary erogenous region, there are at least three such sexual centers and erogenous regions: the clitoris (corresponding to the penis), the vaginal passage up to the womb, and the nipple. In both sexes there are other secondary and reflex centers, but there is good reason for believing that these are more numerous and more wide-spread in women than in men. [. . .]

This great diffusion of the sexual impulse and emotions in women is as visible on the psychic as on the physical side. A woman can find sexual satisfaction in a great number of ways that do not include the sexual act proper, and in a great number of ways that apparently are not physical at all, simply because their physical basis is diffused or is to be found in one of the outlying sexual zones. [. . .]

In conclusion it may be worth while to sum up the main points brought out in this brief discussion of a very large question. We have seen that there are two streams of opinion regarding the relative strength of the sexual impulse in men and women: one tending to regard it as greater in men, the other as greater in women. We have concluded that, since a large body of facts may be brought forward to support either view, we may fairly hold that, roughly speaking, the distribution of the sexual impulse between the two sexes is fairly balanced.

We have, however, further seen that the phenomena are in reality too complex to be settled by the usual crude method of attempting to discover quantitative differences in the sexual impulse. We more nearly get to the bottom of the question by a more analytic method, breaking up our mass of facts into groups. In this way we find that there are certain well-marked characteristics by which the sexual impulse in women differs from the same impulse in men: 1. It shows greater apparent passivity. 2. It is more complex, less apt to appear spontaneously, and more often needing to be aroused, while the sexual orgasm develops more slowly than in men. 3. It tends to become stronger after sexual relationships are established. 4. The threshold of excess is less easily reached than in men. 5. The sexual sphere is larger and more diffused. 6. There is a more marked tendency to periodicity in the spontaneous manifestations of sexual desire. 7. Largely as a result of these characteristics, the sexual impulse shows a greater range of variation in women than in men, both as between woman and woman and in the same woman at different periods.

Married Love (1918)
Marie Stopes

Most women have never realised intellectually, but many have been dimly half-conscious, that woman's nature is set to rhythms over which man has no more control than he has over the tides of the sea. While the ocean can subdue and dominate man and laugh at his attempted restrictions, woman has bowed to man's desire over her body, and, regardless of its pulses, he approaches her or not as is his will. Some of her rhythms defy him – the moon-month tide of menstruation, the cycle of ten moon-months of bearing the growing child and its birth at the end of the tenth wave – these are essentials too strong to be mastered by man. But the subtler ebb and flow of woman's sex has escaped man's observation or his care.

If a swimmer comes to a sandy beach when the tide is out and the waves have receded, leaving sand where he had expected deep blue water – does he, baulked of his bathe, angrily call the sea 'capricious'?

But the tenderest bridegroom finds only caprice in his bride's coldness when she yields her sacrificial body while her sex-tide is at the ebb.

There is another side to this problem, one perhaps even less considered by society. There is the tragic figure of the loving woman whose love-tide is at the highest, and whose husband does not recognise the delicate signs of her ardour. In our anaemic, artificial days it often happens that the man's desire is a surface need, quickly satisfied, colourless, and lacking beauty, and that he has no knowledge of the rich complexities of love-making which an initiate of love's mysteries enjoys. To such a man his wife may indeed seem petulant, capricious, or resentful without reason.

Welling up in her are the wonderful tides, scented and enriched by the myriad experiences of the human race from its ancient days of leisure and flower-wreathed love-making, urging her to transports and to self-expressions, were the man but ready to take the first step in the initiative or to recognise and welcome it in her. Seldom dare any woman, still more seldom dare a wife, risk the blow at her heart which would be given were she to offer charming love-play to which the man did not respond. To the initiate she will be able to reveal that the tide is up by a hundred subtle signs, upon which he will seize with delight. But if her husband is blind to them there is for her nothing but silence, self-suppression, and their inevitable sequence of self-scorn, followed by resentment towards the man who places her in such a position of humiliation while talking of his 'love'.

So unaware of the elements of the physiological reactions of women are many modern men that the case of Mrs. G. is not exceptional. Her husband was accustomed to pet her and have relations with her frequently, but yet he never took any trouble to rouse in her the necessary preliminary feeling for mutual union. She had married as a very ignorant girl, but often vaguely felt a sense of something lacking in her husband's love. Her husband had never kissed her except on the lips and cheek, but once at the crest of the wave of her sex-tide (all unconscious that it was so) she felt a yearning to feel his head, his lips, pressed against her bosom. The sensitive inter-relation between a woman's breasts and the rest of her sex-life is not only a bodily thrill, but there is a world of poetic beauty in the longing of a loving woman for the unconceived child which melts in mists of tenderness toward her lover, the soft touch of whose lips can thus rouse her mingled joy. Because she shyly asked him, Mrs. G.'s husband gave her one swift unrepeated kiss upon her bosom. He was so ignorant that he did not know that her husband's lips upon her breast melt a wife to tenderness and are one of a husband's first and surest ways to make her physically ready for complete union. In this way he inhibited her natural desire, and as he never did anything to stir it, she never had any physical pleasure in their relation. Such prudish or careless husbands, content with their own satisfaction, little know the pent-up aching, or even resentment, which may eat into a wife's heart, and ultimately may affect her whole health.

Often the man is also the victim of the purblind social customs which make sex-knowledge *tabu*.

It has become a tradition of our social life that the ignorance of woman about her own body and that of her future husband is a flower-like innocence. And to such an extreme is this sometimes pushed, that not seldom is a girl married unaware that married life will bring her into physical relations with her husband fundamentally different from those with her brother. When she discovers the true nature of his body, and learns the part she has to play as a wife, she may refuse utterly to agree to her husband's wishes. I know one pair of which the husband, chivalrous and loving, had to wait years before his bride recovered from the shock of the discovery of the meaning of marriage and was able to allow him a natural relation. There have been not a few brides whom the horror of the first night of marriage with a man less considerate has driven to suicide or insanity.

That girls can reach a marriageable age without some knowledge of the realities of marriage would seem incredible were it not a fact. One highly-educated lady intimately known to me told me that when she was about eighteen she suffered many months of agonising apprehension that she was about to have a baby because a man had snatched a kiss from her lips at a dance.

When girls so brought up are married it is a *rape* for the husband to insist on his 'marital rights' at once. It will be difficult or impossible for such a bride ever after to experience the joys of sex-union, for such a beginning must imprint upon her consciousness the view that the man's animal nature dominates him. [. . .]

What actually happens in an act of union should be known. After the preliminaries have mutually roused the pair, the stimulated penis, enlarged and stiffened, is pressed into the woman's vagina. Ordinarily when a woman is not stimulated, the entrance to this canal, as well as the exterior lips of soft tissue surrounding it, are dry and rather crinkled, and the vaginal opening is smaller than the man's distended penis. But when the woman is what is physiologically called tumescent (that is, when she is ready for union and has been profoundly stirred) local parts are flushed by the internal blood supply and to some extent are turgid like those of the man, while a secretion of mucus lubricates the opening of the vagina. In an ardent woman the vaginal orifice may even spontaneously contract and relax. (So powerful is the influence of thought upon our bodily structure, that in some people all these physical results may be brought about by the thought of the loved one, by the enjoyment of tender words and kisses, and the beautiful subtleties of wooing.) It can therefore be readily imagined that when the man tries to enter a woman whom he has *not* wooed to the point of stimulating her natural physical reactions of preparation, he is endeavouring to force his entry through a drywalled opening too small for it. He may thus cause the woman actual pain, apart from the mental revolt and loathing she is likely to feel for a man who so regardlessly uses her. On the other hand, in the tumescent woman the opening, already naturally prepared, is lubricated by mucus, and all the nerves and muscles are ready to react and easily accept the man's entering organ. This account is of the meeting of two who have been already married. The first union of a virgin girl differs, of course, from all others, for on that occasion the hymen is broken. One would think that every girl who was about to be married would be told of this necessary rupturing of the membrane and the temporary pain it will cause her; but even still large numbers of girls are allowed to marry in complete and cruel ignorance.

It should be realised that a man does not woo and win a woman once for all when he marries her: *he must woo her before every separate act of coitus,* for each act corresponds to a marriage as other creatures know it. Wild animals are not so foolish as man; a wild animal does not unite with his female without the wooing characteristic of his race, whether by stirring her by a display of his strength in fighting another male, or by exhibiting his beautiful feathers or song. And we must not forget that the wild animals are assisted by nature; they generally only woo just at the season when the female is beginning to feel natural desire. But man, who wants his mate all out of season as well as in it, has a double duty to perform, and must himself rouse, charm, and stimulate her to the local readiness which would have been to some extent naturally prepared for him had he waited till her own desire welled up.

To render a woman ready before uniting with her is not only the merest act of humanity to save her pain, but is of value from the man's point of view, for (unless he is one of those relatively few abnormal and diseased variants who delight only in rape) the man gains an immense increase of sensation from the mutuality thus attained, and the health of both the man and the woman is most beneficially affected.

Assuming now that the two are in the closest mental and spiritual, as well as sensory harmony: in what position should the act be consummated? Men and women, looking into each other's eyes, kissing tenderly on the mouth, with their arms round each other, meet face to face. And that position is symbolic of the coming together of the two who meet together gladly.

It seems incredible that to-day educated men should be found who – apparently on theological grounds – refuse to countenance any other position. Yet one wife told me that she was crushed and nearly suffocated by her husband, so that it took her hours to recover after each union, but that 'on principle' he refused to attempt any other position than the one he chose to consider normal. Mutual well-being should be the guide for each pair.

It is perhaps not generally realised how great are the variations of size, shape, and position of all the sex parts of the body in different individuals, yet they differ more even than the size and characters of all the features of the face and hands. It happens, therefore, that the position which suits most people is unsatisfactory for others. Some, for instance, can only benefit by union when both are lying on their sides. Though medically this is generally considered unfavourable or prohibitive for conception, yet I know women who have had several children and whose husbands always used this position. In this matter every couple should find out for themselves which of the many possible positions best suits them *both*.

When the two have met and united, the usual result is that, after a longer or shorter interval, the man's mental and physical stimulation reaches a climax in sensory intoxication and in the ejaculation of semen. Where the two are perfectly adjusted, the woman simultaneously reaches the crisis of nervous and muscular reactions very similar to his. This mutual orgasm is extremely important, but in many cases the man's climax comes so swiftly that the woman's reactions are not nearly ready, and she is left without it. Though in some instances the woman may have one or more crises before the man achieves his, it is, perhaps, hardly an exaggeration to say that 70 or 80 per cent. of our married women (in the middle classes) are deprived of the full orgasm through the excessive speed of the husband's reactions, or through some mal-adjustment of the relative shapes and positions of the organs. So deep-seated, so profound, are woman's complex sex-instincts as well as her organs, that in rousing them the man is rousing her whole body and soul. And this takes time. More time, indeed, than the average, uninstructed husband gives to it. Yet woman has at the surface a small vestigial organ called the clitoris, which corresponds morphologically to the man's penis, and which, like it, is extremely

sensitive to touch-sensations. This little crest, which lies anteriorly between the inner lips round the vagina, enlarges when the woman is really
tumescent, and by the stimulation of movement it is intensely roused and
transmits this stimulus to every nerve in her body. But even after a woman's dormant sex-feeling is aroused and all the complex reactions of her
being have been set in motion, it may even take as much as from ten to
twenty minutes of actual physical union to consummate her feeling, while
two or three minutes often completes the union for a man who is ignorant
of the need to control his reactions so that both may experience the added
benefit of a mutual crisis to love.

Men, Women and God (1923)
A. Herbert Gray

In the following pages I propose to write simply and plainly about the
social, personal, and bodily relations of men and women, and about the
ways in which their common life may attain to happiness, harmony, and
efficiency.

I shall deal with matters often handled only with much diffidence, and
thought of with uncomfortable reserve. And I address myself to men and
women alike.

I do it all on the basis of one assumption, namely, that a God of love in
designing our human nature cannot have put into it anything which is
incapable of a pure and happy exercise; and in particular that in making
the sex interest so central, permanent, and powerful in human beings He
must have had some great and beautiful purpose. I start, in fact, with the
faith that the sexual elements in our humanity, once rightly understood
and finely handled, make for the enrichment of human life, for the increase of our health and efficiency, and the heightening of our joy. I believe that nothing is more necessary for the world to-day than that we
should trace out the ways in which this tremendous life force that is im-
planted in us all may be used to forward the higher aims of our common
life, and to help the race on its upward march. [. . .]

Sex is no accident in our humanity. The function of the sexual elements
in our physical frame is so central that unless they be truly managed health
and strength are impossible. Their relation is no less vital to our mental
and aesthetic life, and they appear to control almost absolutely our nervous stability. No man or woman attains to fullness and harmony of life if
the sexual nature be either neglected or mismanaged. No society is strong
and happy unless this part of life is truly adjusted. It may even be said that

the evils that come through the mismanagement of sex relations have beaten every civilization up to the present. And no doubt it is natural enough to shudder over the abominations of prostitution and sex vice in general, and so to turn our minds away from the whole matter. But for all that our emotional energies would be better employed in trying to understand this titanic force, and in learning how it may be utilized for our upward progress. Mere prohibitions have so utterly and entirely failed us that we ought now to realize that there is no hope in them alone. What we need is a positive constructive ideal for this part of life which will indicate the real value of the sexual forces in us, and not leave young men and women partly perplexed, partly ashamed, and partly annoyed because they are as the Creator made them. [. . .]

The ideal which still lingers in many minds, though it is seldom openly confessed, is that boys and girls, young men and women, should be kept in complete ignorance of the truth about their sexual natures until they marry, and that then they should be left to learn all that they need to know from Mother Nature direct. That at least would seem to be a fair inference from the fact of the conspiracy of silence in which ninety per cent. of parents have engaged towards the beings they love best.

Unfortunately in order to carry out the policy thus implied it would be necessary to keep children from associating with other children, to forbid them to read the Bible, the great classics of literature, and the daily papers – to keep them from the theatre, and from the study of nature – in fact to bring them up in a world which does not exist. For in all the ways I have suggested do boys and girls now collect garbled, half-true, and distorted notions about sexual life. And even if it were possible to carry out the policy it would still not be desirable. Marriage is not the simple and easy thing which the policy would imply. Mother Nature does not teach young couples all that they need to know. Often they make serious mistakes in the first few days. Often they mishandle and spoil the beautiful relationship on which they have entered to their own disgust and disappointment. Uncounted couples to-day have reason for the bitterness with which they complain that nobody ever taught or helped them.

In fact the policy of silence is as cruel as its assumptions are untrue. Ignorance is an impossibility for the young. Our choice lies between garbled, distorted, and defiled knowledge and a knowledge that shall be clean, innocent, and helpful. It has often happened that men and women brought up on the policy of silence have first learnt the facts about life through some contact with vice or sin, and those who know what horrible sufferings sudden discoveries of that sort may mean for sensitive natures cannot possibly have any doubts remaining on this point. There are few more cruel things possible than to bring a girl up in the ignorance which is mistaken for innocence and then to allow her to go out into the world to learn the truth by chance, or through some unclean mind. [. . .]

If mere lust is the vilest thing on earth, pure love is the most beautiful. And when pure love dominates a life all the sexual activities of the body may be transmuted and redeemed until a complete life is attained in which all the primal forces of our beings find a happy exercise under the control of a passion that is at once physical, mental, and spiritual. But the body is not in this process denied. It is accepted, understood, and made to play its true part. If passion be truly handled it provides the driving force for a life that is effective, courageous, and joyous. He is most truly living a spiritual life who has learnt to use all the powers of his incarnate nature in a life of strenuous activity and loyal love.

I do not mean of course that there is no place in the highest type of life for renunciation. Nor do I mean for a moment that only in marriage can greatness and fullness of life be attained. It is hard to use words correctly at a time when special meanings have come to be attached to such words as repression and suppression. What the psychologists have discovered is that unconscious, or incomplete, or unaccepted repression of bodily instincts leads to a dangerous condition. He who has not really surrendered desire, but simply tried to drive it underground, may indeed reap troubles enough and to spare.

But it needs no psychological training to know that deliberate, sincere, and courageous renunciation of this or that bodily desire for the sake of some compelling ideal may lead to the very finest kind of life. Only in this process the body is not ignored. It is taken into account. Nor are its forces neglected. Through the process technically described as sublimation, a way is to be found whereby life force restrained in one direction finds other and most valuable ways of expression.

Hypatia or Woman and Knowledge (1925)
Dora Russell

Persuade the single women that the married woman is an unfair competitor, terrify them so far as you can into believing that to succumb to sex is something unbecoming and disgraceful and punishable with misery everlasting, whether in marriage or outside it, and you can prevent the women combining against you.

But not if Aspasia will speak. If she but would, and put an end to this lie for ever. She could tell us how, especially during the years of war, young women took the last step towards feminine emancipation by admitting to themselves and their lovers the mutual nature of sex-love between man and woman. It sounds a platitude, but is, in fact, a revolution. [. . .] While poverty and parents forbade the certainty of marriage, with nothing but instability and death around them, our modern Aspasias took the love of man and gave the love of woman, and found this union, free and full on either side, the most priceless gift the immortal gods can bestow. There is nothing new in this, the moralist will say – it is just wickedness. Yes, there is this that is new: that, though these younger women may be driven from fear of starvation to the outward acceptance of old codes and conventions, inwardly they know they have done no wrong and will not admit a conviction of sin. Sex, even without children and without marriage, is to them a thing of dignity, beauty, and delight. All Puritans – and most males so long as they can remember – have tried to persuade women that their part in sex is pregnancy and childbirth, and not momentary delight. As well tell a man his part is the hunting and skinning of animals for food and clothing. To enjoy and admit we enjoy, without terror or regret, is an achievement in honesty. We will go further and say that polygamy, proffered by the male as a solution to our sexless lives, is no solution at all when we are polyandrous. It is useless to go on pretending, as both sexes do, about this question. The plain truth is that there are as many types of lover among women of all classes as among men, and that nothing but honesty and freedom will make instinctive satisfaction possible for all. Grant each man and woman the right to seek his or her own solution without fear of public censure. Moral questions of this kind cannot be decided by some abstract rule. [. . .] The wrong lies in rules that are barriers between human beings who would otherwise reach a fuller and more intense understanding of one another. And any man or woman of intelligence and vitality can testify that to have known each other as lovers is to have completed mental and spiritual, as well as physical, understanding, and to have permanently enriched each other's lives, capacities, energies, imaginations. There is no need to make these divisions into mind and body. There is no difference. A way of walking, laughter, thoughts spoken or written, gestures of love or anger, colour and light of eyes or hair – these are the human being, man or woman. It is thus that modern individuals think of one another. When we think so it seems absurd to argue whether or no love between man and woman should stop short of a certain kind of physical expression. It is useless to say that a mental exchange is sufficient. On the contrary, lovers know that it is through sexual understanding they best apprehend the quality of each other's minds. It is equally futile to argue that woman is cheated of her full rights if children do not result. That is not true.

It is said that modern human beings, by dint of not valuing the body, are physically degenerate and lose the finest ecstasies of love. Their digestions are poor, we are told, their breath foul, their teeth bad. [. . .] Health, to be sure, is essential; but health is to be secured in the modern world, not by a return to savagery, but by the use of intelligence. I believe the bodies of young people to-day to whom fair opportunities have been given are more healthy within and without than they were in past times. And I believe that the disappearance of religious and moral dualism between mind and matter – not by an oppressive victory of either, neither by rational and moral control, nor by abandonment of sensual materialism, but by a better understanding of psychology and physiology based on the discoveries of physical science – is bringing to the whole of life, but especially to sex-love, maternity, the rearing and education of children, joy and rapture and promise surpassing anything known to the purely instinctive life of the past. [. . .]

It is for modern women and for men who can understand the problem to make an end to secrecy, shame, and starvation where sex is concerned.

Ideal Marriage (1928)
Theodore Van de Velde

And I also address myself to married men, for they are naturally educators and initiators of their wives in sexual matters; and yet they often lack, not only the qualifications of a leader and initiator, but also those necessary for equal mutual partnership!

They have no realisation of their deficiencies. For the average man, of average 'normal' genital potency, who performs his 'conjugal duties' regularly and with physiological satisfaction to himself, still imagines that he has thereby met all the requirements his wife can make. And if she is not satisfied, and remains in a permanent condition of 'suspended gratification,' then, with regret or indignation according to his own type of temperament, he simply puts her down as one of those 'sexually frigid' women (from 20 to 80 per cent. of all women are supposed to be sexually frigid – a conveniently and conspicuously wide margin of error!), laments his bad luck, and drifts further and further apart from her.

If he has been fortunate enough to wed a woman of warmer and more spontaneous temperament, who is obviously not indifferent to the rites of marriage – if those rites take place in the same invariably scheduled manner, with no varieties of local stimulation or sensory adornment – sexual satiety will in a few short years intrude itself into the consciousness of both, and equally imperil their marriage. For monotony can only be relieved by variation, and, to the uninstructed man, the only possible variation seems to be in the *object* of his efforts; and the rift in the lute is there, and widens.

The thought that the defect and the failure might be on *his* side, that he himself might have prevented the alienation which he truly deplores – this enlightening and humbling truth never dawns upon him!

For he does not know that there are numberless delicate differentiations and modifications of sexual pleasure, all lying strictly within the bounds of *normality*, which can banish the mechanical monotony of the too well-known from the marriage-bed, and give new attractions to conjugal intercourse. Or, if he guesses this truth, he thinks it implies degeneracy and debauchery, for he fails to understand that what is physiologically sound may also be considered ethically sound. He thinks his wife is 'far above that sort of thing', leaves her more and more to herself, seeks the diversity of stimulation he needs outside his home, and often ends in *real* debauchery in consequence!

This average husband does not even know that his wife's sexual sensations develop and culminate to a slower rhythm than his own. He does not know *at all* that he must *awaken* her with delicate consideration and adaptation. He cannot understand why the Hindoo women, used to the sexual assiduity and skill of their own men, mock the clumsy Europeans as 'village cocks'; nor does he appreciate the point of view of those Javanese who boast, not of the joy they received, but of the delight they gave. [. . .]

The essence and significance of Don Juan is a mystery to most men, or is grossly misinterpreted. They should read Marcel Barrière's 'Essai sur le Don-Juanisme Contemporain', and learn that the soul of this arch-lover was not seeking the base triumph of snatching and throwing away, but ever and only the ecstasy of giving the joy of love.

And in this sense the husband should act the part of Don Juan to his wife over again. Then, in giving delight, he will himself experience it anew and permanently, and his marriage will become *ideal*.

And if *erotic genius* does not characterise him, the man needs *explicit knowledge* if he is to be capable of inspiring such desire and imparting such joy.

He must *know how to make love*.

The ensuing chapters may be of help to him here. They can, in certain portions, be read by educated laymen without any difficulty. Other portions, however, need close and careful study. For I aim at giving my instructions and deductions an entirely scientific tone and basis, though at keeping free from superfluous pedantry. This manner of treatment, as well as the nature of the theme, make it impossible to avoid the use of many foreign words and technical terms. Readers who do not exactly comprehend any of these words can ask a doctor to explain their precise meaning.

For, to achieve our purpose, is well worth study. [. . .]

By the term sexual intercourse, we herewith designate the full range of contact and connection, between human beings, for sexual consummation. But let us first of all make unmistakably clear that by 'sexual intercourse', unqualified by any adjectives, we refer *exclusively to normal intercourse between opposite sexes*. If we cannot avoid occasional reference to certain abnormal sexual practices, *we shall emphatically state that they are abnormal*. But this will only occur very seldom, for, as postulated above, it is our intention to keep the Hell-gate of the Realm of Sexual Perversions firmly closed. On the other hand, Ideal Marriage permits normal, physiological activities the fullest scope, in all desirable and delectable ways; these we shall envisage, without any prudery, but *with deepest reverence for true chastity*. All that is morbid, all that is perverse, we banish: for this is Holy Ground.

In order to obviate confusion, let us first define what we regard as normal sexual intercourse. It is not altogether easy. All rigid definitions and sharp distinctions are particularly difficult in sexual matters. I think the most comprehensive and exact definition is as follows: That intercourse which takes place between two sexually mature individuals of opposite sexes; which excludes cruelty and the use of artificial means for producing voluptuous sensations; which aims directly or indirectly at the consummation of sexual satisfaction, and which, having achieved a certain degree of stimulation, concludes with the ejaculation – or emission – of the semen into the vagina, at the nearly simultaneous culmination[1] of sensation – or orgasm – of both partners.

Complete sexual intercourse comprises: the prelude, the love play, the sexual union; and the after-play or epilogue (postlude). Its summit and its purpose alike, blend in the *third stage*. The accepted technical term for this third stage is *coitus;* but I shall call it *communion*. This has the associations of union, consummation and copulation: and has the further advantage that it does not emphasise the activity of the man and the passivity of the woman, which in Ideal Marriage should merge into a melodious *mutuality* of interaction and response. Communion-mating – merging together – implies *equal rights and equal joys in sexual union*.

This mating or communion – which may also, in the narrower and more precise sense, be termed sexual union – begins with the introduction of the male organ into the vagina, reaches its summit in the twofold *acme* and its purpose in the outpouring and reception of the seed of life. It concludes, strictly speaking, when the phallos is withdrawn from the vagina. Its *biological purpose* is attained in *fertilisation* or *impregnation*, but impregnation is not necessarily a part of the process of sexual union, nor is sexual union always an indispensable preliminary condition for impregnation. [. . .][2]

But the most simple and obvious substitute for the inadequate lubricant is the natural moisture of the salivary glands. It is always available; of course it has the disadvantage of very rapid evaporation. This makes it insufficient in cases where actual communion is prevented by lack of distillation. And during a very protracted local or genital manipulation, this form of substitute must be applied to the vulva, not once, but repeatedly. And this may best, most appropriately, and most expeditiously be done without the intermediary offices of the fingers, but through what I prefer to term the *kiss of genital stimulation,* or *genital kiss:* by gentle and soothing caresses with lips and tongue.[3]

This type of stimulation has many advantages. First of all the lack of local secretion ceases to be a drawback, and even becomes an advantage. Secondly, the acuteness of the pleasure it excites and the variety of tactile sensation it provides, will ensure that the previous deficiency is made good; i.e., that sexual excitement and desire reach such a point that – either by these means alone or aided by other endearments – distillation takes place, heralding psychic and bodily readiness for a sexual communion, successful and satisfactory to both partners.

The genital kiss is particularly calculated to overcome frigidity and fear in hitherto inexperienced women who have had no erotic practice, and are as yet hardly capable of specific sexual desire.

But – the husband must exercise the *greatest gentleness,* the *most delicate reverence!* The old proverb says: from the sublime to the ridiculous is but a step. In the lore of love, this proverb means that *supreme beauty and hideous ugliness are separated by a border-line so slight that our minds and senses may transgress it, unawares!*

We may assume that it is unnecessary to describe the technique of this form of genital stimulation. It may be constructed from what has already been said in detail, about the kiss in general, and about the special structure of the feminine organs.

The same obtains as regards the *analysis* of this procedure. I will only emphasise that the sensations of taste and smell are more likely to be of greater importance here than in the mouth kiss! Therefore, and as the special situation and secretions of the genital organs present difficulties in this respect, let the passive partner take care, to prevent repulsive and unfortunate impressions by the most scrupulous and meticulous personal cleanliness! [. . .]

For the *active* partner, the pleasures of the genital kiss are *wholly psychic.* They centre round the joy of giving joy to and rousing desire in the beloved, and the imaginative realisation of this pleasure and desire. (Of course, this psychic and emotional pleasure may be intense, and transmit itself to the *periphery,* in the form of increased tumescence.) The feelings of the passive partner, on the other hand, however strong their emotional undertones, are predominantly peripheral, i.e., physical.

The fact that in this particular form of caress more than any other, the man is generally the active partner, is because of his naturally greater initiative, and also because of the difference in the *tempo* of the respective erotic reactions, which is usual while the woman is still a novice.

On occasions when the man's reactions are less rapid, the woman may with advantage take the more active part during the second act of the love-drama, and *herself, most successfully, give – instead of receiving – the genital kiss.*

Is it necessary, however, to emphasise the need for aesthetic delicacy and discretion here? To advise her to abstain entirely from such contacts during the early stages of married life, and only to venture on them later, and experimentally? To remind her that she runs greater risks than he does, in approaching that treacherous frontier between supreme beauty and base ugliness? I think there is *no* need; for she knows this intuitively, she feels it with all a woman's instinctive modesty.

But, of course, the psychic situation is very different when, through mutual memories of joy and love, a happy adaptation has been achieved, and given her the artistry of experience.

Then a certain feminine initiative and aggression brings a refreshing variety. Let her be the wooer sometimes, not always the wooed. She can be so while quite retaining her distinctive dignity and sweetness. This *role* of wooer can express her love in a very desirable way, and be intensely gratifying to the husband, who feels that he not only feels desire, but inspires it, too.

In this more evolved and richer harmony of relationship, the use and enjoyment of genital stimulation and the genital kiss, will depend wholly on inclination, temperament, individual sensibility and practice of both partners. They may be enjoyed alternately or sometimes simultaneously.

For in every form of sport or art, every adept makes full use of every aspect and possibility, in order to perfect and vary his achievement. He neglects neither the grand effects nor the delicate details. And so, how should it be otherwise in the art of love which is the richest and subtlest of all?

[handwritten margin note: art of love not just science of sex]

Notes

1 The term *culmination* or *acme* is used preferably to *orgasm*.

2 *Note on pregnancy without previous coitus.* There are numerous though, of course, exceptional instances on record of impregnation or conception following the penetration of sperm-cells into the female genitalia without complete *immissio penis* or entrance of the male organ. Such cases are of great practical importance.

3 As all expert readers will easily understand, I have intentionally *not* employed

the more or less technical terms for the attainment of orgasm through bucco-lingual contact with the genitals, for *this* reason: I refuse to use these expressions which almost always refer to pathological practices, when I treat of manifestations which are, in their present context, *absolutely unobjectionable and legitimate,* ethically, aesthetically and hygienically. (Of course, their hygienic and aesthetic value depends entirely on the spotless cleanliness and wholesomeness of the bodies of both husband and wife.)

The Sex Factor in Marriage (1930)
Helena Wright

Every complete act of love follows a definite scheme; it should be an epitome in miniature of the whole relationship of the two lovers. A wife needs to be courted and wooed afresh every time her husband seeks her. It is necessary to have an atmosphere of peace and leisure; hurried love-making cannot be successful. Words play the first part; the husband tries to show his wife how much he loves and desires her, and so evokes in her mind the feeling of being desired. It is a pity that darkness is so constantly the setting chosen. In a subdued light the lovers can watch each other's faces, and the husband can tell by the expression of his wife's eyes whether he is fulfilling her wishes or not. Next comes a time for all sorts of love-play, the husband definitely seeks to arouse his wife's feelings by caressing her body in every way that occurs to him.

It has been discovered that in the majority of women the most complete response follows if they are stimulated in a definite sequence. Touching and caressing certain areas on the skin surface of the body powerfully excite sex desire. These areas seem to be related to one another, so that if the order of stimulation is followed, the response becomes more and more ardent. First, and most obvious, is the region of the mouth and face, and with them are the base of the neck and the lobes of the ears. The earliest sign of response is flushing of the cheeks, and if this occurs ultimate success generally follows. The second responsive area is the skin covering the breasts, and particularly the nipples. Stimulation here is very powerful, because the nipples are constructed of delicate and very sensitive tissue, and they are capable of becoming firm and erect under the caresses of a lover's lips or fingers.

By this time the woman's whole body will have become awake and responsive, and she will welcome contact anywhere on the skin surface. She ought to be ready for the beginning of direct stimulation of the sex organs themselves. It is here that rhythm plays an essential part. Sensation in the clitoris and the immediately surrounding mucous membrane can only be aroused by the application of constantly changing pressure. Continuous pressure very soon becomes painful. Fingers are by far the most delicate instruments for arousing definite local sex-sensations. There is an infinite variety in the number of possible movements, and every husband should discover the kinds of pressure and the rhythms of moving which give his wife most pleasure. Probably no two women are exactly alike.

During this stage of the sex-act comes the moment which shows that the wife is ready for full reception of her husband. In describing the anatomy of the genital region we mentioned two little glands, called Bartholin's glands, and we said that their purpose is to supply a slippery fluid. As soon as the clitoris is sufficiently excited, these glands work, and pour out their fluid over the walls of the vagina. This appearance of moisture is the sign that the vagina is prepared for the penis.

If during the preliminary stages the man keeps his attention on the effect he is producing on his wife, and concentrates all his mental power on a desire to please her, he will find it quite possible to control his own feelings until the right moment.

The question of the positions of the husband and wife during the completion of the act is very important. There are many possible positions, and some of them are described below. Most of the successful positions fulfill at least two essential conditions: contact can be maintained with the clitoris, and both partners can move their hips freely.

The sensations aroused by stimulation of the walls of the vagina are generally more difficult to excite than those of the clitoris. Sensation in the clitoris seems to be natural to every normal woman, but it often takes considerable time and patience to establish a vivid degree of sensitiveness in the vagina. The relative intensity of sensation in the vagina and in the clitoris varies very much in different women, and in different moods of the same woman. Theoretically it might be said that the ideal type of feminine sensation is concerned with the vagina alone, but that ideal is seldom realized. As a general rule it is true to say that a woman has not attained full sex maturity until she is able to feel pleasure as acutely in the vagina as in the region of the clitoris.

The suggestions which are here given are intended mostly for the help of those who are beginning to establish sex relations, and it is for that reason that stress is laid on the importance of maintaining clitoris stimulation. Nearly all women find vaginal sensation through, as it were, the gateway of clitoris sensation. When they have fully experienced both, they will vary their sex-life according to mood and temperament. For the full experience of the orgasm or sexual climax, intense feeling must generally be present in both places.

The last part of the act, after penetration has taken place, is usually, though not necessarily, the shortest. The wife is now in full co-operation;

by the movements of her hips, and consequently of the vagina, she helps to add to her husband's pleasure, at the same time she ensures that at each downward movement of her husband's the clitoris shall be adequately stimulated. This last matter is very important; many wives are unable to reach the climax because their husbands fail to realize that rhythmic friction of the clitoris is necessary right up to the end of the act.

It sometimes happens that even with the greatest care the husband has his ejaculation before the wife has arrived at the climax, he must therefore always make sure that his wife has complete satisfaction. With a little experience and sympathetic observation he will know this without being told; at the moment of orgasm there are characteristic muscular movements of the wife's sex organs, and several deep, quick breaths, which have only to be watched for, to be recognized easily. In any case, if there is mutual confidence the husband will find no difficulty in ascertaining whether his wife is satisfied or not.

If her orgasm has not occurred, it can easily be produced if stimulation of the clitoris is continued. This can be done in many ways, one of the simplest is to effect a change of position. If the wife comes uppermost, and lies face downwards, she can find the hard bone just above the root of the penis, and, by pressure of the clitoris on this bone and by movements directed as she needs, induce her own orgasm. Or if the husband has learned delicacy and skill, he will, by movements of his fingers in the region of the clitoris, be able to help his wife to attain her orgasm. None of these devices is ideal, and no couple should be content until they have learnt how to experience orgasm together. As the acuteness of sensation grows in the vagina, so gradually will the difficulty of reaching orgasm together disappear.

It is a curious fact that sex maturity has opposite effects on the man and woman with respect to the time each needs to reach full excitement and the orgasm. Inexperienced men find it difficult not to come to the climax too soon. In the course of time, and with the establishment of habit, they are able to lengthen the interval before the climax. With woman it is the reverse; as she becomes experienced she can be roused to the climax more and more quickly. So does nature work towards a complete harmony in sex relationships.

Variety is as important in the sex-life as it is in everything else. What is the commonest cause of the breakdown of the marriage-tie? Surely it is a desire for something new. Monotony is the deadliest enemy of love. No one can be expected to eat the same food every day, or to wear the same clothes indefinitely. Why should not the same common-sense rule be applied to love? It ought to be the aim of every pair of lovers who know love to be an art, to study the question, and to think out new ways of loving, so that their mutual sex-experience will always have the element of freshness and novelty.

Nowadays many husbands and wives work together, and so see a good deal of each other in sober, working moods. These wives would do well not to let their husbands forget that they also have a feminine, decorative, even 'frilly' side to their natures. After working all day with an efficient and businesslike companion, a husband feels a new thrill of pleasure if the evening brings him a charmingly dressed playmate, the same woman, yet not the same, ready for fun instead of work. As the years go by, different stages occur in married life. The chief problem at the beginning is generally the husband's, he cannot be content until he has charmed his bride out of all shyness, and made her a joyful and enthusiastic partner. Later comes a time when it is often the wife's turn to take the initiative. Nothing can be more pleasing to a husband than to know that he is the centre of his wife's desires, especially if that wife has learned the art of being a dozen women in one.

However active a man's nature may be, times inevitably come when he is tired, and lacks, for the moment, the energy for taking the initiative in love-making. These times are the wife's opportunity to show her many-sided nature, when she may woo her husband and charm him out of his fatigue. Usually he is the energy-giver in their love-play, now it is her turn. The more masculine the man is, the more subtle will be his pleasure in these occasional and temporary reversals of the sex-roles. In these moods he needs to be wooed, to be gradually awakened. A woman radiant with health and energy has the power of giving strength and rest to her lover, she can banish his fatigue, and in some mysterious way bring him back to life and radiance.

Part V

Reproductive Control

Introduction

Lesley Hall

Effective contraception was clearly an essential element in sexology's un-coupling the link between sexuality and reproduction with which sexol-ogy was concerned, and a desideratum of the conjugal sex promoted by such texts as those discussed in part IV. Malthusian propagandists had been advocating 'prudential restriction' of births within marriage on eco-nomic grounds since the middle of the nineteenth century. However, pub-lishing books of practical advice often led such idealists into the courtroom.

Nonetheless, from 1870 the British birth-rate, and that of most Euro-pean nations, perceptibly declined, due to a variety of factors, of which the deliberate employment of contraception was one. The extent to which it was effective, given the marginal and unscrupulous nature of most manu-facturers and retailers of birth-control devices (who also sold purportedly abortifacient 'women's pills'), is still debated. The rise of eugenic anxie-ties about the quality as well as the quantity of the nation's population from the 1890s initiated discussions about and investigations into the whys and wherefores of restriction of births. The vast majority of eugenic thinkers in Britain deplored birth control for creating a dangerous differential be-tween the birth-rate of the middle classes and that of the less desirable elements within society. The latter were not felt capable of the forethought involved in taking contraceptive precautions, though some of the more extreme eugenists mooted the possibilities of sterilization.

While Havelock Ellis advocated the improvement of the nation through the generation of fit children, unlike many eugenists he was not convinced that everything on the subject of breeding was already known and simply needed to be put into practice. In his 1911 pamphlet on *The Problem of*

Race-Regeneration, he pleads for a 'cautious and sceptical attitude in the face of undue dogmatism', and indeed, cautions against 'a life regulated by codes and statutes'.

Feminists had been divided on the question of birth control. Some nineteenth-century pioneers had seen allegiance to the Malthusian cause as consistent with feminism, but the general feeling had been that contraception would merely encourage the male licence feminists were anxious to restrain. However, increasingly during the early twentieth century birth control was coming to be seen as having an essential role in the improvement of maternal health. Marie Stopes strikes this note in her 1919 *Letter to Working Mothers*, appealing to the desire of women themselves to have healthier children (the boundary between this and a more explicit eugenic agenda was often extremely fuzzy). One of her arguments for birth control was that it would prevent the enormous amount of illegal abortion and attempted abortion which was taking place, with deleterious effects on women's health.

In 1920 the bishops of the Church of England, in *A New Gospel for All Peoples*, rejected Stopes's plea to give their approval to the use of contraception in marriage. However, many religious thinkers, such as A. Herbert Gray, were revaluing marriage and the place of sex within it and felt that a case could be made for birth control as consistent with Christian marriage. Gray in *Men, Women and God* argues for the emotional and health benefits of intercourse and makes a case for sexual intimacy in itself being 'right and good' aside from its procreative purpose.

Doctors were somewhat behind the clergy in giving at least such theoretical approval to the benefits of birth control within marriage. The subject was omitted from the medical school curriculum and seldom discussed in medical journals, and few doctors knew much about it. Women doctors were rather more sympathetic, and general practitioners and public health doctors often held views at variance with the vociferous elite of the profession. 'Michael Fielding' (pseudonym of Dr Maurice Newfield (1893–1949)) in *Parenthood: Design or Accident?* makes the case for birth control as an essential contribution to 'preventive medicine', but also as a 'positive means of advancing health and happiness'. He cites the statistic, first brought into the debate by the Workers' Birth Control Group consisting of Labour Party women trying to get this issue onto the Party platform, that child-bearing was more dangerous than coal-mining. He queries the assumption that doctors are necessarily well qualified to speak on the subject. Like Gray, Fielding counters the accusations that contraception is 'unnatural' by pointing to other 'devices not in Nature' which have 'secure[d] general approval' in the modern world.

All these writers deal with contraception implicitly as relating to the spacing and limitation of the number of children within marriage. In contrast, Naomi Mitchison (b. 1897), a writer and part of a Bohemian circle, deals also with those couples who 'have at all costs to avoid having babies' as well as the married. Addressing birth control in a wide context of heterosexual relationships, both inside and outside marriage, she explores the practical and emotional drawbacks to the contraceptive methods available at that time, including non-penetrative sex.

Few of these writers (except, fleetingly, Mitchison, in a passage not quoted) mention abortion except as a dangerous practice which contraception should obviate, or, in the case of Fielding, as a last resort in certain medical extremities. Stella Browne, however, states in this 1935 paper on 'The Right to Abortion' what she had been saying for twenty years, that women had a right to abortion under hygienic conditions at their own choice, not just in certain carefully defined cases. The case is made on feminist grounds, by-passing claims of women as mothers or as victims of crimes, to position them as autonomous beings.

An antithetical case is put by A.M. Ludovici (1882–1971), who makes a trenchant case against both birth control and abortion in his contribution to the same collection of essays. Ludovici is a rare case of an opponent of reproductive control arguing from a point of view other than that of religion. While he bases his case on physiological theory, Ludovici was not a doctor and few contemporary doctors, however opposed to birth control and abortion, would have wholly concurred with his controversial opinions.

The Problem of Race-Regeneration (1911)
Havelock Ellis

There, indeed, is one of the main problems when we seek to regenerate the race. How can we be reasonably sure that we are likely to produce fit children? The best efforts of scientific men to answer this question have not yet resulted in answers which can be applied to given cases with certainty. Scientific eugenics is still in an early stage, and the more mature knowledge of animal breeders, who breed for points, furnishes little help when we are dealing with men and women. Even some of the conclusions which have been formulated by scientific workers will probably need revision, or at all events interpretation, in the light of further facts and researches. There are some conclusions which may be set forth with a reasonable certainty, but they are not many. For some time to come it will be necessary to retain a cautious and sceptical attitude in the face of undue dogmatism in this field. More knowledge, we may be sure, will come in time. In the meanwhile we may be thankful that the questions which that knowledge will answer are being so anxiously put. For, there can be no doubt, the sense not only of social responsibility but of responsibility for the future of the race, the duty towards the next generation, really is growing among us, though cynics doubt whether such considerations can ever influence the selfish desires of men and women. But they are tending to do so, as many doctors can bear witness. Galton, during the last years of his life, believed that we are approaching a time when eugenic considerations will become a factor of religion, and when our existing religious conceptions will be re-interpreted in the light of a sense of social needs so enlarged as to include the needs of the race which is to come. Certainly, for those who have been taught to believe that man was in the first place created by God, it should not be difficult to realise the Divine nature of the task of human creation which has since been placed in the hands of men, to recognise it as a practical part of religion, and to cherish the sense of its responsibilities. Moreover, it is not true that men have ever felt free to choose their mates for life at random. The savage and the civilised are alike bound by restrictions which few dare to overpass. There have always been castes and classes into which a man was free to marry, and a much greater number of castes and classes which by rigorous custom, or even severe penalties, he was prohibited from marrying into. There is no great hardship involved in the injunction to marry into the caste of the well-born, the class of the healthy, and the less hardship since those castes and classes will always be, on the whole, the most attractive.

It is part of our problem to consider how best we may reconcile the claims of the race with the claims of individual freedom. The ground for such reconciliation is prepared if we remember that, as we have seen, the development of the sense of personal responsibility is implied in the growth of our civilisation. The finer breeding of the race is a matter that is primarily settled in the individual conscience. It is childish to suppose that it can be regulated by mere Act of Parliament. The law is a dead letter, disregarded or evaded, if it is not the outcome of the personal conviction of the people; and if it is merely, as it ought to be, the formal registration of that conviction, it is still a comparatively unimportant matter. It is in the developed individual conscience, guided by a new sense of responsibility, and informed by a new knowledge, that any regeneration of the race must be rooted. [. . .]

For we have to be on our guard – and that is our final problem, perhaps the most difficult and complex of all – lest our efforts for the regeneration of the race lead us to a mechanical and materialistic conception of life, to the conception of a life regulated by codes and statutes, and adjudicated in law courts. Better an unregenerate life than such a regeneration! For freedom is the breath of life, joy is the prime tonic of life, and no regeneration is worth striving for which fails to increase the total sum of freedom and of joy. Those who are working for racial regeneration must make this very clear, or they discredit their own aims. This is why it is necessary, in connection with racial regeneration, to deal with literature, with art, with religion, for it is only in so far as these things, and such as these, are rendered larger and freer and more joyous that a regenerated life will have its heightened value. It is useless to work for the coming of a better race if we impose upon it the task of breaking the fetters its fathers have forged. Licence, indeed, is always evil, for it involves a reckless indifference to the good of others. But licence, so far from being the ally of freedom, is its deadliest foe. To permit licence to the few is to make freedom impossible for the many. Order, self-control, sympathy, intelligent regulation, are necessary in all the matters that concern society and the race, because without them there can be no freedom. In the great garden of life it is not otherwise than in our public gardens. We repress the licence of those who, to gratify their own childish or perverted desires, would pluck up the shrubs or trample on the flowers, but in so doing we achieve freedom and joy for all. If in our efforts to better social conditions and to raise the level of the race we seek to cultivate the sense of order, to encourage sympathy and foresight, to pull up racial weeds by the roots, it is not that we may kill freedom and joy, but rather that we may introduce the conditions for securing and increasing freedom and joy. In these matters, indeed, the gardener in his garden is our symbol and our guide. The beginning of the world is figured as an ordered and yet free life of joy in a garden. All our efforts for the regeneration of the race can be but a feeble attempt to bring a little nearer that vision of Paradise.

A Letter to Working Mothers (1919)
Marie Stopes

I expect your first child was a great joy to you and your husband, but you went on having children so rapidly that you got very tired and worn out by the third or fourth child, or miscarriage. Also, if they came about every year, you had not time properly to nurse one before another was on the way, and you noticed that they seemed not to be so strong as you would like. You wanted a good family, but you did so want time to rest and get strong yourself between their coming, and you so wanted that every child you bore should be strong enough to live and grow up. No one told you how to give yourself a good long interval to pick up between the children; I am going to tell you how to do this so that you may bear *strong* children, and be happy bearing the children, because you have them when you are really *well*, and want them yourself. It gives you much pain and sorrow and loss to bear many weak children which die early, and it is also a terrible waste all round. What you would like, and what the country needs, are strong happy children who live and grow up to be fine men and women.

Also, many of those to whom I am writing this letter in particular are mothers who have already several children, and whose husbands, for one reason or another, are not able to earn very big wages; or, even worse, have gone in for drink, or who have become ill. You have a hard struggle to keep your children, and when the weekly wage is spent on rent and food, there is very little, perhaps nothing, left for many other things you need. But you are still young, and you are living with your husband, and there is always the shadow of fear hiding in the corner of your bedroom that, if you let him have his way, there will be more babies, and that will stop you working and will bring another child to feed, and you feel you cannot face it. The last one you had was very 'peeky', and you cannot afford to give it enough milk.

So you begin to dread what used to be your chief joy, that is to have your husband with you. On the other hand, if you are a strong-minded woman and you rule your husband and prevent him having his way, there is another fear, however much you may hide it deep in the bottom of your heart, and that is that you will not keep him, and that some bad girl will get him, for men who are husbands need what is wrongly called the 'husband's right'.

This makes things very difficult for you, and very often it happens that you get 'caught', and you know that the baby that you feared might come has really begun. Then your mind is full of anxiety because you fear all the extra poverty and trouble, perhaps even the hunger that it will mean, and as you love children you fear also the cruelty of bringing a little child into the world without being able to feed it, and give it the clothes it needs. So you do, or you try to do, a desperate thing: you try to get rid of that baby before it has 'gone too far'. Your neighbours or some old woman you know may tell you of various dodges which they have tried, and which may get rid of the beginning of a baby, and perhaps you try one after the other; but either it may have gone too far, or in that way you may be strong, and you may find that the little unwanted baby continues to grow.

Now I want you to think what this means, and I want you never again to try to get rid of a baby if it has begun. Many, many times the things women have done to themselves to try to get rid of a coming baby have made both themselves and that baby weaker than it would have been, perhaps even have deformed it. But babies that are coming are wonderfully strong little creatures, and possibly you may appear to have done very little harm to it; but though the harm may not show for a long time, it is there, because you have harmed yourself, and the coming baby gets everything through you. Anything which weakens you or strains you, injures you and through you affects your child in some way, even though it may not show at first.

In this letter I am going to begin by telling you of one or two things which many of you do, and which you ought *not* to do. But the reason I am speaking of these 'ought nots' is only in order to show you a much better and healthier way to get just the results which you have been trying to get in the wrong way, because people have not shown you the right way.

Men, Women and God (1923)
A. Herbert Gray

Not only because the subject of Birth Control occupies a very great place in the public attention just now, but also because it does raise very important and real questions for married persons I wish to speak shortly of it here.

Some day, perhaps, the medical profession will do the public the great service of issuing some authoritative statement about the physical aspects of the matter, for there are issues with which only medical men can deal wisely.

And yet it is far from being only or even mainly a medical question. The moral and social issues involved in it are of great importance.

It is now a matter of common knowledge that it is possible for two persons to live together in sexual intimacy and yet avoid having children. And this has created new problems for the married and new dangers for the unmarried. Probably it has had a great deal to do with the recent increase of irregular sexual relationships outside marriage. The women whose sole motive for chastity was the fear of having children and so of being openly disgraced are now set free to sin against the truth without fear of that particular penalty.

I am not, however, in the meantime concerned with them. It is the problem raised for married persons that concerns me. About two main points I am quite clear.

In the first place, for two healthy young persons to marry with the definite intention of having no children is, I believe, an unchristian thing. If they cannot afford to have children they cannot afford to marry. If at the beginning they interfere with nature they spoil their first experiences of sexual intimacy, which should be spontaneous and untrammelled. I even believe that artificial attempts to postpone the arrival of a first child are a deplorable mistake. The first consummation of love should be closely followed by parentage. Some couples having followed the plan of postponing parentage have, when it was too late, found that by this course they had forfeited the possibility of that great privilege. Of course children mean very hard work. Of course they restrict the freedom of parents to pursue their own pleasure, and use up a large proportion of the family income. But these things are a blessing in disguise. Comparative poverty for young couples is a bracing and a useful discipline. Probably the cream of the nation consists of men and women reared in families of four or five, where the parents gave much individual attention to each child, and by self-denial helped them to a good start in life. When birth control is resorted to in order to avoid the labours of family life it is a purely selfish and quite indefensible thing.

I am thinking of course of healthy parents. Unhealthy parents probably ought not to have children at all.

The second point I am clear about is that for most couples to have as many children as is possible is equally indefensible. Most healthy couples could have far more children than they can do justice to. In fact the plan of unrestricted families results in a threefold wrong. It is nothing less than cruel to women. The overburdened mothers who were confined once a year or once in eighteen months, never allowed to regain full strength between confinements, and made prematurely old, are, I hope, a thing of the past. Marriage on those terms did mean servitude. Further, the plan is cruel to children. They cannot on these terms receive sufficient attention. They are not given a fair start in life, and in many cases do not even receive sufficient healthy nourishment. These things are of course in part due to the artificial conditions of modern life. But the conditions are there and cannot be ignored. And thirdly, the plan involves a wrong to society. We have great need of healthy well-trained children, but society as a whole suffers when children are brought into the world who cannot be properly cared for.

About this point I conceive there really cannot be any doubt whatever. And thus the problem of birth control forces itself upon our attention. It is a duty to women, to children, and to the state. The really difficult question is, 'How is it to be achieved?'

One great Church in Christendom replies, 'By continence, and by no other method.' And there are many who arrive at the same position because they hold that sexual intimacy is only justified, and is only holy, when the deliberate purpose of producing children enters into it. As I see the matter we come here to the central ethical issue of this whole matter. Is it true that sexual intimacy is only right and beautiful when it is entered upon with a creative purpose, or is it also right and sacramental as an expression of mutual affection? Or put differently – granting that two persons have allowed their love to lead to parentage, and have loyally accepted the burdens of family life, may they rightly continue to live in intimacy after the point has been reached at which they know they ought not to have any more children? It is at this point that people of unquestionable moral earnestness differ acutely. I am compelled to take my stand with those who believe that sexual intimacy is right and good in itself as an expression of affection. It has, as a matter of fact, a good many other consequences than the production of children. It constitutes a bond of very great worth between two persons. It is in many interesting ways beneficial to a woman's physical system; and it brings to men a general balance and repose of being which is of enormous value. I believe, in fact, that in actual experience it does justify itself as a method of expressing affection.

The alternative for thousands of couples is not merely the cessation of sexual intimacy, but also abstinence from all the endearing intimacies which are natural and spontaneous in married life. They must not only sleep apart, but in many ways live apart. And this not only means pain of heart such as would take a very great deal to justify it, but also often leads to serious nervous trouble because of the strain which it involves. I have insisted again and again in these pages that continence is perfectly possible for unmarried men. But continence for a man living in the same house with a woman whom he loves, and with whom he has had experience of sexual intimacy, is a very different thing. [. . .]

As to how that control should be achieved I have no special fitness to speak. I would advise any couple, faced by the problem, to consult some doctor of repute till they understand the matter, and then to find out for themselves what is for them the right course to adopt.

Parenthood: Design or Accident? (1928)
Michael Fielding

In this book an attempt is made to explain clearly what is meant by birth-control, why it is being advocated, and how it may best be practised. It contains very little information that may not also be found in the works of other writers who have contributed to the subject. But it differs from most of these works in a number of important respects. First of all, it is completely free from the sentimentality with which many writers find it necessary to invest any theme that involves consideration of the sexual function. No attempt is made to conciliate any reader's prudery; no concession is made to prurience. Physiological facts are stated baldly and without emotion. It is considered sufficient to mention in its proper place the fact that sex intercourse is usually pleasurable or that sexual relations may be beautiful. But it is not deemed necessary to express any ecstasy that in a prosaic world such things should be.

Secondly, all the information is strictly accurate. There are a number of widely circulated books on birth-control in which some of the information is reliable but a great deal is not. Those not written by doctors, with personal experience of contraceptive technique, suffer particularly from this defect. The writers, it would appear, indiscriminately jumble together all the methods of which they have ever heard, without any regard to whether they have anything to commend them apart from the fact that some people at some time have made use of them. Unfortunately, the lay reader is not in a position to sift out what may be valuable and efficient in this glut of methods offered for his selection and may find himself adopting one which would be condemned out of hand by any medical or psychological authority. Many methods that have been extensively used are given no mention at all in this book; some are merely mentioned to be condemned. Nothing is described fully that has not been taught by the writer to his patients in the course of a wide practice extending over several years. Nothing is advocated that has not passed the test of experience and proved itself to be completely reliable as well as physiologically and aesthetically adequate. It is considered better to describe two or three reliable methods, covering a great variety of needs, accurately and in detail, than to create confusion, and incidentally insecurity, by giving a kind of annotated catalogue of all birth-control procedures. [. . .]

I think there must be very few enlightened people left in the world who believe that the doctor's chief function is to cure disease. For one thing he usually cannot do it. He can patch and mend, and remove a tumour here and a diseased organ there; he can, in certain types of acute illness, lend a helping hand to the natural resistances of the body that are trying to cope with the disease process; he can ameliorate symptoms; but he cannot present a chronically sick patient with the brand-new set of organs and tissues that would be required to produce the only restoration of health that merits the name of cure. This truth is being realised even by the medical profession: the function of the doctor is being recognised more and more to be not the cure of fully-formed disease but the prevention of its small beginnings. 'Prevention is better than cure' is an expression of popular wisdom; prevention is usually easy – cure impossible, is a summary of the outlook of modern medicine.

It is as a contribution to preventive medicine that I wish to deal with birth-control in this section. It is very easy indeed to defend contraception when, owing to a woman's state of health, pregnancy may mean the loss of life; or when a man or woman is afflicted with a transmissible disease that is almost certain to blight from the very beginning the life of the child resulting from such pregnancy. No doctor would fail to warn a woman suffering from certain forms of heart disease, from pulmonary tuberculosis, and certain types of kidney disease, of the grave danger to health and probably life that is involved in any pregnancy she may dare to undertake. Indeed, these are conditions in which, to save the life of the mother, doctors frequently feel they must take the serious step of terminating, as early as possible, an already accomplished pregnancy. Similarly, most people would justify almost any step taken to prevent men and women afflicted with syphilis from reproducing children inevitably destined to suffer from the same terrible disease. There are, it is true, some exceptionally high-minded people whose uncompromising zeal for the uplift of the human race demands the withholding of any information destined to prevent the conception of congenitally diseased babies; but, on the whole, in such cases even a most determined opponent of birth-control will concede that some advice on the prevention of conception may be given. It is highly probable, however, that the advice he would give would not be the same as that which would come from an advocate of birth-control.

But birth-control has other uses than to serve as a desperate remedy for desperate diseases. I wish to advocate it not as a medicine for the sick but as an invaluable contribution to the physical and mental well-being of normal men and women: not merely as a preventive of sickness but as a positive means of advancing health and happiness.

There are a number of disorders arising out of excessive child-bearing. They are so common that most people have come to regard them as the inevitable lot of woman and are prepared to face them with a degree of resignation and fortitude which those who believe in such things must find most inspiring. The tragedy of it is that this complacent attitude is not wholly confined to men; one meets such resigned acceptance of premature decrepitude and chronic invalidism even among the women who fill the out-patient departments of our hospitals and make work in our operating theatres entirely on account of disease and disablement contracted from having children more frequently than their bodies can endure.

Because child-bearing is a normal physiological process it must not be assumed that therefore it is one free from danger. Every year, in the United Kingdom, more than four confinements in every thousand end fatally. These figures represent an average for all classes, rich and poor; in industrial areas they are much higher, amounting in some to no less than eight deaths per thousand. It is true that many of these deaths are preventable; one need only study the variations of statistics from district to district to realise this. Better housing conditions, a more efficient midwifery service, adequate ante-natal and post-natal care for every child-bearing woman are all factors that would contribute to a lowering of this appalling maternal death-rate. But there are grounds for believing that even under the

best conditions a fatal accident rate of nearly two per thousand confinements may be expected. I do not think that anybody has yet suggested the
scheduling of maternity as a dangerous trade; but it is as well that one
should realise that even coal-mining, which is generally regarded as one
of the most dangerous occupations for men, has a fatal accident rate of
just over one per thousand – about half of that involved every time a
woman undergoes the normal physiological process of child-bearing *under the best possible conditions.*

But there is more to it than that; this normal physiological process makes
an enormous demand on the health and body of even the best constituted
woman. At the end of her great task of building up, nourishing, and supporting a life other than her own, the mother is in a state of great exhaustion; her abdominal muscles are weak and flabby from prolonged
over-stretching; the muscles and ligaments that help to keep the womb in
its place have lost their tone and her whole body is crying out for rest and
recuperation. If the woman is healthy and the labour has been normal,
this recuperation will in time be complete. The muscles and ligaments will
once more become tense and efficient and the abdomen again be adequate
to the task of supporting a pregnant womb.

When, however, pregnancies follow each other without a sufficient interval between them, recovery never takes place. On each occasion a terrific strain is put on the still exhausted organism; on each occasion the
residue of exhaustion is a little greater than it was the last. Misplacements
of the womb now become so serious that a whole train of symptoms
beginning with chronic backache and ending often in complete invalidism
is initiated; progressively, the abdominal muscles become flabbier and flabbier until there is no hope of their ever recovering themselves. The pregnant uterus can no longer assume its correct position in the body, for this
position is largely determined by the tenseness of the abdomen, and all
kinds of abnormal positions of the embryo involving difficult and prolonged labour result; tears of the neck of the womb, a common accompaniment of difficult labour, become increasingly frequent; a new danger
arises, in that such tears are recognised to favour the development of can-
cer of the womb; and the departments of our hospitals specialising in the
diseases of female organs of generation are filled with women, weary and
old before their time, suffering from chronic pain and disablement brought
about entirely by a too rapid succession of so-called normal physiological
events.

A healthy woman, who desires to do so, may have six or even more
children; and, as long as her pregnancies are properly spaced, suffer no
ill-effects thereby; but the same number of pregnancies in six or seven
years is the shortest cut possible to premature old-age and infirmity. [. . .]

But the differential birth-rate, none the less, presents serious problems because it shows clearly that the classes who are economically least capable of bearing the burden of large families are the very ones who are producing them. It is undesirable to breed, even from a stock that is all that the most exacting eugenist could wish, children who, for economic reasons, will never be given a proper chance in life. One advocates the prevention of excessive child-bearing among the poorest classes not on the ground that they are the 'worst stocks', but in order to put a stop to the tragedy of fine children doomed to inadequate lives solely on account of parental poverty.

Wherever one finds a high birth-rate one also finds a corresponding high infantile death-rate. That is not the worst, however: it is a tragedy for the parents, but not necessarily for the infants. But a high death-rate is also associated with a high sickness rate, and that means that a large percentage of the surviving children are fated, by cause of infantile disease, to grow up into frail, suffering men and women whose lives are a burden to them, practically from the cradle to the grave.

A civilised regard for the happiness and well-being of children demands the practice of birth-control; it demands that the rights of the child should be taken into account. As we must decide for ourselves what those rights may be, there is, of course, no need to be very exacting: but it does not seem excessive to suggest that no child should be brought into the world unless he is wanted, unless there is sufficient food, clothing and shelter available for his physical needs, and enough loving care to tide him over his early helpless years. The question of education is no less important. In our complex society the man or woman who has been denied education in childhood and adolescence, who by reason of poverty has been pushed straight from an inadequate school-life into any sort of blind-alley occupation, is likely to go to the wall. He joins the great mass of semi-skilled and unskilled persons for whom there are never enough jobs to go round; he becomes part of the margin of superfluous persons available for use by those whose unfailing contribution to the solution of our economic difficulties is to beat down still further the standard of life of the mass of the people.

Not only is birth-control the child's charter, safeguarding his right to affection and nurture; but it also provides for the great mass of people the only solution to the domestic and financial problems of the marriage state. There is, to begin at the very beginning, the question of early marriage. Innumerable young people who want to marry and who could make each other very happy, are deterred by the knowledge that their income, though sufficient for themselves, could not bear the strain of decently maintaining another person. A knowledge of contraception would make it possible for them to undertake marriage without a sense of guilt or fear; and they could defer the producing of children till their income was adequate to the demands that such an undertaking would make on it.

Many people, it is true, believe that early marriage involves a premature focussing of interest on the sexual life, to the detriment of spiritual and intellectual development. I do not think that such a belief corresponds with the psychological facts that anyone, who is prepared to distinguish clearly between what is and what he would like to be, can observe for himself. Most normal young people feel very urgent sexual needs which distract their minds and draw their energies away from the practical purposes of life. They find that they cannot, as it were, get on with the job, when in spite of their very best intentions, sexual longings insist on obtruding themselves and diverting their attention from practically everything else. Sexual starvation means not only that terrific efforts (that could be far more profitably directed to intellectual ends) have to be made to suppress desires that are as primitive and as natural as hunger for food, but, only too often, a yielding to temptations which involve the risk of infection by venereal disease. Early marriages with contraception seem to me to be by far the best alternative open to young people whose economic circumstances permit no proper provision for children. [. . .]

Doctors are singled out especially from members of other professions apparently on the assumption that a doctor's view on birth-control *necessarily* has greater value than that of anybody else. I emphasise the word 'necessarily' because it can be conceded that when an argument for or against birth-control is based on purely medical considerations a doctor's view does merit more consideration than that of a person without his advantages of training and experience. But anyone who cares to read the polemics against birth-control written by doctors will find that in the majority of them the argument is not based on medical considerations at all; it is based on the particular ethical, religious or political views the doctor in question may hold, any medical argument being dragged in to make a show of technical justification of views that have been arrived at on entirely different grounds.

Now, clearly, a doctor's views on ethics, religion and politics may be very important indeed; they may, for instance, be the most important thing about the doctor himself; but they do not merit any more or any less consideration in a discussion on birth-control than the moral, religious or political views of a member of any other profession [. . .] It is very rare indeed for a doctor to make his first approach to birth-control through his medical studies; that is largely the fault of the medical schools in which there is no organised teaching of this vital subject. In most instances his initiation dates from some moral speculation such as whether it is ever right to have sexual relations except for the specific purpose of reproducing; or some political one such as the Empire's need for larger populations. He has, in fact, often to relate birth-control to his concepts of the good, the beautiful and the true long before he has given adequate thought to any medical considerations that might help him to form his judgment. It is very gratifying indeed to note that his speculations lead him far more often in favour of birth-control than against it.

But there *are* medical writers against birth-control who attempt to build up a medical case; and I think it is important that some of their more alarming statements – those, for instance, that may deter anyone hesitating on the brink of a decision in his own life – should receive a certain amount of consideratition. [. . .]

Bacteria and parasites still infect and destroy the human subject; the threat of war is not lifted; periodic famines still wipe out populations; but these 'natural' expedients no longer appear effectively to avert the risk of over-population and, what is more, a lot of people do not like them, and even find themselves in conflict with Nature's methods of securing the (admittedly) beneficent end of limiting population. They are not deterred by the fact that the alternative is the substitution of an expedient that is not in Nature.

It is not usual to regard the scientist labouring to track down and destroy the micro-organisms of disease as an 'unnatural' monster. It is not even a mortal sin to put on oilskins to avert one of the natural consequences of rain. The confusion arises from the curious assumption that 'natural' is synonymous with good, and 'unnatural' with evil. The world of Nature is neither good nor evil: it is material upon which man must work to produce expedients and ends the goodness or badness of which may then be judged in terms of his own moral nature. These expedients are unnatural only in the sense that they do not already exist in Nature, and one may freely admit that if everything man needed for his use, happiness and development were performed in Nature, there would be some real point in stigmatising as unnatural and immoral any modification of Nature he dared to make.

But many devices not in Nature have contributed to human happiness and well-being, and, as such, have managed to secure general approval. They have been called inventions, and range from houses, clothes, electric light, cooked foods and mass production motor-cars, to such useful devices as braces to overcome the natural force of gravity. But general approval has not been achieved easily. Each conquest of Nature has been greeted with uneasy suspicion – with the pious assertion that these new-fangled ideas are unnatural and no good can possibly come of them. Such was the case when chloroform was introduced as an anaesthetic against the pains of child-bearing; pain, it was held, is a natural accompaniment to child-bearing with which it is impious to interfere. Similarly, aeroplanes were unnatural, because 'if we were intended to fly we should have been provided with wings.' Those who fought to abolish slavery were attacked on the grounds that they were wickedly attempting to interfere with a law of Nature.

Comments on Birth Control (1930)
Naomi Mitchison

Birth control methods are used by three sorts of couples. By temporary or semi-permanent lovers who have at all costs to avoid having babies. By young married couples (it seems simpler to consider the young couple always as 'married', though I only intend to imply a man and woman living in a union of love which is intended to be permanent) who want to space their babies, or, more rarely, to avoid having any. And by couples married for some time who wish to have no more babies, or, more rarely, to go on spacing them.

For the first of these three classes, the only alternative is abortion, which is apt to be dangerous, expensive and unpleasant, and is at present illegal. They must practice birth control. When two people are burning for one another, and anyhow probably having to get round or over all sorts of material obstacles before they can get their desire, this is only one more, and not perhaps a very important one. The flames can leap it.

At present there is a good deal of discussion going on about the advisability of pre-marital sexual experience, of course with the use of contraceptives. There is much to be said both for and against this. Especially with a girl, the first serious love affair is bound to have rather devastating psychological and physiological effects, and it is no use allowing her to believe that she can hop in and out of these troubled waters without any kind of difficulty. Personally, I think there is something to be said for the view that the Nordic young should normally be allowed to have romantic affections for persons of their own sex up to the end of adolescence; these probably engage the emotions less violently and are more easily recovered from, but those who practice them must take care to grow up at the right moment and turn to the other sex when their bodies are fully developed, and that is sometimes difficult.

There is also, I think, a great deal to be said for the Northern custom of hand-fasting, the unofficial betrothal which only becomes binding when a baby is certainly on the way. It is painful to think of a man or woman, over the age, say, of twenty-five, unless they are living a peculiarly exciting life of the mind, who has had no experience of love, and one would prefer it to be a happy and mutual experience without too much or too long repression. But I am inclined to think also that it is possible to overdo the business of casual affairs, as practised for instance, according to Judge Lindsay, by many of the American young. It seems to show a certain poverty of imagination to have to plunge at once into the final expression of emotion. No wonder they write so little good poetry. The honest lover, whether or not she marries, is one thing, the amateur prostitute is another, and the girl who considers marriage the only respectable profession and uses her hard virginity as a carrot for donkeys, is another still.

The young married couples have more to think about. If two normal people want to live together permanently the probability is that one, or more likely both of them want children. As I have said already there is a certain amount of propaganda about, advising that they should always wait first for a year or two in order to get used to one another. Quite apart from the desire for children – the desire to come fully out of adolescence and seize on that new bit of life which parenthood is – the suggestion seems to me most rash. The time for getting used to one another, in all conscience, is before marriage. It is too late to discover afterwards – especially with our present divorce laws – that they cannot manage it.

Until lately there has been another difficulty, besides this emotional one of wanting a child at once, in store for the young couple who decide to wait. This was that a virgin girl, even when she faced the situation, could not think it possible that she would be able to wear any kind of check pessary. And most newly married lovers would prefer the risk of starting a baby at once, which is not perhaps so great as the normal risk, to having their delight and beauty marred by the use of any obvious contraceptive device by the man, a preference not merely of romantic sentimentality, but a moral and aesthetic choice of some importance. Up till the last few years no doctor could give much advice, but there is now a technique which can be taught beforehand to a young bride and used with complete success. Even for this, a quite young girl may still have to overcome her traditional shamefastness; much will depend on the doctor consulted and more on whether she has had a reasonably scientific education.

But with the best will in the world, it is always possible that a newly married wife cannot easily and comfortably adjust a pessary; some women find them difficult enough to use until after the birth of the first child. If this is so, there are, of course, other possibilities, some of them not so safe, but at least avoiding part of the risk. There is no small soluble pessary at present on the market which is really reliable when used by a naturally fertile woman, and several kinds have uncomfortable properties which make them particularly unsuitable. I am not going to discuss two of the obvious alternatives to real contraception. One is *coitus interruptus*, which has been sufficiently criticized already by doctors and books, both as risky and also as having disastrous nervous effects on both man and woman. The other is the so-called safe period. This may work with some women, but as it can only be arrived at in any individual by a process of trial and error it is not of much practical use. All that can be said is that for a majority of normal women if they are leading normal lives, there are certain times during the month in which they are more likely to conceive than at others. But who is to know – in the present state of biological knowledge – whether she actually belongs to this majority?

However, even if contraceptive methods are difficult for a time, one thing is tolerably clear. There are many kinds of mutual caresses and pleasures. It seems probable that it is better for the young couple, both as a matter of health and enjoyment – may I perhaps even say morals? – that they should not have more actual copulation than they both really want to the bottom of their hearts, for it is a thing which develops fantastically easily into a mere pleasant habit of marriage. Here as usual, the Aristotelian – perhaps merely the Hellenic – ethic turns out to be only common sense.

Now one of the problems which the young married couple must face (and it is not an immediately obvious problem) is this: are they the sort of people who want their children only when they are intended, or as happy and surprising accidents? It is quite easy to say that it is braver and nobler and more civilized to have only intentional children (this is especially true of a woman who has had one or two already and knows what she is in for), that they should be loved even before conception and that there is a particular thrill in saying: 'Now is the time, to-day or to-night, in such and such a city or forest, we will beget our child.' That does splendidly for some kinds of people. But there are others (whether we like it or not) who prefer the other thrill of the accident, people who like to live casually like the cows and the lilies of the field, who probably have no fixed hours or terms of work, but belong to the professions like painting or pure science, which can be pursued violently or slackly according to the needs of the moment and the actual job they are on. They will at any rate have the grace and courage to find it amusing and not merely bitterly annoying when their contraceptive methods fail, as they are apt to sooner or later for all of us, and will be less inclined to rush off to Russia or Dr. . . . to get something done about it.

The young couple must also consider that it is not always possible to have a baby when one wants it, and it is extremely painful when the intentional conception fails again and again. And yet another moral problem which our ancestors did not have to cope with, is this terrible responsibility of the deliberate creation or denial of life. Once we start considering: we willed this life, are we justified? Once we begin to say: ought we to deny life to a being, to a potential child who might be alive and happy? We may find ourselves let in for such hideous pains and entanglements of thought, such contradictions and misunderstandings between husband and wife – optimist and pessimist perhaps – that we had better almost have had the earlier problems of health and economics, but with a kindly providence above seeing to the filling of the quiver.

But as the couple age, another set of problems present themselves. Very few normal couples with their own jobs and their own intellectual interests, keep up a devouring passion for one another all their lives. Love is not static, however much one might like it to be; it must almost necessarily move away from, as well as towards, passion. Why then, one might ask, do the hypothetical couple want to go on copulating? Because, if it was discovered that after all they did not really want it, then they had better stop; there will be no need to bother about the control of conception. But there seem to be a good many reasons why they should both want and need it.

First, if they still love one another, they have a great tenderness and amity towards one another, a mutual trust and security, which usually manifests itself, perhaps for want of a more definite way, and because most people are not clever with words, in their old expression of physical passion. Secondly they have feelings about children. Very often a woman is aware with a deep tenderness that the man is her children's father; she gets a particular satisfaction from him when she feels that he may be putting another into her, she may even manage to transfer this satisfaction to the best protected copulation, with perhaps, a curious secret hope in the moment of crisis that something may after all have gone wrong. The man may share this to some extent, but it is not so usual. Also, of course, they probably have some physical passion for one another, even after many years and much use, if they are reasonably healthy and beautiful; they find it pleasant to dance and flirt with one another still, and obvious to go on from that to their full satisfaction.

'The Right to Abortion' (1935)
F.W. Stella Browne

The woman's right to abortion is an absolute right, as I see it, up to the viability of her child. It does not depend upon certainty of death for her if the child is carried to term, though such a certainty or probability is, of course, a double claim to this relief. It does not depend on damage or permanent injury to her physical or mental health, whether certain or probable, if her child is born at term. It does not depend on the number of her previous confinements: the suggestion, put forward by some vigorous and veteran agitators for abortion law reform, that the woman should first supply a quota of at least two children, seems to me to disregard the individual needs, nature, and conditions of women. Neither does the right to refuse an unwanted child depend on economic conditions, though these supply an almost universal argument in this era of unemployment. Neither does the right we claim depend on having obtained the sanction of the Law and the Church to live with some special man, to bear his name, and share his home and means. Abortion legal for married women only would be the final climax of the illogical absurdity of our respectability complex; but it is certain to be advocated in some quarters, and it is a perfect example of the narrowest Trade Union spirit. After all, is not contraception for married women only the slogan of much organized feminist respectability?

The right to abortion does not depend on crimes which the conventions of romantic tradition deem worse than death, and which laws justifiably treat as second only to murder. (It is an interesting question how far the reprobation of rape is a defence of women's dignity and personality and how far it is subconscious 'compensation', communal jealousy, and property defence.) These crimes are barbarous and tragic, but the victim, even the girl in her early teens, is legally compelled to carry and bring to birth the results of sexual violence, whose begetter is punished with the full rigour of the law. Cannot chivalry here be tempered with reason, justice, and common sense?

Neither does the right to abortion *depend* on the uncertain and unpredictable result of possible genetic patterns in the child. Heredity is a much more intricate problem than pre-Mendelian Darwinism supposed. Before birth, heredity – or at least *maternal* inheritance – and environment are hardly distinguishable, and the mother's food, habits, and mental and emotional reactions must have profound effects, through the metabolic rhythms which pass through her child's body from her own. Abortion must be the key to a new world for women, not a bulwark for things as they are, economically nor biologically. Abortion should not be either a perquisite of the legal wife only, nor merely a last remedy against illegitimacy. It should be available for any woman, without insolent inquisitions, nor ruinous financial charges, nor tangles of red tape. For our bodies are our own.

But what of the practical realization of this principle? It seems to me that our case is as strong empirically as ethically, and that a severely circumscribed permission to terminate pregnancy would be attended by so many difficulties and cause so many injustices and absurdities that it would soon be found unworkable; just as the present law, for all its severity, is broken all over the country every day and by thousands of women, poor and rich, and by their helpers or exploiters, qualified or quacks.

Let us examine possible *restricted concessions* of the right to termination of pregnancy; in every case, be it well understood, by means of qualified and skilled medical and surgical help. No supporter of the right to abortion wishes to hand women over to the clumsy, uncleanly, often futile and often fatal interferences of those who, in Mr. George Bedborough's apt phrase, 'trade on the tragedy of despair', though there are cases of women who, whether with some midwifery training or a natural turn for practical medicine, have come to the aid of their friends and neighbours in this way, almost habitually, and earned thanks and blessings instead of bringing disaster. Nevertheless the attendant risks, without exact knowledge of the patient's circumstances and peculiarities and general constitution, and without the fullest opportunities for antiseptic and aseptic precautions, are too great. They need never occur under a law which honestly faced and humanely provided for the need to avert unwanted motherhood.

The mere fact that operations could be performed thoroughly and need not be scrambled through with eyes and ears alert for possible interruptions would save thousands of lives. So would the mercy of the *right* to a few days' rest in bed, with cleanliness and quiet, drowsing and light food; without inquiries and subterfuges, feverish fears, and those dread sudden chills. The trail of disease and crippling injuries, displacements, discharges, haemorrhages, inflammations, after unskilled – or even skilled but subsequently neglected – 'illegal operations' is as much a human sacrifice as the more spectacular death-roll itself.

An adequate abortion law would also encourage *constructive* research. There is no reason to suppose that we are at more than the mere alphabet of chemistry and psycho-biology in this matter. It is true that nearly all the vegetable potions used in traditional and current folk-lore to procure abortion are only effective in dosages which may inflict permanent injury, especially on heart, kidneys, and organs of elimination. But individual differences – 'idiosyncrasies' – here are very great. Throughout the islands of the Pacific, and in Mexico and Central America as well as Indonesia, there is a highly skilled and carefully guarded technique which attains results without slaughtering or crippling women. Missionaries have failed to extirpate this accomplishment, and anthropologists have testified to its admirable efficacy. Is it perhaps – together with the whole erotic art of the islands – a heritage from the Areoi or from a past far more remote? In any case, the invention and circulation of a perfectly reliable and otherwise tolerable abortifacient – especially if it could be self-administered, either by the mouth or as injections, intravenous or intramuscular – would be the greatest gift science could give to women. This triumph is perhaps possible within measurable time – unless indeed such civilization as Europe has achieved should pass away under a deluge of the high explosives and poison gases which afford so lucrative and respectable a branch of research and industry. The right to abortion is a key-point, going deep down to the roots of social philosophy and economic reality.

'The Case Against Legalized Abortion' (1935)
A.M. Ludovici

Another flagrant instance of the sexual monomorphic bias (which now happens to be masculine) is the Birth-Control Movement, which has aimed at securing for the woman the male's adaptation to sex without the so-called 'worst consequences' (the baby), and at warding off the menace of over-population, without any consideration whatsoever for the functions and needs of the female body.

Seeing that the average woman's active sexual life lasts from her four-teenth to her forty-sixth or fiftieth year, by limiting her to two or three children as the birth controllers wish to do (and in an enormous number of homes the one-child family – a purely male arrangement – is now es-tablished) means that for whole decades of her sexual life she is not func-tioning normally as a woman at all, but has merely done the service to her male of securing his sexual adaptation, and, in so doing, has assimilated her sex to his, the complete cycle of which begins and ends with sexual congress.

There is, unfortunately, no space to enter into the grave consequences of this inhuman treatment of woman; but I can assure those who imagine that her specific sexual cycle can, for the greater part of her sexual life, be thus assimilated to the male's without damage to her, are guilty of the most serious error.

Nevertheless, under the influence of our masculine and monomorphic view of sex, there appears superficially to be so little wrong with birth control that an enormous number of its advocates are actually women, and women eagerly embrace its teaching. Surely this is proof enough of the extent to which current values can corrupt even instinct!

True, many of the advocates of birth control are not scientists or in a position to appreciate the enormity of their propaganda. On the other hand, there are many medical people among them, and even these seem to be unaware of their monomorphic view of sex.

I cannot quote all the medical experts who are guilty of this uncon-scious subservience to the paramount values of the age. But by quoting the greatest of them all, I again leave it to the reader to concede my point regarding the remainder.

Writing in 1917, Havelock Ellis said: 'The method of birth-control by one of the contraceptive measures is the one and only method which places in the hands of the whole population possessed of ordinary care and providence the complete power to regulate, limit, or, *if necessary altogether prevent,* the production of offspring, while yet enabling the functions of married life to be exercised.'

Whose functions of married life? Obviously, only the man's! And we are thus back again at our modern obsession, the masculine and monomorphic view of sex.

When it is remembered that this modern, monomorphic view of sex is now backed in women's minds by all the panic created through the tragic muddle into which the normal function of parturition has been allowed to fall; when it is remembered that its plausibility seems superficially obvious in the face of the economic struggle and the recent emancipation and industrialization of women; when, moreover, the reader appreciates the temptation to accept it, owing to the pacificist, international fraternizing and other ideals of the age – over and above women's academic and professional ambitions, which in their turn assimilate the female to the male – it will be seen that, morbid and anti-feminine as this male monomorphic Feminism is, it is to some extent comprehensible, and that it requires the utmost independence of thought and concentration upon realities not to fall a victim to its spell.

Imagine another state, in which the function of parturition was the delight it should be (and often is to-day, in spite of everything the masculinized population may say); imagine a state in which men envied (as they should) woman's far richer sexual life, in which the parturient female was the emblem of the Joy of Life, and in which all woman's characteristics – her earlier maturity, her peculiar morphology, her whole relationship to the child – were regarded as the acme of desirability, and you would find aesthetes like Goethe laughed at, birth controllers reviled as jealous Puritans, and doctors who advise anaesthetics for childbirth stigmatized as the ascetic kill-joys of the age. [. . .]

Turning now to an all too brief enumeration of the reasons why I oppose the legalization of abortion, I say it should be resisted –

(i) Because it is a measure appealing to and calculated to accommodate only the masculinoid female, and when any other more desirable woman urges it she does so in ignorance of what it means and what it involves. Why is the masculinoid woman prone to avail herself of legalized abortion and to support the movement favouring it? Because her masculinoid morphology and psyche indicate that she is the victim either of gonadal insufficiency, which makes her female impulses feeble; of genital hypoplasia (under-development of her generative equipment), which makes her indifferent to the psychophysical experiences of maternity, or of a definite male bias in her physiology (a metabolic rate or endocrine balance – or both – approaching the male type) which inevitably makes her wish to escape her essentially female destiny.

(ii) Because only Puritans and kill-joys can wish to exploit the panic that has seized upon the womanhood of Western civilization in order, by starting a new fashion or tradition, to deprive the only desirable examples of that womanhood of their full sex expression and experience, to limit it to a paltry few years in the long span of sexual life Nature has given them, and possibly to deprive them of the very capacity to enjoy that sexual life and to feel its thrills and desires. This panic has arisen through the mismanagement of gestation and parturition by our civilization and its science, and through the recruitment to motherhood every year of thousands of degenerate women who have no business to become parous and who therefore give female sex functions a bad name. As, however, this is only a bad phase, which wise measures can and will overcome, it would be insane to alter our institutions and laws just to meet the requirements of this bad phase, and thus perpetuate a degenerate patch in our history.

(iii) Because it cannot and will not suppress criminal or surreptitious abortion; but by causing artificial abortion to seem more rational and proper (owing to its new odour of official sanctity) make it much more difficult – as they are discovering in Russia – to instruct the population as a whole concerning its grave disadvantages and dangers.

(iv) Because the only way to deal with surreptitious and criminal abortion and to put a stop to the agitation for legalized abortion is to attempt what has never yet been attempted in England or France, but which they are now (only too belatedly!) trying in Russia – to educate the female population in the elements of the whole problem, so that they may know the gravity and dangers of interrupting a pregnancy. At present the very agitation in favour of legalized abortion leads thousands of ill-informed women (chiefly married, although much is made by my opponents out of the tragically pathetic plight of the unmarried mother) to think that the operation is as simple and safe as a hair-cut. And many of the less scrupulous advocates of legalized abortion must be held responsible for this widespread belief.

Even in the most wildly revolutionary state, however, certain operations for abortion at certain times cannot be legalized. There will always, therefore, be a surreptitious service to meet desperate cases, who prefer death to the alternative. But, even in these cases, much good could be done by spreading knowledge of the gravity and danger of interrupting a pregnancy. Legalizing abortion, as we have seen, could not touch such cases.

(v) Because *ton corps n'est pas à toi* and never can be *à toi,* and Victor Margueritte was talking sentimental twaddle. Your body cannot be your own to do as you like with so long as you live with other people in a state of more or less mutual dependence, in which there is a tacit agreement (now ratified by law) that you will support them, and they you, in case of mishap. In such circumstances, when you yourself and everyone else insists in adversity on getting the last ounce of your neighbour's pity, there cannot possibly be a right deliberately to make yourself a permanent burden on the community by gratuitously interfering with a natural process.

(vi) Because, as usual in these agitations, only a misguided minority is demanding this reform. The wiser, sounder, and more normal among the women of the nation are not interested in it.

Part VI

Eugenics

Introduction

Carolyn Burdett

Francis Galton coined the term 'eugenics' to describe what he wanted to become a new, guiding religion for a secular, rational age: namely knowledge of, and control over, human procreation. Galton's studies of eminent men in the 1860s had convinced him that both physical and mental characteristics are *inherited*. The only way to improve human life is to ensure that the best – the fittest – members of the population reproduce more than the less fit. Galton believed that in modern, 'civilized' societies, the struggle for resources had become less and less efficient, as humans sought kinder and more humane ways of ordering their lives. In consequence, weaker members of society were protected and able to pass on weaknesses to their offspring, thus imperilling improvement and progress. The only answer, Galton argued, was for humans to take control of the processes of selection, and this is precisely what he proposed eugenics should do. Eugenics aimed, through the use of scientific knowledge and methodology, to go to the heart of what Victorian ideology had made the most intimate and private part of nineteenth-century lives: marriage, sexual relations, and the birth of children.

Galton's most important successor was Karl Pearson (1857–1936), a trained mathematician. Pearson headed what became the major research centre for eugenic work, the Galton Eugenics Laboratory at University College, London, where he and his co-workers developed a statistical methodology called biometrics. By categorizing the human population in terms of different physical and mental characteristics, and correlating them between parents and offspring, 'fitness' and 'unfitness' could be identified and traced back through family lines of heredity. Politically, Pearson identified himself as a socialist. He strongly opposed the doctrine of laissez-faire which characterized liberal thinking in the nineteenth century, arguing that the state was the only body capable of ordering the community towards a common good. But whatever tasks the state carried out, its body, the nation, would not thrive if its major raw material, its people, were weak. Therefore Pearson saw the *primary* responsibility of the state as the overseeing of what had hitherto been accepted as the privacy of sex and family, because they were of foremost importance to the strength and stability of the nation. The major players in ensuring the continued health and progress of the nation would be the professionals, scientists, and experts who were uniquely able to determine human quality through their objective, scientific investigations. The pieces by Pearson included here demonstrate this central role of the nation, and suggest, too, how his eugenics supported an enthusiasm for imperial expansion based upon a belief in racial superiority.

Pearson's major aim, however, was to establish the scientific credentials of eugenics. He was, and remained, suspicious of popularizers of eugenics, which is how he viewed the Eugenics Education Society, even though this body became the most influential conduit for eugenic ideas in the first half of the century. The Society was founded in November, 1907, changing its name to the Eugenics Society in 1926. It published *Annual Reports*, which were incorporated into the Society's journal, *The Eugenics Review* (from which several extracts here are taken), established in 1909. The Society's membership counted many well-known names amongst its ranks, drawn from intellectual, professional and radical circles, including Havelock Ellis, G.B. Shaw, H.G. Wells, Sydney and Beatrice Webb, A.J. Balfour, Neville Chamberlain and Maynard Keynes. In 1912, the Society organized the first International Eugenics Congress, held at the University of London; it also contributed to many parliamentary reports and Royal Commissions in the first decades of the century, and was supported financially by bodies such as London's County Council and the Medical Research Council. In general, it aimed to set forth 'the national importance of Eugenics', to create a sense of civic responsibility, and to further knowledge of the laws of heredity and eugenic teaching in as wide a sense as possible.

The Society's 'Aims and Objects', published in 1935, are included here. They illustrate how eugenics was conceived as a body of scientific knowledge *and* a policy programme. The aims of the latter are couched in terms of the commonly used distinction between positive and negative eugenics: the first encourages 'superior, healthy and useful stocks' to give birth to more children (through, for example, favourable taxation and family allowances), while the second seeks to restrict the birth-rate of those deemed to suffer hereditary infirmity. Negative eugenics was primarily directed at the 'feeble-minded', an indistinct term which grouped together many different types of mental condition as well as forms of socially deviant behaviour. The extract from Havelock Ellis's *The Task of Social Hygiene* illustrates the position favoured by the Society, which drew back from advocating compulsory methods of eugenic intervention, such as enforced sterilization, stressing instead the importance of fostering a 'eugenic conscience' in the community at large.

In the first decades of the twentieth century, however, and again during the depression of the 1930s, the eugenic movement was beset by fears of racial degeneration, and the question of compulsion was never far away – as is evidenced in the comments made in the 'Aims and Objects' about birth control, segregation, sterilization, the prohibition of marriage and abortion. Nevertheless, the Eugenics Society was keen to distance itself from what it saw as the excesses of Nazi policy: *The Eugenics Review* 'Notes of the Quarter' included here cautiously assent to Hitler's 1933 Eugenic Sterilization Law, except where it espouses the enforced sterilization of Jews and other, vilified, 'foreign races'. The extract from Julian Huxley's (1887–1975) 'Eugenics and Society' illustrates how the rise of fascism began to concentrate the minds of some members of the scientific community. Huxley, a biologist, was an advocate of eugenics, but felt that mainstream eugenic thinking had become clogged by class and race prejudices. Here he argues for a transformed social system and a new spirit of internationalism as the means to an improved and progressive life, freed from the threat of aggression between nations.

From its beginning, eugenics drew support from a spectrum of political opinion which frequently found the sharpest disagreements over issues of sexuality. Indeed, the position of women was always at the heart of eugenic debate, as Ellis argues here. The centrality of sex was, perhaps, a major lure for radicals, like George Bernard Shaw. It also unleashed some fervently reactionary responses, exemplified here by W.C.D. Whetham (1867–1952) and C.D. Whetham. Caleb Saleeby (1878–1940), too, although arguing for the importance of women's suffrage, puts political rights for women firmly within the context of their domestic duties. At the other end of the spectrum, Herbert Brewer, another self-proclaimed socialist, advocated artificial insemination to control biological inheritance in a radically more efficient way, freed as it would be from the panoply of emotions and desires associated with sex, which could, in their turn, be satisfied with impunity. Socialism would provide the good social environment, and 'eutelegenesis' the 'superman' fit for it.

Some feminists were attracted to eugenics because of the centrality it accorded to women and mothering, although few, particularly in the earlier part of the century, would have found much to support in Brewer. Many women, feminists included, saw in eugenics a scientifically valid basis for an improved sexual morality. Even a feminist such as Olive Schreiner (1855–1920), who was broadly opposed to the 'social purity' movement of the late nineteenth century, makes the issue of women's submission to the greater good central to her argument for women's emancipation. In her influential *Woman and Labour*, Schreiner counters eugenic fears that feminist aspirations will displace sexual and maternal ones – and therefore threaten the fertility of the middle classes – with an argument which itself draws on a eugenic rhetoric of race responsibility. It demonstrates how the attempt to imagine women's emancipation was intimately bound up with the new scientific languages of sexuality, which so often put the nature of femininity at the centre of their concerns.

The Sexual Question (1906)
August Forel

Our strong sexual appetite is no longer in proportion to the exigencies of procreation, nor to the means of providing food for our descendants, nor to the right of the latter to better or even tolerable existence, for the simple reason that the weak, the diseased and the children are no longer eliminated as in former times among primitive races by infanticide, epidemics, wild-beasts, neglect or war (it is now the strong and courageous who are eliminated by the latter). But it is not in our power to modify our instinctive and hereditary sexual appetite, while we have always at hand the necessary means to regulate and improve procreation. [. . .]

I repeat here that it is not our object to create a new human race of superior beings, but simply to cause gradual elimination of the unfit, by suppressing the causes of blastophthoria, and sterilizing those who have hereditary taints by means of a voluntary act; at the same time urging healthier, happier and more social men to multiply more and more. [. . .]

What then are the types of men which we should endeavor to produce?

Types to Eliminate. – First of all we must understand that negative action is much easier than positive. It is more easy to mention the types which should not be allowed to multiply than those which should. These are, in the first place, all criminals, lunatics, and imbeciles, and all individuals who are irresponsible, mischievous, quarrelsome or amoral. These are the persons who do the most harm in society, and introduce into it the most harmful taints. It is the same with alcoholics, opium-eaters, etc., who, although often capable in other respects, are dangerous by their blastophthoric influence. Here the only remedy consists in the suppression of the use of narcotics, for it is no use eliminating a few narcotized individuals as long as a greater number is always being produced.

Persons predisposed to tuberculosis by heredity, chronic invalids, the subjects of rickets, hemophilia, and other persons incapable of procreating a healthy race owing to inherited diseases or bad constitution, form a second category of individuals who ought to avoid propagation, or do so as little as possible.

Types to Perpetuate. – On the other hand, men who are useful from the social point of view – those who take a pleasure in work and those who are good tempered, peaceful and amiable should be induced to multiply. If they are endowed with clear intelligence and an active mind, or with an intellectual or artistic creative imagination, they constitute excellent subjects for reproduction. In such cases certain taints which are not too pronounced may be passed over.

True will-power, i.e., perseverance in the accomplishment of rational resolutions, and not the tyrannical and obstinate spirit of domination, is also one of the most desirable qualities which ought to be reproduced. Will-power must not be confounded with impulsiveness, which is rather the antinomy of it, but often deceives superficial observers, and makes them believe in the existence of a strong will, because of the violent manner in which it tries to realize momentary impulsive resolutions.

The Scope and Importance to the State of the Science of National Eugenics (1909)
Karl Pearson

If we attempt to define the scope of statecraft we enter no doubt the field of controversy, but may we not extend the condition which so fitly expresses the primary need of the individual – the healthy mind in healthy body – to the swarm of individuals with which the statesman has to deal? Taking the word 'sanity' in its broadest sense of health and soundness, the primary purpose of statecraft is to insure that the nation as a whole shall possess sanity; it must be sound in body and sound in mind. This is the bedrock on which alone a great nation can be built up; by aid of this sanity alone an empire once founded can be preserved. There are secondary important conditions – too often regarded as primary – which are undoubted parts of statecraft. The nation must have the instruments and the training needful to protect itself and its enterprises; it must hold the sources of raw material and the trade routes requisite to develop the wealth upon which its population depends; it must have the education necessary to makes its craftsmen, its traders, its inventors, its men of science, its diplomatists, and its statesmen the equals at least of those of its rivals on the world-stage. Nay, perhaps as important as all these, it must have traditions and ideals so strong that the prejudices of individuals and the prerogatives of classes will fall before urgent national needs; it requires teachers, be they pressmen, poets, or politicians, who grasp the wants of the nation as a whole; who, independent of class and party, can remind the people at the fitting moment of their traditions, and their special function amid nations.

Yet if we come to analyse the secondary conditions, we shall find in each case that their realization depends on the fulfilment of our primary condition. Without high average soundness of body and soundness of mind, a nation can neither be built up nor an empire preserved. Permanence and dominance in the world passes to and from nations even with their rise and fall in mental and bodily fitness. No success will attend our attempts to understand past history, to cast light on present racial changes, or to predict future development, if we leave out of account the biological factors. Statistics as to the prevalence of disease in the army of a defeated nation may tell us more than any dissertation of the genius of the commanders and the cleverness of the statesmen of its victorious foe. Lost provinces and a generation of hectoring may follow to the conquered nation whose leaders have forgotten the primary essential of national soundness in body and mind.

Francis Galton, in establishing a laboratory for the study of National Eugenics in the University of London, has defined this new science as 'the study of agencies under social control that may improve or impair the racial qualities of future generations, either physically or mentally'. The word *eugenic* here has the double sense of the English *wellbred*, goodness of nature and goodness of nurture. Our science does not propose to confine its attention to problems of inheritance only, but to deal also with problems of environment and of nurture. It may be said that much social labour has already been spent on investigating the condition of the people; there have been Royal Commissions, Parliamentary and Departmental Committees, and much independent effort on the part of philanthropists, medical men, and social reformers. I would admit all this, and would try to appraise it at its true value. Some of it has provided useful material for eugenic study; much of it is the product of wholly irresponsible witnesses with comments by commissioners equally untrained in dealing with statistical problems. Witnesses, commissioners, philanthropists, social reformers, as a rule, and medical men only too frequently, sadly need that technical education, that power of reasoning about statistical data, which I think will become general when Eugenics has been made a subject of academic study, and minds specially trained to this branch of scientific inquiry are placed at the disposal of our statesmen. I do not, of course, say that there was no eugenic research before Francis Galton invented the word and named the new science. But I believe the day not distant when we shall recognize that he seized the psychological moment to assert its claim to academic consideration; and that in the time to come the nation will be more than grateful to the man who said that the university is the true field for the study of those agencies which may improve or impair our racial qualities. To become a true science, you must remove our study from the strife of parties, from the conflict of creeds, from false notions of charity, or the unbalanced impulses of sentiment. You must treat it with the observational caution and critical spirit that you give to other branches of biology. And when you have discovered its principles and deduced its laws, then, and then only, you can question how far they are consonant with current moral ideas or with prevailing human sentiment. I myself look forward to a future when a wholly new view as to patriotism will be accepted; when the individual will recognize more fully and more clearly the conflict between individual interests and national duties. I foresee a time when the welfare of the nation will form a more conspicuous factor in conduct; when conscious race-culture will cope with the ills which arise when we suspend the full purifying force of natural selection; and when charity will not be haphazard – the request for it being either a social right, or the granting of it an anti-social wrong. But if we are to build up a strong nation, sound in mind and body, we shall have to work in the future with trained insight: I feel convinced that real enlightenment will only follow a scientific treatment of the biological factors in race development.

The Family and the Nation (1909)
W.C.D. Whetham and C.D. Whetham

While, among certain sections of the upper classes, women have been impeded in their true duties by the desire to share the amusements to which their husbands and brothers have become too much addicted, among another section they have suffered as much, or perhaps even more, from the wish to take an equal part in man's work instead of his play.

The intellectual and political development of the last half-century has been accompanied by an unfortunate tendency to belittle the home duties for which women, by their essential nature, are specially responsible. For this tendency men are to blame at least to the same extent as women. Both sexes have failed to appreciate the high honour which should attach to the successful performance of the true womanly duties. To bring forth, nourish, and educate children is, for the future of the race, more important work than any that falls to the lot of man. To regulate well a household, to keep in order, cleanliness, and health the home, on the comfort of which the welfare of the whole family depends, is highly skilled work, and at least as essential a function in life as man's external profession or political activities.

The recent demands of certain women for a share in social, political, philanthropic, and educational work are hard to resist, since they are often greatly to the immediate benefit of the community. But it cannot be doubted that the quiet home life necessary for the right birth and management of a large family is incompatible with many external activities, and with the gratification of a desire to seek an apparently larger sphere of immediate work and influence in social, industrial, and political life.

For young married women, such external activities are a direct menace to the future welfare of the race. Even for unmarried women, the indirect danger is great, especially in setting a false ideal of life before the rising generation. Indications are not wanting that a position of industrial independence, or the wider, if more superficial, interests of active public life, with the demoralizing accompaniment of publicity and notoriety, exert such a fascination on the minds of some women that they become unwilling to accept the necessary and wholesome restrictions and responsibilities of normal marriage and motherhood. Woe to the nation whose best women refuse their natural and most glorious burden!

In considering the physiology and psychology of the race, it seems clear that the stock of human life, our most valuable national asset, must, as in every sound economic system, be divided into two parts representing capital and income. Men represent the income, to be used and spent freely by each succeeding generation as need arises. Women must be considered as capital, to be spent sparingly in the present, to be husbanded carefully for the future. [. . .]

In towns and other areas where many women are employed in manual labour, such as places where textile industries are carried on, the birth-rate is abnormally low. Northampton, Halifax, Burnley, Blackburn, Derby, Leicester, Bradford, Oldham, Huddersfield, and Bolton – all places in which an exceptionally large proportion of married women are engaged in factory work – are the ten towns in all England in which the relative fall in the birth-rate between 1881 and 1901 is most startling. On the other hand, in mining districts, where the employment of women is rare, the birth-rate remains high.

We see, then, that a direct correlation can be traced between the freedom of women from industrial occupations and the number of children they produce. [. . .]

For the benefit of the children, the absence of the mother from the home is to be deplored. Employment that takes her away should be discouraged by every means in our power. At present, when a respectable, hard-working woman with several children loses her husband by accident or disease, the Poor Law Guardians usually give relief which is quite inadequate for support. The widow is forced to neglect her children in order to earn their bread. For the good of the community, even to prevent economic waste, we should in this respect adopt the recommendation of the Report of the Minority of the Poor Law Commission and give adequate support, when the conditions of the family and home are good, on the agreement that the mother gives her whole time to her children. The knowledge that such action would be taken in worthy cases would remove one motive which tends to favour restriction of family among the best and most provident of the labouring class. The direct effect of the action would be an ultimate gain to the community, for, as economists have come to realize, 'the most valuable of the year's crops, as it is the most costly, is not the wheat harvest or the lambing, but the year's quota of adolescent young men and women enlisted in the productive service of the community; . . . the due production and best possible care of this particular product is of far greater consequence to the nation than any other of its occupations.'

Woman and Labour (1911)
Olive Schreiner

What if, the increased culture and mental activity of woman necessary for her entrance into the new fields, however desirable in other ways for herself and the race, should result in a diminution, or in an absolute abolition of the sexual attraction and affection, which in all ages of the past has bound the two halves of humanity together? What if, though the stern and unlovely manual labours of the past have never affected her attractiveness for the male of her own society, nor his for her; yet the performance by woman of intellectual labours, or complex and interesting manual labour, and her increased intelligence and width, should render the male objectionable to her, and the woman undesirable to the male; so that the very race itself might become extinct through the dearth of sexual affection? What, and if, the woman ceases to value the son she bears, and to feel desire for and tenderness to the man who begets him; and the man to value and desire the woman and her offspring? Would not such a result exceed, or at least equal, in its evil to humanity, anything which could result from the degeneration and parasitism of woman? Would it not be well, if there exist any possibility of this danger, that woman, however conscious that she can perform social labour as nobly and successfully under the new conditions of life as the old, should yet consciously, and deliberately, with her eyes open, sink into a state of pure intellectual torpor, with all its attendant evils, rather than face the more irreparable loss which her development and the exercise of her gifts might entail? Would it not be well she should deliberately determine, as the lesser of two evils, to dwarf herself and limit her activities and the expansion of her faculties, rather than that any risk should be run of the bond of desire and emotion between the two sexual halves of humanity being severed? [. . .]

It must be at once frankly admitted that, were there the smallest possible danger in this direction, the sooner woman laid aside all endeavour in the direction of increased knowledge and the attainment of new fields of activity, the better for herself and for the race.

When one considers the part which sexual attraction plays in the order of sentient life on the globe, from the almost unconscious attractions which draw amoeboid globule to amoeboid globule, on through the endless progressive forms of life [. . .]; till in the highly developed male and female it assumes its aesthetic and intellectual but not less imperative form, couching itself in the songs of poet [sic], and the sometimes deathless fidelity of richly developed man and woman to each other, we find it not only everywhere, but forming the very groundwork on which is based sentient existence; never eradicable, though infinitely varied in its external forms of expression. When we consider that in the human world, from the battles and dances of savages to the intrigues and entertainment of modern Courts and palaces, the attraction of man and woman for each other has played an unending part; and, that the most fierce ascetic religious enthusiasm through the ages, the flagellations and starvations in endless nunneries and monasteries, have never been able to extirpate nor seriously to weaken for one moment the master dominance of this emotion; that the lowest and most brutal ignorance, and the highest intellectual culture leave mankind, equally, though in different forms, amenable to its mastery; that, whether in the brutal guffaw of sex laughter which rings across the drinking bars of our modern cities, and rises from the comfortable armchairs in fashionable clubs; or in the poet's dreams, and the noblest conjugal relations of men and women linked together for life, it plays still to-day on earth the vast part it played when hoary monsters ploughed after each other through Silurian slime, and that still it forms as ever the warp on which in the loom of human life the web is woven, and runs as a thread never absent through every design and pattern which constitutes the individual existence on earth, it appears not merely as ineradicable; but it is inconceivable to suppose that the attraction of sex towards sex, which, with hunger and thirst, lie, as the triune instincts, at the base of animal life on earth, should ever be exterminable by the comparatively superficial changes resulting from the performance of this or that form of labour, or the little more or less of knowledge in one direction or another.

That the female who drives steam-driven looms, producing scores of yards of linen in a day, should therefore desire less the fellowship of her corresponding male than had she toiled at a spinning-wheel with hand and foot to produce one yard; that the male should desire less of the companionship of the woman who spends the morning in doctoring babies in her consulting-room, according to the formularies of the pharmacopoeia, than she who of old spent it on the hillside collecting simples for remedies; that the woman who paints a modern picture or designs a modern vase should be less lovable by man, than her ancestor who shaped the first primitive pot and ornamented it with zigzag patterns was to the man of her day and age; that the woman who contributes to the support of her family by giving legal opinions will less desire motherhood and wifehood than she who in the past contributed to the support of her household by bending on hands and knees over her grindstone, or scrubbing floors, and that the former should be less valued by man than the latter – these are suppositions which it is difficult to regard as consonant with any knowledge of human nature and the laws by which it is dominated. [. . .]

While, if the statement that the female entering on new fields of labour will cease to be lovable to the male be based on the fact that she will then be free, all history and all human experience yet more negates its truth. The study of all races in all ages, proves that the greater the freedom of woman in any society, the higher the sexual value put upon her by the males of that society. The three squaws who walk behind the Indian, and whom he has captured in battle or bought for a few axes or lengths of tobacco, and over whom he exercises the despotic right of life and death, are probably all three of infinitesimal value in his eyes, compared with the value of his single, free wife to one of our ancient, monogamous German ancestors; while the hundred wives and concubines purchased by a Turkish pasha have probably not even an approximate value in his eyes, when compared with the value which thousands of modern European males set upon the one comparatively free woman, whom they may have won, often only after a long and tedious courtship.

So axiomatic is the statement that the value of the female to the male varies as her freedom, that, given an account of any human society in which the individual female is highly valued, it will be perfectly safe to infer the comparative social freedom of woman; and, given a statement as to the high degree of freedom of woman in a society, it will be safe to infer the great sexual value of the individual woman to man.

Finally, if the suggestion, that men and women will cease to be attractive to one another if women enter modern fields of labour, be based on the fact that her doing so may increase her intelligence and enlarge her intellectual horizon, it must be replied that the whole trend of human history absolutely negates the supposition. There is absolutely no ground for the assumption that increased intelligence and intellectual power diminishes sexual emotion in the human creature of either sex. The ignorant savage, whether in ancient or modern societies, who violates and then clubs a female into submission, may be dominated, and is, by sex emotions of a certain class; but not less dominated have been the most cultured, powerful, and highly differentiated male intelligences that the race has produced. A Mill, a Shelley, a Goethe, a Schiller, a Pericles, have not been more noted for vast intellectual powers, than for the depth and intensity of their sexual emotions. And, if possible, with the human female, the relation between intensity and sexual emotion and high intellectual gifts has been yet closer. The life of a Sophia Kovalevsky, a George Eliot, an Elizabeth Browning have not been more marked by a rare development of the intellect than by deep passionate sexual emotions. Nor throughout the history of the race has high intelligence and intellectual power ever tended to make either male or female unattractive to those of the opposite sex.

The Problem of Practical Eugenics (1912)
Karl Pearson

[Our statesmen and social reformers] first penalised parentage – forgetting that to the masses the child is a commodity produced according to its economic value and the result is that in fifty years they have almost halved the national birthrate, thus cutting off from Dame Nature much of her selective power; they overlooked the fact that the smaller the family the greater is the chance of degeneracy for we are limited to the less efficient elder born. By the foundation of innumerable charities and municipal institutions they further penalised the fitter parent, who had to support his own fit offspring, as against the unfit parent who passed his degenerate offspring into asylums and homes. The fertility at a given age which in 1851 was greater for the districts with desirable characteristics, became in 1907 markedly greater in the districts associated with undesirable characteristics. An artificial birthrate has been created in the fitter classes, which may become habitual, and if so spells ultimate racial destruction.

Practical eugenics demand in the first place that the economic value of the child shall be restored, that parentage shall no longer be penalised;

and in the second place the reversal of the present system by which the fit parent is handicapped as against the unfit. If both are in the same trade they receive the same wages, but the one is burdened by, the other relieved of, his offspring. The essential principle should be to handicap the unfit parent, not to relieve him of his encumbrances. The differential endowment of fit parentage relatively to unfit parentage and to childlessness, is the fundamental demand of the eugenist. Personally, I do not yet see light towards its practical solution, except in a system of national insurance, in which employer, state and workman shall combine to insure against invalidity, motherhood and the nurture of offspring – such provision being differentiated by the fitness of the parentage. Meanwhile, we have spent the millions at present available, millions which might have produced lasting influence on the race, in the fleeting good of an environmental effect; it is the old story repeated in the most recent evil by which unthinking philanthropy has crippled our power of modifying race fitness. The last inducement to fit parentage, the support in old age of a sturdy offspring, is removed by the state support alike of the fit and the unfit parent.

The view of human society which has been given in this lecture, will I fear prove unpopular – that is not in my mind an argument against its truth. I would not ask you to accept it without much criticism, and without viewing it from every possible side. To some of you who do this it will become a real possession, which will unify your conceptions of our present difficulties as to the apparent incompatibility of the highest forms of civilisation with continuous race progress. Why do we find degeneracy and race suicide arise as human sympathies and emotions are widened? I think the answer lies in the fact that environment appeals directly to our senses, but the indefinitely more potent heredity only to our reasoning. We rush to modify the former, regardless of the laws of the latter. The relief of pain and suffering is so obvious a duty, the penalisation of parentage is so disguised and so distant in its effects. When we say: 'You must protect the child from unhealthy or cruel environment', the best of the nation is with us with vote and even with purse. When we say: 'You must preserve the economic value of the child', we evoke no sympathy; none see at once the whole tale of penalised parentage, lowered birthrate, cacogenic reproduction, race degeneracy and the ultimate race suicide involved in the breach of that principle. Yet of the two statements I do not hesitate to say that the latter is far more fundamental; it is the search-light, which illumines the inmost recesses of history, and explains the fall of great world-civilisations. For those, who are desirous of judging legislation and social habit from the standpoint of practical eugenics, I feel certain that the fundamental questions are: (i) Do they preserve or create economic value for the child, and (ii) Do they emphasise the economic value of the child of fit parentage over that of unfit parentage? The first affirmed insures that the bulk of men will have children at all; the second affirmed that those children will be progressively better born.

The child as a commodity whose supply is regulated by economic value may sound a harsh doctrine. But truth – whether of natural selection or of social evolution – is not created by man; he has only to discover it, be it palatable or bitter. Social stability depends upon the extent to which we allow even unpalatable truth to guide our legislation and our conduct.

The Task of Social Hygiene (1912)
Havelock Ellis

Eugenics constitutes the link between the Social Reform of the past, painfully struggling to improve the conditions of life, and the Social Hygiene of the future, which is authorized to deal adequately with the conditions of life because it has its hands on the sources of life. [. . .]

A problem which is often and justly cited as one to be settled by Eugenics is that presented by the existence among us of the large class of the feeble-minded. No doubt there are some who would regret the disappearance of the feeble-minded from our midst. The philosophies of the Bergsonian type, which to-day prevail so widely, place intuition above reason, and the 'pure fool' has sometimes been enshrined and idolized. But we may remember that Eugenics can never prevent absolutely the occurrence of feeble-minded persons, even in the extreme degree of the imbecile and the idiot. They come within the range of variation, by the same right as genius so comes. We cannot, it may be, prevent the occurrence of such persons, but we can prevent them from being the founders of families tending to resemble themselves. [. . .]

Closely related to the great feeble-minded class, and from time to time falling into crime, are the inmates of workhouses, tramps, and the unemployable. The so-called 'able-bodied' inmates of the workhouses are frequently found, on medical examination, to be, in more than fifty per cent cases, mentally defective, equally so whether they are men or women. [. . .]

These classes, with their tendency to weak-mindedness, their inborn laziness, lack of vitality, and unfitness for organized activity, contain the people who complain that they are starving for want of work, though they will never perform any work that is given them. Feeble-mindedness is an absolute dead-weight on the race. It is an evil that is unmitigated. The heavy and complicated social burdens and injuries it inflicts on the present generation are without compensation, while the unquestionable fact that in any degree it is highly inheritable renders it a deteriorating poison to the race; it depreciates the quality of a people. The task of Social Hygiene which lies before us cannot be attempted by this feeble folk. Not only can they not share it, but they impede it; their clumsy hands are for ever becoming entangled in the delicate mechanism of our modern civilization. Their very existence is itself an impediment. Apart altogether from the gross and obvious burden in money and social machinery which the protection they need, and the protection we need against them, casts upon the community, they dilute the spiritual quality of the community to a degree which makes it an inapt medium for any high achievement. It matters little how small a city or a nation is, provided the spirit of its people is great. It is the smallest communities that have most powerfully and most immortally raised the level of civilization, and surrounded the human species (in its own eyes) with a halo of glory which belongs to no other species. [. . .]

It is here that the ideals of Eugenics may be expected to work fruitfully. To insist upon the power of heredity was once considered to indicate a fatalistic pessimism. It wears a very different aspect nowadays, in the light of Eugenics. [. . .] The two measures which are now commonly put forward for the attainment of eugenic ends – health certificates as a legal preliminary to marriage and the sterilization of the unfit – are excellent when wisely applied, but they become mischievous, if not ridiculous, in the hands of fanatics who would employ them by force. Domestic animals may be highly bred from outside, compulsorily. Man can only be bred upwards from within through the medium of his intelligence and will, working together under the control of a high sense of responsibility. The infinite cunning of men and women is fully equal to the defeat of any attempt to touch life at this intimate point against the wish of those to whom the creation of life is entrusted. The laws of marriage even among savages have often been complex and strenuous in the highest degree. But it has been easy to bear them, for they have been part of the sacred and inviolable traditions of the race; religion lay behind them. And Galton, who recognized the futility of mere legislation in the elevation of the race, believed that the hope of the future lies in rendering eugenics a part of religion. The only compulsion we can apply in eugenics is the compulsion that comes from within. All those in whom any fine sense of social and racial responsibility is developed will desire, before marriage, to give, and to receive, the fullest information on all the matters that concern ancestral inheritance, while the registration of such information, it is probable, will become ever simpler and more a matter of course. And if he finds that he is not justified in aiding to carry on the race, the eugenist will be content to make himself, in the words of Jesus, 'a eunuch for the kingdom of Heaven's sake', whether, under modern conditions, that means abstention in marriage from procreation, or voluntary sterilization by operative methods. For, as Giddings has put it, the goal of the race lies, not in the ruthless exaltation of a super-man, but in the evolution of a super-mankind. Such a goal can only be reached by resolute selection and elimination.

The breeding of men lies largely in the hands of women. That is why the question of Eugenics is to a great extent one with the woman question. The realization of eugenics in our social life can only be attained with the realization of the woman movement in its latest and completest phase as an enlightened culture of motherhood, in all that motherhood involves alike on the physical and the psychic sides. Motherhood on the eugenic basis is a deliberate and selective process, calling for the highest intelligence as well as the finest emotional and moral aptitudes, so that all the best energies of a long evolution of womanhood in the paths of modern culture here find their final outlet. The breeding of children further involves the training of children, and since the expansion of Social Hygiene renders education a far larger and more delicate task than it has ever been before, the responsibilities laid upon women by the evolution of civilization become correspondingly great.

The Eugenic Prospect (1921)
C.W. Saleeby

The gaining of the vote by the women of Great Britain and the United States in 1918 and 1920, respectively, is a great political event. But it is also much more. Many years ago I ventured on the definition that a politician is one who is ever thinking of the next election, but a statesman is one who is ever thinking of the next generation. There will be an abundance, if not a surfeit, of discussion and action by the politicians thus defined. Let us here attempt a more difficult and immeasurably more worthy task – the service of statesmanship – by asking what the political enfranchisement of woman, involving as it must and will, her economic freedom also, may signify for the race – the future, the unborn, the life of this world to come.

We must try to define our first principles, and in doing so here I am merely recapitulating the doctrine laid down a decade ago in my volume on 'Woman and Womanhood'.

First. – In the evolution of sex, in both the vegetable and animal world, from the beginning of aeonian antiquity, the female sex has ever been *the* sex, alike the main highway and the essential vehicle of life. Incomparably the highest product of this sex is woman. In her physique and her psyche she is nature's supreme organ and trustee of the future. If she should fail in this function the race must fail, and history, rightly read, teaches that where she has failed, from whatever cause, the race has there failed, nought else conceivable availing. So long as the individual is mortal, parenthood must determine the destiny of any living race – and therefore, in the case of mankind, the destiny of all nations. Parenthood is dual, and I am the last man to understate the importance of fatherhood; but nature has decreed that motherhood shall be much more important still. Its racial significance and imperiousness are transcendent, and ever were and will be. In thus asserting the pre-eminence and racial sacro-sanctity of motherhood, I am not 'dictating to women' – undoubtedly a gross impertinence, and properly resented, from anything in trousers – but simply indicating the supreme part which nature has allotted to her. No higher compliment to her sex is conceivable.

Second. – The old view, which we find indicated in the dogmas of certain world-religions, that the mother is merely the vessel and nurturer of her child, whereas the father is its real parent and creator, is false. She is creatrix as he is creator. Each of us is derived equally – with the strictest mathematical accuracy – from both of our parents. We should not deceive ourselves because we usually choose to name the family after its father. Though only the paternal cognomen be transmitted, we inherit equally from both parents. The maternal stock, epitomized in the maternal germ-cell, is as important as the paternal. In the interests of good breeding it is as important to recruit the future from the mothers of fine stock as from such fathers. The leading idea of the volume above-named is that, on genetic grounds, the race needs the finest women to be the mothers of the future, and that no development of feminism will ultimately justify itself if that eugenic principle be ignored or outraged.

The problem of the home is how to reconcile the unquestionable claims of woman as an individual, and the no less unquestionable claims of the race upon her. There are certain apparent solutions of that problem, now in practice, which do not solve, but simply evade it. We seem to be on the way toward the hope that the beehive may serve as a suitable model for mankind, and the structure of an enduring human society. In the bee society, the highest development of the individual, by far, is found in females who are not mothers. They have renounced maternity, as it were, and have become masterpieces of life in their marvellous instincts, their courage, their devotion and unselfishness. The so-called 'queen', the only mother in the hive is, to speak frankly, a fool, incapable of looking after herself, and, so far from being a queen, does not direct or control the least of her own activities, to say nothing of those of the hive or any individual in it.

Mankind might, perhaps, evolve some analogous form of socio-racial structure. The highly educable and educated women, the most intelligent, provident, and active, might put maternity on one side, leaving that function to the inferior members of their sex. Something of which that is no unfair description is what we increasingly see around us to-day in the leading nations of the world. My own oft-reiterated belief is that along these lines happiness is the least of the greatest number of individuals and the poorest prospect for the future quality of the race. The future of the hive is no safe indication for a race that relies not upon instinct but upon intelligence, which varies widely in different individuals, and is most markedly hereditary. Whatever may be well for bees, mankind needs the finest women to be the mothers of its future.

Observation of individuals shows, further, that nature is not so perverse or ambiguous in her demands as we might suppose. For the vast majority, not least of the finest women, motherhood not only serves the race through them, but serves them as individuals – their personal happiness and completeness, their physical and psychical health, and length of days. Only too many women have learnt this truth too late.

Surely we must stick to our principles, and mayhap we shall find ourselves coming out right in the end, both for the individual and the race. Woman can, must, and will use the vote for the protection of the home and the family, of youth and the race. If she finds – as indeed needs no finding – that present economic practice heavily handicaps her in many ways, but never so heavily as when she is discharging her supreme function of maternity, she must and will rectify the economics which are, indeed, so uneconomic, so spendthrift of individual and racial welfare.

Asserting the truths above defined, she must and will say that, if money rightly exists for anything at all, it exists for the protection of motherhood, upon which national and racial destiny depend. She will say, and '*say it with votes*', that, if any service be paid for, if any labourer be worthy of his hire, the supreme national and racial service of motherhood must be paid for. Perhaps we may question whether the term, 'endowment of motherhood', is best to indicate this principle. We do not speak of the endowment of generalship or of statesmanship or of the bench or of the priesthood or of medicine when we pay salaries, wages or fees to the men whom we choose to direct our armies, make our laws, administer justice, guide our churches or tend our bodies. We pay these people for the useful work they do. Similarly mothers should be paid.

We have seen, however, that this just, necessary, and long overdue reform in economics will not solve all the problems which are posed for us in the present rightful demand for freedom and personal development of the individual woman. It is not for any man to attempt to solve a problem which is woman's, and which she alone can solve. Any man may, however, be permitted to remind woman of her supreme importance to the race, which she sometimes appears to forget, rating herself far too lowly in that regard, even when she thinks that she is making high claims for herself. And it may be permitted a man who can never forget that all great nations in history have fallen in their turn, and who believes that decay of parenthood – of which motherhood is the better half – is the mortal disease of nations, to ask here again the question which Walt Whitman, seer of seers, asked nearly half a century ago:

> With all thy gifts, America, . . .
> Power, wealth, extent, vouchsafed to thee . . .
> What if one gift thou lackest? (the ultimate human
>   problem never solving:)
> The gift of Perfect Woman fit for thee –
> What if that gift of gifts thou lackest?
> The towering Feminine of thee?
> The beauty, health, complexion fit for thee?
> The Mothers fit for thee?

'Notes of the Quarter [on Nazism]' (1934)
The Eugenics Review

The Nazi Government has lost little time in making it plain that both the quality and quantity of the German people is to be one of its principal cares. In our correspondence columns here Mrs. Grant Duff describes the deep concern over the low birth rate; and other reports show that the Ministry for National Enlightenment and Propaganda has not only appointed a consultative committee of experts on population and race policy, but has also instructed the Press to foster the cult of the large family. [. . .]

The article mainly consists of a draft Bill (for Prussia; Saxony seems to be following suit) not only for making voluntary sterilization legal, but for actually pressing it upon aments, the insane, epileptics, the unsocial (criminals), deaf-mutes, and physical weaklings (tubercular). There is also a clause declaring sterilization desirable when 'three eugenically minded doctors, one of them an official, recognize the danger of severe harm to possible offspring'. In view of the frequency with which defects are recessive or semi-recessive, this is an excellent clause that may very well do as much good as all the others put together. Finally, the draft Bill gives the authorities power to forbid sterilization in particular cases. Dr. Vellguth emphasizes that negative eugenics, with which he is mainly concerned, must be secured by making sterilization *attractive*; and he outlines several ways in which this may be done. He also points out that purely eugenic indications are not absolutely necessary, since for social and humane reasons the mentally diseased should be freed of family responsibilities.

The clause making it possible to forbid sterilization is interesting as show-ing the typical German preoccupation with the positive side of eugenics, and the recognition in that country of the need for a widespread eugenic conscience. 'Our people', writes Dr. Vellguth, 'has lost its pride in health'. And, 'You who carry healthy germplasm in you, know you that it belongs not to you, but to the German people! Make no mistake about that!'

Though some of the details might not meet with general approval in this country, the broad outlines, as so far sketched, of the German Bill will certainly command the assent of all experienced eugenists. It is therefore doubly deplorable that the scientific tenor of the proposals should be en-tirely vitiated by the inclusion of 'foreign races' among the potential sterilizees. Dr. Vellguth writes, 'We wish as far as possible to hinder the infiltration of foreign blood into the organism of our nation; Jews, Ne-groes, Mongols, and similar peoples could therefore with their consent be legally sterilized whether they are healthy or ill.'

There may be something to be said for not encouraging such risky racial experiments as colour-hybrids; but we have not for many years had so dis-turbing an example of a great nation making itself ridiculous as the whole German campaign against the Jews. Herr Hitler has still not realized, apparently, that in declaring that the small number of Jews in Germany have achieved an altogether disproportionate measure of success – in the arts, sciences, and learned professions – he has publicly acknowledged their superiority to the bulk of the nation that wishes to get rid of them!

'Aims and Objects of the Eugenics Society'
(1935)
The Eugenics Review

Eugenics aims at improving the inborn qualities of future generations.

Ethical and scientific bases
The *ethical* basis of eugenics consists in duties not only to our neigh-bours but also to posterity. These duties include the provision, not only of the best possible environmental conditions, but also the best physical and mental endowment.

The *scientific* basis of eugenics must be one of sound biological knowl-edge. Racial changes have hitherto occurred without conscious human direction. Eugenics seeks to find the means by which the blind forces of Nature may be controlled by a consciously directed policy based on scientific study of transmissible biological factors.

Among animals and primitive peoples, racial changes occur through natural selection, i.e. by unrestricted reproduction of all types, causing a struggle for existence in which the less capable are eliminated by early death. Modern civilized man revolts against submission to this crude process and usually resorts to the restriction of families. This may involve the preservation and increase of weak types – a racial deterioration which improvements in the environment alone are powerless to check. Rational eugenic selection aims at diminishing the fertility of all persons below the average in valuable heritable qualities and at maintaining a sufficient reproduction of those above the average to ensure that their contribution to the next generation should become progressively larger.

Eugenics: A study and a practice

The term 'Eugenics' implies both a scientific study and a social practice. By further study, an attempt should be made to give precision to our knowledge of the part played by heredity in regard to physical and mental superiority, to human defects and diseases and to human inefficiency in any form of society. In particular an attempt should be made to elucidate the respective influences of heredity and environment upon the human type, and to define more clearly such terms as good and bad stock, and superior, average and inferior endowment.

But as well as being a study, eugenics is a social practice. In practice it seeks to realize the aims of (A) *positive* and (B) *negative eugenics* respectively by:

(A) promoting the fertility of superior, healthy and useful stocks; and by
(B) restricting through voluntary measures the multiplication of those who suffer from hereditary infirmities.

An indispensable preliminary to the application of either of these principles is to create throughout the community a 'eugenic conscience'. This is to be attained not only by the education of the young in the principles of biology, but also by spreading among all an appreciation of the effects of their actions upon future generations. Except in regard to the segregation of lunatics, mental defectives and certain criminals, the *Society* does not advocate the compulsory application of the principles of negative eugenics. It seeks to awaken a eugenic or racial conscience which will influence:

1   The individual in the choice of a mate and in the decisions as to parenthood, and
2   the community so as to bring to bear on issues of eugenic importance the forces of scientifically informed public opinion.

The study of eugenics

The *Society* encourages the study of all aspects of human heredity and differential fertility. It considers that the following subjects are specially in need of further investigation:

Population problems
    Further knowledge is needed (*a*) concerning the relative rates of multiplication of the different sections of the population, (*b*) as to whether a definite relation exists between the inherited qualities of different sections of the community and their social and economic status, and (*c*) as to the eugenic or dysgenic tendencies of different types of social structure.

Human abilities and disabilities
    The *Society* favours the study of the inheritance of good health and physique and of special abilities and aptitudes of social value to the community. It is also anxious to promote the organized study of hereditary deficiencies, diseases and defects, with a view of ascertaining their prevalence and distribution, and of rendering more accurate our forecasts of their incidence in affected families. The co-operation of the medical profession in this task is essential.

The 'Social Problem Group'
    This term was employed by the Mental Deficiency (Wood) Committee, 1930, to denote a group of people who are asserted to exhibit 'social problem' characteristics such as insanity, mental defect, epilepsy, occupational instability, recidivism, inebriety and social dependency. The *Society* seeks to determine if such a group can be distinguished and defined, and if any of its characteristics are of a hereditary nature.

Human evaluation and registration
    The *Society* desires to see changes made in the methods of keeping the relevant statistical records so that data may be available for eugenic study. This principle should apply to the registration of births and marriages and to records of medical inspection of school children, so as to make possible the detection of changes in the physical condition of the population.

Family records
    Galton stated that every intelligent person should study his family pedigree. The *Society* has prepared a schedule to facilitate such study and looks forward to the establishment of facilities for the preservation and study of pedigrees.

Research into contraceptive methods

The *Society* favours the promotion of clinical, statistical and laboratory research with a view to ascertaining the reliability, the practicability and the effects on health (both of parents and children) of existing contraceptive methods; it also encourages research with a view to the discovery of methods sound in these respects.

Family allowances

The *Society* favours the study of the eugenic value or danger of different forms of Family Allowances.

Race mixture

In certain circumstances, race mixture is known to be bad. Further knowledge of its biological effects is needed in order to make it possible to frame a practical eugenic policy. Meanwhile, since the process of race mixture cannot be reversed, great caution is advocated.

Immigration

In view of the possible effects on the national stock of admitting persons of varying quality, the biological aspects of the regulations governing immigration, and the plans for emigration within the Empire should be regarded as a matter of urgent study.

The practice of eugenics

As above stated, this can be divided into negative and positive aspects.

Negative eugenics

The following measures have, at various times, been suggested as likely to diminish the fertility of sub-average persons: birth control, sterilization, segregation, legal prohibition of marriage and artificial termination of pregnancy.

Birth control

Instruction on methods of birth control, under medical supervision, should be provided by local authorities. Such instruction should stress both its value and danger from a eugenic point of view, and should not be restricted to women suffering from gynaecological illnesses.

Sterilization

The *Society* advocates that facilities for voluntary sterilization be provided, under appropriate safeguards, for persons suffering from or carrying transmissible defects seriously impairing physical or mental efficiency.

It considers that without introducing compulsion, valuable results can be achieved by awakening throughout the community an enlightened eugenic conscience.

Segregation

In cases of mental defect and mental disorder, the *Society* does not regard sterilization as an alternative to segregation but as an accessory or ancillary procedure. The *Society* concurs with the recommendations of the Wood Committee that facilities should be extended and perfected for segregating and 'socializing' mental defectives. Voluntary sterilization would, from the eugenic standpoint, be a necessary adjunct to this policy.

Legal prohibition of marriage

It has been proposed that the marriage of mental defectives should be prohibited by law. So far as this is intended as a eugenic measure it is ineffective and undesirable, as it does not prevent, and may even incite, propagation by promiscuous unions with their dysgenic possibilities and other evils. Its aims can be realized more effectively and humanely by providing defectives desiring to marry with facilities for obtaining their own sterilization and by encouraging marriage when this safeguard has been adopted.

Termination of pregnancy

The *Society* advocates the provision of legalized facilities for voluntarily terminating pregnancy in cases of persons for whom sterilization is regarded as appropriate, and in cases of incest and rape.

Positive eugenics

The *Society* holds that married couples of sound stock who deliberately have fewer children than they can adequately bring up, do an injury to the race. It opposes restrictions on marriage which now discriminate against sound stocks.

The following measures are suggested in order to promote the fertility of such people.

Family allowances

The *Society* favours the provision of family allowances by the establishment of graded equalization pools and other systems calculated to have a eugenic effect. It regards as wholly dysgenic the provision of allowances through flat rate payments by the State.

Taxation

In order to ease the burden of taxation where the expenses of bringing up children are very heavy in relation to the income, the present system of income tax allowance should be amended, extended and rendered more effective.

Education

The *Society* favours for children of superior ability the extensive provision of scholarships sufficient to ease financial burdens, and thereby promote the further reproduction of the parents.

Birth control

The *Society* holds that, since the practice of birth control in the last seventy years has acted dysgenically rather than eugenically, birth control should be practised by persons of superior biological endowment only with a view to spacing births.

Marriage certificates

The *Society* favours the exchange before marriage of certificates providing information of eugenic significance.

'Eutelegenesis' (1936)
Herbert Brewer

The present concern of eugenics is with the elimination of defect. Its greater mission, however, lies in the creation of excellence. If man has arisen from a simian stock then we may be the forerunners of beings as superior to ourselves as we are to the apes. It is difficult to give precision to the idea of such exalted beings. Nevertheless the idea exists and gives to eugenics its most powerful inspiration.

Yet superman remains a dream, as elusive as that of Messiah. 'When shall Messiah come?' asked the Jewess of Braniza. 'When all the Jews have become either altogether virtuous or altogether vicious,' was the reply. The biologist is apt to reply in somewhat similar terms to the eugenicist. Mankind may one day create something better than itself. But first it is necessary to unravel the complexities of Mendelian inheritance in man, and to assess a myriad genes as good or bad. Even H.G. Wells, so daring elsewhere, gives no encouragement here. 'The deliberate improvement of man's inherent quality', he says, 'is at present unattainable.'

Yet facts from wide fields of experience support a challenge to these views. Few great advances of any kind have waited upon sure calculations and complete knowledge for their inception. If action is dependent on knowledge the converse is also true. The physicist might have waited in vain for his data but for the trial and error initiatives of the workshop. Racial advance may be regarded as an adventure entailing risks commensurate with the great reward which success would give.

The difficulties indeed appear immense. Intensity of selection must govern the rate of biological change. Since man is a slow breeder, any appreciable rate of advance requires a selection not less effective than that which is applied to domesticated animals. The creation of superior breeds of livestock has only been possible by preferring a few out of thousands or more. In the best strains of highly bred animals 40 to 60 per cent. may have to be culled merely to prevent the standard from deteriorating. Similar selection in the human species might well seem possible only by a ruthless overriding of individual preference and by annihilating most of what is connoted by love and marriage.

But entirely new possibilities exist in the application of invention to the mechanism of reproduction. Contraception has already begun to show how far-reaching may be the effects of such inventiveness. Through contraception the emotional satisfactions of sexual union have become dissociated from the ends which that union was evolved to fulfil – i.e. the fusion of male and female germ cells. Here it may be noted that it is through coitus that reproduction is involved in the turbulent emotions of sex. Yet coitus is but a means, the real end being fertilization. The intense consciousness aroused by the means is in contrast with the entire lack of it in relation to the end itself. The emotions which might appear to constitute insuperable obstacles to radical departures in human reproduction therefore are linked to accessory rather than to fundamental factors.

Contraception makes physical love independent of fertilization, but not the reverse. In the mind of primitive and semi-civilized man conception [...] was frequently believed to be independent of sex union. Positive eugenic advance may well depend upon whether civilized man can recapture the outlook of our forebears who held these beliefs. For science has transformed primitive fiction into modern reality. To-day generation without antecedent sexual union is not only an experimental fact but a practice which is being widely and successfully applied to stockbreeding. [...]

Have these facts [recording the successful artificial insemination of mammals] any implications for eugenics? It is suggested that they have and that it is worth considering tentatively what these implications may be. For the process of reproduction from the germ cells of individuals between whom is no bodily contact, I propose the name telegenesis. The possible application of this process to the eugenic breeding of man may be termed eutelegenesis. Many psychological objections may be aroused at the mere mention of such a project. But for the moment only its physical aspects will be considered.

In the human male reproductive system, as in that of other mammals, there is an enormous margin of wastage. The spermatozoa in a single emission average about 226 millions, a normal man producing, between the ages of twenty-five and fifty-five, something like 339,385 millions. Since coital capacity is set aside as a limiting factor, artificial insemination renders feasible an immensely increased multiplication in relation to the male. If only one spermatozoon out of each thousand were utilized, this great wastage would yet enable one man in a year to fertilize five million women. Such a standard is not yet technically possible with animals. But there seems no reason why with improved technique it should not ultimately be so.

We may consider the results which might follow an experiment in human reproduction carried out by using the germ cells of a few highly selected males to impregnate the general body of females. Such a process might produce a great and rapid improvement in the hereditary qualities of the race. [. . .]

Where with random mating a defect dependent on a duplicated recessive factor is exhibited in one per ten thousand, 198 per ten thousand will be heterozygous (i.e. carriers) for the same defect. Though mating may not be entirely at random, it is evident that the existence of a great reservoir of latent defectiveness is responsible for the frequent appearance of unpredictable degeneracy. To attempt the elimination of such degeneracy by sterilizing it as it appears is like clearing a river of fish by catching the few which jump from the water. The method now in view would meet the problem by sweeping out of existence the whole inextricable tangle of latent defect in a few generations, replacing it concurrently with hereditary material of the highest excellence. The carrier female, on this view, need not be denied the gratification of her maternal impulses, which with women in general must be regarded as fundamental to self-realization and happiness. A vast store of maternal energy would thus be conserved and canalized for racial progress.

Applied to the purpose of creating homozygous types of the highest excellence in respect of heredity, and to the rapid diffusion of advantageous mutations as they occur, eutelegenesis might accomplish in a few generations what otherwise would require millennia. 'What is now most wanted from science', said Major Leonard Darwin, 'is that she should demonstrate that a comparatively wide and rapid advance in nearly all human qualities is now at all events a possibility.' Eutelegenesis would appear to furnish an answer to that question.

It is frequently assumed that any far-reaching scheme for the eugenic breeding of humanity can only be accomplished by compulsory measures. Compulsion, in the opinion of the writer, is both wrong and unnecessary. Eugenic advance must be the voluntary adventure of free men and women, or nothing. Eutelegenesis might be such an adventure. All it need ask of society is that people with courage and imagination enough to make a new experiment for human progress should be left alone. Compared with Plato's eugenic methods, eutelegenesis is mild and conservative. It does not require the abolition of marriage and the family. Men and women who, mutually attracted in the customary ways, desired to marry and to have children would not be denied. The difference would be that when a child was decided upon, man and wife would act upon the simple moral principle that the welfare of the child must be the first consideration. The logical consequence of that principle is that the best hereditary endowment possible should be chosen for the child. All that would be needed to finally implement the decision would be a simple manipulation, less painful than drawing a tooth and no more unchaste than an ante-natal examination, carried out by a qualified physician.

At this point one may meet the objection that eutelegenesis means breeding human beings like animals. Exactly the contrary is the case. Eutelegenesis means that, instead of reproduction being the blind consequence of an animal mating, it is an act of deliberate creativeness to which animal life holds no parallel. It is hardly necessary to add that, though in eutelegenesis there is a conscious dissociation of reproduction from coitus, this does not imply that sexual love has no part to play in satisfying the deep emotional needs of mankind. [. . .]

The information in the hands of the eutelegenetic organization would form the basis on which prospective parents would exercise their choice. No personal contact between the putative parents and the superior men chosen would be either desirable or necessary. The investigation of the genetic qualifications of the superior men who were willing to co-operate would necessarily involve them in certain inconveniences. But if a eugenic conscience and aspiration may not be found in the intellectual leaders of men, it must be vain to seek it elsewhere.

An important work of the organization would be the keeping of records and pedigrees. If for no other reason, this would be necessary to avoid conflicting with the marriage laws regarding consanguinity. Reasons of expediency would render it desirable to obviate the marriage of half-sibs through a eutelegenetic father. On such lines as these, I suggest, eutelegenetic reproduction might be applied to humanity.

Objections and difficulties would appear to centre chiefly round a possible reluctance on the part of the ordinary man to delegate, so to speak, his procreative functions. Masculine egotism and jealousy have undeniably played an important part in sex relations, both animal and human. In mankind, however, these impulses seem extremely variable and anthropology yields many examples where they have been attenuated or submerged. Ethically, jealousy must be regarded as a quality appropriate to the animal rather than to the human. 'Il y a dans la jalousie plus d'amour propre que d'amour', said de La Rochefoucauld. In relation to eutelegenesis, it would appear absurd for a man to feel jealous of one with whom his wife enters into no consciously personal and emotional contact whatever.

Much is likely to be said about the possibility of the putative father feeling that the eutelegenetic child is in a real sense his own. There is reason to believe, however, that in so far as the paternal sentiment rests upon an instinctive basis, it is entirely a matter of association. The germinal continuity of sire and offspring could not possibly have been appreciated in the mind of the anthropoids from which man arose. Hartland has shown that ignorance of the dependence of birth upon sexual intercourse was general in primitive man. Various Australasian and Melanesian peoples have retained their ignorance until modern times. Definitely paternal behaviour patterns, however, are present in these cases. Even in apes and monkeys adult males display a friendly and protective attitude to the infant members of their group, and this seems a rudimentary form of paternal behaviour. That association plays a major part in evoking the paternal sentiment in civilized society is supported by facts relating to child adoption. So far as the instinctive basis of the paternal sentiment is concerned, therefore, it would appear that eutelegenesis would leave it unaffected.

As regards the ideological aspect of paternity, the putative father might feel himself bound to the eutelegenetic child in an even deeper sense than if the child were derived materially from himself. For, conjointly with the mother, he might feel himself to have created, by the deliberate exercise of his will and thought, a being in whom his ideal aspirations were embodied. In coming to understand its true relation to its creative father a unique gratitude and love might be evoked in the child towards those who had given it the most precious of all gifts, a splendid hereditary nature. [. . .]

If egotism, prejudice and the blind behaviour patterns inherited from our animal ancestors are destined for ever to dominate sex and parenthood, then indeed eutelegenesis has no chance. It will be dismissed as contrary to common sense and human nature, as an idea capable of taking root only in the minds of cranks and perverts. But if mankind comes to realize its imperative mission to create out of itself something infinitely nobler and better, if sex can be envisaged as the instrument of a profoundly religious purpose, if mankind can perceive the full implications of the truth that biologically, as otherwise, we are members of one body, then eutelegenesis will become a new evangel. And in applying it to the creation of its children, mankind will journey, with pride and joy, along a short road to superman.

'Eugenics and Society' (1937)
Julian Huxley

The Dysgenic Character of our Present Social System

When we think along these lines, we shall find, I believe, that a system such as ours, a competitive and individualist system based on private capitalism and public nationalism, is of its nature and essence dysgenic. It is dysgenic both in the immediate respect of failing to utilize existing reservoirs of valuable genes, and also in the long-range tasks of failing to increase them, failing to trap and encourage favourable mutations, and failing to eliminate harmful mutations.

Under our social system, the full stature or physique of the very large majority of the people is not allowed to express itself; neither are the full genetic potentialities of health permitted to appear except in a small fraction of the whole, with a consequent social waste of individual happiness which is formidable in extent; and finally, innate high ability is encouraged or utilized only with extreme inadequacy. For the first two wastes, ignorance is partly responsible, but in the lower economic strata, poverty is the chief cause. For the latter, our inadequate educational system is chiefly responsible.

Then R.A. Fisher has brilliantly and devastatingly shown the relentless way in which such a system as ours promotes both infertility and certain types of talent, and in so doing ties together the genetic factors responsible. In the course of the generations genes making for small families become increasingly bound up with those making for social and economic success; and conversely those making for social and economic failure become bound up with those making for high reproduction rates. Eugenically speaking our system is characterized by the social promotion of infertility and the excess fertility of social failure. [. . .]

Then, in so far as our system remains nationalist, the demand for man-power and quantity will continue to interfere with the higher aim of quality. Furthermore, modern war itself is dysgenic. This has often been pointed out as regard its direct effects. It appears, however, also to hold for its indirect effects; many among the more imaginative and sensitive types are to-day restricting their families, sometimes to zero, because they feel that they cannot bear to bring children into a world exposed to such a risk of war and chaos.

As eugenists we must therefore aim at transforming the social system. [. . .]

The Eugenic Approach to Control of the Social Environment

What sort of practical changes, then, should we as eugenicists try to encourage in the social and economic system? In the first place – what we have already noted as desirable on theoretical grounds – the equalizing of environment in an upward direction. For this, by permitting of more definite knowledge as to the genetic constitution of different classes and types, will at once give us more certainty in any eugenic selection, negative or positive, upon which we may embark; and secondly, we must aim at the abandonment of the idea of national sovereign states, and the subordination of national disputes to international organization and supernational power.

But we need something more radical than this – we must try to find a pattern of economic and communal life which will not be inherently dysgenic; and we must also try to find a pattern of family and reproductive life which will permit of more rapid and constructive eugenics.

On the first point, it seems clear that the individualist scramble for social and financial promotion should be dethroned from its present position as main incentive in life, and that we must try to raise the power of group incentives. Group incentives are powerful in tribal existence, and have been powerful in many historical civilizations, such as the old Japanese. What interests us chiefly, however, is to find that they have been to a large extent effective in replacing individualist money incentives, or at least diminishing their relative social importance, in several modern States, notably Germany and the U.S.S.R.

It is not for a biologist to discuss the purely social merits of different political philosophies: but he may be allowed to point out that not all group-incentives are equally valuable from the eugenic standpoint. Those of Nazi Germany, for instance, presuppose an intensification of nationalist feeling and activity instead of their diminution: and this, we have concluded, is actually anti-eugenic. It may of course be urged that it is in its immediate effect eugenic; and there will be many to uphold the value of the eugenic measures recently adopted in Germany under the stimulus of National-Socialist ideas and emotions, even if some of them be crude and unscientific. But if in the long run it leads to overpopulation and war, it is essentially dysgenic, and in matters of evolution we must, I think, take the long view.

Further, if the social environment is such as to give satisfaction to the possessors of social traits such as altruism, readiness to co-operate, sensitiveness, sympathetic enthusiasm, and so forth, instead of, as now, putting a premium on many antisocial traits such as egoism, low cunning, insensitiveness, and ruthless concentration, we could begin to frame eugenic measures for encouraging the spread of genes for such social virtues. [. . .]

Another important point to remember, especially in these days when the worship of the State is imposing a mass-production ideal of human nature, is the fact and the significance of human variability. The variability of man, due to recombination between divergent types that have failed to become separated as species, is greater than that of any wild animal. And the extreme variants thrown up by the constant operation of this genetic kaleidoscope have proved to be of the utmost importance for the material and spiritual progress of civilization. Whatever bias or prejudice may beset the individual eugenist, eugenics as a whole must certainly make the encouragement of diversity one of its main principles. But here again the environment comes in. If extreme types are to be produced, especially gifted for art, science, contemplation, exploration, they must not be wasted. The social system must provide niches for them. [. . .]

Eugenics and Reproductive Morality and Practice

Still more important for the comparatively immediate future is the relation of the dominant group-incentive to reproductive morality, law, and practice. We all know that certain schools of Christian thought to-day are opposed on grounds of religious principle to birth-control, that indispensable tool of eugenics as well as of rational control of population, and even to the very notion of eugenics itself. But even if this opposition could be overcome, there would remain in this field grave obstacles, both to the spread of the eugenic idea and to the rate of its progress in practice. These are the prevailing individualist attitude to marriage, and the conception, based on this and on the long religious tradition of the West, of the subordination of personal love to procreation. The two influences together prevent us collectively from grasping the implications of the recent advances in science and technique which now make it possible to separate the individual from the social side of sex and reproduction. Yet it is precisely and solely this separation that would make real eugenics practicable, by allowing a rate of progress yielding tangible encouragement in a reasonable time, generation by generation.

The recent invention of efficient methods on the one hand of birth-control and on the other of artificial insemination have brought man to a stage at which the separation of sexual and reproductive functions could be used for eugenic purposes. But it is of real interest to note that these inventions represent merely the last steps in an evolutionary process which started long before man ever existed. [. . .]

This has already led in point of fact to the widespread separation of the personal function of sexual union from its racial consequences, of love from reproduction. It is true that some persons and bodies on theological or metaphysical grounds either ostrich-like deny the existence of this separation, or assert that it ought not to be practised; but this does not alter the fact.

The perfection of birth-control technique has made the separation more effective; and the still more recent technique of artificial insemination has opened up new horizons, by making it possible to provide different objects for the two functions. It is now open to man and woman to consummate the sexual function with those they love, but to fulfil the reproductive function with those whom on perhaps quite other grounds they admire. [. . .]

Here it must suffice to point out that unless we alter the social framework of law and ideas so as to make possible the divorce between sex and reproduction, or if you prefer it between the individual and the social sides of our sexual functions, our efforts at evolutionary improvement will remain mere tinkering, no more deserving the proud title of eugenics than does the mending of saucepans deserve to be called engineering.

That consummation, you will perhaps say, is impossibly remote from our imperfect present, hardly to be affected by any of our little strivings to-day. That may be so: but I am not so sure. [. . .]

It is to my mind not only permissible but highly desirable to look far ahead. Otherwise we are in danger of mistaking for our eugenic ideal a mere glorification of our prejudices and our subjective wish-fulfilments. It is not eugenics but left-wing politics if we merely talk of favouring the survival and reproduction of the proletariat at the expense of the bourgeoisie. It is not eugenics but right-wing politics if we merely talk of favouring the breeding of the upper classes of our present social system at the expense of the lower. It is not eugenics but nationalist and imperialist politics if we speak in such terms as subject races or miscegenation. Our conclusions in any particular case *may* be on balance eugenically correct (though the correlation between broad social or ethnic divisions and genetic values can never be high), yet they will not be based primarily upon eugenic considerations, but upon social or national bias. The public-school ideal, or that of the working-class movement, or that of colonial imperialism, may be good ideals; but they are not eugenic ideals.

The Danger of Man's Genetic Degeneration: Conclusion

Before concluding, I should like to draw attention to one eugenically important consequence of recent progress in pure genetics. In all organisms so far investigated, deleterious mutations far outnumber useful ones. There is an inherent tendency for the hereditary constitution to degrade itself. That man shares this tendency we can be sure, not only from analogy but on the all-too-obvious evidence provided by the high incidence in 'civilized' populations of defects, both mental and physical, of genetic origin.

In wild animals and plants, this tendency is either reversed or at least held in check by the operation of natural selection, which here again proves itself to be, in R.A. Fisher's words, a mechanism capable of generating high degrees of improbability. In domestic animals and plants, the same result is achieved by our artificial selection. But in civilized human communities of our present type, the elimination of defect by natural selection is largely (though of course by no means wholly) rendered inoperative by medicine, charity, and the social services; while, as we have seen, there is no selection encouraging favourable variations. The net result is that many deleterious mutations can and do survive, and the tendency to degradation of the germ-plasm can manifest itself.

To-day, thanks to the last fifteen years' work in pure science, we can be sure of this alarming fact, whereas previously it was only a vague surmise. Humanity will gradually destroy itself from within, will decay in its very core and essence, if this slow but relentless process is not checked. Here again, dealing with defectives in the present system can be at best a palliative. We must be able to pick out the genetically inferior stocks with more certainty, and we must set in motion counter-forces making for faster reproduction of superior stocks, if we are to reverse or even arrest the trend. And neither of these, as we have seen, is possible without an alteration of social system.

Part VII
Race

Introduction

Siobhan Somerville

'The question of sex – with the racial questions that rest on it – stands before the coming generations as the chief problem for solution.' So wrote Havelock Ellis in 1897 in the general preface to his multi-volume *Studies in the Psychology of Sex*, which became one of the most important texts of late nineteenth-century sexology in Europe and the United States. Ellis's statement suggests that 'racial questions' held a central place in the endeavours of these early sexologists, but the precise ways in which notions of race both shaped and were constructed by sexologists were not obvious. What exactly did Ellis mean by 'racial questions'? More significantly, what was his sense of the relationship between racial questions and the 'question of sex'? In scientific and medical studies from this period, 'race' could refer to groupings based variously on geography, religion, class or colour. Occasionally sexologists invoked racial difference as an explicit factor in their formulations, but, more often, unspoken beliefs and assumptions about race shaped medical models of sexuality and gender, as was the case in the culture at large.

Perhaps the apparent centrality of 'racial questions' to sexology should not surprise us, given that it developed as a field during a period of increased attention to and rigidification of racial and national boundaries in Europe and the United States. This era saw the ascendancy of European and American imperialism, increased anti-black violence in the United States, immigration limits and exclusion acts, and anti-semitism in Europe. The use of the term 'race' to refer to a division of people based on physical (rather than genealogical or national) differences had originated in the late eighteenth century, when Carl von Linnaeus and Johann Friedrich

Blumenbach first classified human beings into distinct racial groups. Blumenbach's work in turn became a model for the nineteenth-century fascination with anthropometry, the measurement of the human body. Behind these anatomical measurements lay the assumption that the body was a legible text, with various keys or languages available for reading its symbolic codes. In the logic of biological determinism, the surface and interior of the individual body rather than its social characteristics, such as language, behaviour or clothing, became the primary sites of its meaning. Scientists debated which particular anatomical features (skin, facial angle, pelvis, skull, brain mass, genitalia) carried racial meanings, but the theory that anatomy predicted intelligence and behaviour remained remarkably constant. As a result, because of the cultural authority of an ostensibly objective scientific method, these mappings of racial difference were produced as facts of nature and were used to justify the economic and political disenfranchisement of various racial groups within systems of slavery and colonialism.

One of the most important ways in which the discourses of race and sexuality intertwined during this period was through the concept of degeneracy, understood as a kind of reverse evolutionary process, in which the usual progression towards more 'civilized' mental and physical development was replaced with regression instead, resulting in a weakened nervous system and the emergence of 'primitive' physical and mental traits. In texts authored by German, British and American sexologists, African, Jewish and Asian bodies were most often seen to represent this primitive racial body. Darwinian models of evolution also held that, as organisms evolved through a process of natural selection, they showed greater signs of sexual differentiation. As a result, sexual characteristics became a key site for establishing 'normal' and 'degenerate' anatomy and a perceived lack of sexual differentiation between male and female signalled degeneracy. Such a notion had striking political consequences, working to demonize women and men who stepped out of cultural norms of gender. In particular, the notion of inversion, understood as a man's soul in a woman's body, or vice versa, was regularly linked to degeneracy within a discourse that saw homosexuality as a reversion to a sexually undifferentiated past. In this framework, evident in selections by August Forel, Cesare Lombroso and Guglielmo Ferrero, Ellis and others, the bodies of sexual degenerates (homosexuals and prostitutes) were analogous to criminals and 'primitive' races. Yet, in effect, what these accounts produced was not so much the 'truth' about the homosexual, the prostitute, the criminal or the person of colour, but rather the implicit normal body against which the 'abnormal' might be constructed.

The racial discourse of early sexology had numerous and contradictory political intentions and effects. Many sexologists, such as Ellis and Magnus

Hirschfeld, saw themselves as advocates for those labelled sexual degenerates. Their accounts of congenital sexual pathologies attempted to dislodge these 'perversions' from the realms of morality and religion and move them to the purview of science and medicine, but in doing so they reinforced, perhaps unwittingly, the concepts of immutable difference which were the backbone of racial hierarchies and justifications for segregation and imperialism. Others developed theories of acquired pathologies, in which perversions might be caused by environmental causes rather than by heredity, but these models also tended to reinforce stereotypes that linked 'perverse' sexual practices with exotic peoples and climates. Victorian explorer Sir Richard Burton (1821–1890), for example, developed a theory of the Sotadic Zone, a specific geographical area with precise longitudinal co-ordinates, in which he believed 'there is a blending of the masculine and feminine temperaments' responsible for a greater propensity to commit the 'Vice' of homosexuality. While Burton's theory was not based on scientific methodologies, it appealed strongly to sexologists, who cited it widely as a plausible way to map 'uncivilized' sexual behaviour.

The texts included here sample a range of early sexologists' ideas and assumptions about race and sexuality, from the viciously misogynistic and anti-semitic theories of Otto Weininger to the pioneering work of Magnus Hirschfeld, some of whose interventions anticipated more recent feminist, anti-racist and anti-homophobic work on the construction of race and sexuality. It would be a mistake, however, to read any of these texts, including those of C.G. Seligmann (1873–1940) and Margaret Otis (b. 1871), as reliable accounts of the 'truth' about the bodies of those whom they describe. They are instead contradictory documents that reveal much about their authors, as well as the cultural and historical fascinations, anxieties and desires that produced race and sexuality as inextricable and that made sexology thoroughly imbricated in the discourse of race.

The Sotadic Zone (1886)
Sir Richard Burton

Subsequent enquiries in many and distant countries enabled me to arrive at the following conclusions: –

1   There exists what I shall call a 'Sotadic Zone', bounded westwards by
    the northern shores of the Mediterranean (N. Lat. 43°) and by the
    southern (N. Lat. 30°). Thus the depth would be 780 to 800 miles

including meridional France, the Iberian Peninsula, Italy and Greece, with the coast-regions of Africa from Morocco to Egypt.

2   Running eastward the Sotadic Zone narrows, embracing Asia Minor, Mesopotamia and Chaldaea, Afghanistan, Sind, the Punjab and Kashmir.

3   In Indo-China the belt begins to broaden, enfolding China, Japan and Turkistan.

4   It then embraces the South Sea Islands and the New World where, at the time of its discovery, Sotadic love was, with some exceptions, an established racial institution.

5   Within the Sotadic Zone the Vice is popular and endemic, held at the worst to be a mere peccadillo, whilst the races to the North and South of the limits here defined practise it only sporadically amid the opprobrium of their fellows who, as a rule, are physically incapable of performing the operation and look upon it with the liveliest disgust. [. . .]

The only physical cause for the practice which suggests itself to me and that must be owned to be purely conjectural, is that within the Sotadic Zone there is a blending of the masculine and feminine temperaments, a crasis which elsewhere occurs only sporadically. Hence the male *féminisme* [femininity] whereby the man becomes *patiens* [passive] as well as *agens* [active], and the woman a tribade, a votary of mascula [man-like] Sappho, Queen of Frictrices or Rubbers. [. . .]

As Prince Bismarck finds a moral difference between the male and female races of history, so I suspect a mixed physical temperament effected by the manifold subtle influences massed together in the world climate. Something of the kind is necessary to explain the fact of this pathological love extending over the greater portion of the habitable world, without any apparent connection of race or media, from the polished Greek to the cannibal Tupi of the Brazil.

Psychopathia Sexualis [1886] (12th edn, 1903)
Richard von Krafft-Ebing

The foregoing facts concerning acquired antipathic sexual instinct and effemination find an interesting confirmation in the following ethnological data: –

Herodotus already describes a peculiar disease which frequently affected the Scythians. The disease consisted in this: that men became effeminate in character, put on female garments, did the work of women, and even became effeminate in appearance. As an explanation of this insanity of the Scythians, *Herodotus* relates the myth that the goddess Venus, angered by the plundering of the temple at Ascalon by the Scythians, had made women of these plunderers and their posterity.

Hippocrates, not believing in supernatural diseases, recognized that impotence was here a causative factor, and explained it, though incorrectly, as due to the custom of the Scythians to have themselves bled behind the ears in order to cure disease superinduced by constant horseback riding. He thought that these veins were of great importance in the preservation of the sexual powers, and that when they were severed, impotence was induced. Since the Scythians considered their impotence due to divine punishment and incurable, they put on the clothing of females, and lived as women among women.

It is worthy of note that, according to *Klaproth* [...] and *Chotomski*, even at the present time impotence is very frequent among the Tartars, as a result of riding unsaddled horses. The same is observed among the Apaches and Navajos of the western continent who ride excessively, scarcely ever going on foot, and are remarkable for small genitals and mild *libido* and virility. *Sprengel, Lallemand* and *Nysten* recognize the fact that excessive riding may be injurious to the sexual organs.

Hammond reports analogous observations of great interest concerning the Pueblo Indians of New Mexico. These descendants of the Aztecs cultivate so-called 'mujerados', of which every Pueblo tribe requires one in the religious ceremonies (actual orgies in the spring), in which pederasty plays an important part. In order to cultivate a 'mujerado', a very powerful man is chosen, and he is made to masturbate excessively and ride constantly. Gradually such irritable weakness of the genital organs is engendered that, in riding, great loss of semen is induced. This condition of irritability passes into paralytic impotence. Then atrophy of the testicles and penis sets in, the hair of the beard falls out, the voice loses its depth and compass, and physical strength and energy decrease. Inclinations and disposition become feminine. The 'mujerado' loses his position in society as a man. He takes on feminine manners and customs, and associates with women. Yet, for religious reasons, he is held in honour. It is probable that, at other times than during the festivals, he is used by the chiefs for pederasty. *Hammond* had an opportunity to examine two 'mujerados'. One had become such seven years before, and was thirty-five years old at the time. Seven years previous, he was entirely masculine and potent. He had noticed gradual atrophy of the testicles and penis. At the same time he lost *libido* and the power of erection. He differed in nowise, in dress and manner, from the women among whom *Hammond* found him. The genital hair was wanting, the penis was shrunken, the scrotum lax and pendulous, and the testicles were very much atrophied and no longer sensitive to pressure. The 'mujerado' had large *mammae* [breasts] like a pregnant woman, and asserted that he had nursed several children whose mothers had died. A second 'mujerado', aged thirty-six, after he had been ten years in the condition, presented the same peculiarities, though with less development of *mammae*. Like the first, the voice was high and thin. The body was plump.

The Female Offender (1893)
Cesare Lombroso and Guglielmo Ferrero

The primitive woman was rarely a murderess; but she was always a prostitute, and such she remained until semi-civilised epochs. Atavism, again, then explains why prostitutes should show a greater number of retrogressive characteristics than are to be observed in the female criminal.

Various as are these solutions of a singular problem, we may, I think, seek yet another. In female animals, in aboriginal women, and in the women of our time, the cerebral cortex, particularly in the psychical centres, is less active than in the male. The irritation consequent on a degenerative process is therefore neither so constant nor so lasting, and leads more easily to motor and hysterical epilepsy, or to sexual anomalies, than to crime. For a similar reason genius is more common in men than in women; and the lower animals remain insensible to narcotics, which intoxicate the human species, and are not subject to delirium or mania when attacked by fever.

We have now got to the reason why criminality increases among women with the march of civilisation. The female criminal is a kind of occasional delinquent, presenting few characteristics of degeneration, little dulness, &c., but tending to multiply in proportion to her opportunities for evil-doing; while the prostitute has a greater atavistic resemblance to her primitive ancestress, the woman of pleasure, and, as we shall see, has consequently a greater dulness of touch and taste, a greater propensity for tattooing, and so on.

In short, the female criminal is of less typical aspect than the male because she is less essentially criminal; because in all forms of degeneration she deviates to a less degree; because, being organically conservative, she keeps the characteristics of her type even in her aberrations from it; and finally because beauty, being for her a supreme necessity, her grace of form resists even the assaults of degeneracy.

But it cannot be denied that when depravity in woman is profound, then the law by which the type bears the brand of criminality asserts itself in spite of all restraint, at any rate as far as civilised races are concerned [. . .]; and this is particularly true of the prostitute, whose type approximates so much more to that of her primitive ancestress.

Atavism. – Atavism helps to explain the rarity of the criminal type in woman. The very precocity of prostitutes – the precocity which increases their apparent beauty – is primarily attributable to atavism. Due also to it is the virility underlying the female criminal type; for what we look for most in the female is femininity, and when we find the opposite in her we conclude as a rule that there must be some anomaly. And in order to understand the significance and the atavistic origin of this anomaly, we have only to remember that virility was one of the special features of the savage women. [. . .]

The criminal being only a reversion to the primitive type of his species, the female criminal necessarily offers the two most salient characteristics of primordial woman, namely, precocity and a minor degree of differentiation from the male – this lesser differentiation manifesting itself in the stature, cranium, brain, and in the muscular strength which she possesses to a degree so far in advance of the modern female. Examples of this masculine strength may still be found among women in country districts of Italy, and especially in the islands.

Studies in the Psychology of Sex, vol. II: *Sexual Inversion* [1897] (3rd edn, 1915)
Havelock Ellis

Traces of homosexual practices, sometimes on a large scale, have been found among all the great divisions of the human race. It would be possible to collect a considerable body of evidence under this head. Unfortunately, however, the travellers and others on whose records we are dependent have been so shy of touching these subjects, and so ignorant of the main points for investigation, that it is very difficult to discover sexual inversion in the proper sense in any lower race. Travellers have spoken vaguely of crimes against nature without defining the precise relationship involved nor inquiring how far any congenital impulse could be distinguished.

Looking at the phenomena generally, so far as they have been recorded among various lower races, we seem bound to recognize that there is a widespread natural instinct impelling men toward homosexual relationships, and that this has been sometimes, though very exceptionally, seized upon and developed for advantageous social purposes. On the whole, however, unnatural intercourse (sodomy) has been regarded as an antisocial offense, and punishable sometimes by the most serious penalties that could be invented. This was, for instance, the case in ancient Mexico, in Peru, among the Persians, in China, and among the Hebrews and Mohammedans. [. . .]

There is abundant evidence to show that homosexual practices exist and have long existed in most parts of the world outside Europe, when subserving no obvious social or moral end. How far they are associated with congenital inversion is usually very doubtful. In China, for instance, it seems that there are special houses devoted to male prostitution, though less numerous than the houses devoted to females, for homosexuality cannot be considered common in China (its prevalence among Chinese abroad being due to the absence of women) and it is chiefly found in the north. When a rich man gives a feast he sends for women to cheer the repast by music and song, and for boys to serve at table and to entertain the guests by their lively conversation. The boys have been carefully brought up for this occupation, receiving an excellent education, and their mental qualities are even more highly valued than their physical attractiveness. The women are less carefully brought up and less esteemed. After the meal the lads usually return home with a considerable fee. What further occurs the Chinese say little about. It seems that real and deep affection is often born of these relations, at first platonic, but in the end becoming physical, not a matter for great concern in the eyes of the Chinese. In the Chinese novels, often of a very literary character, devoted to masculine love, it seems that all the preliminaries and transports of normal love are to be found, while physical union may terminate the scene. In China, however, the law may be brought into action for attempts against nature even with mutual consent; the penalty is one hundred strokes with the bamboo and a month's imprisonment; if there is violence, the penalty is decapitation; I am not able to say how far the law is a dead letter. [. . .]

If we turn to the New World, we find that among the American Indians, from the Eskimo of Alaska downward to Brazil and still farther south, homosexual customs have been very frequently observed. Sometimes they are regarded by the tribe with honor, sometimes with indifference, sometimes with contempt; but they appear to be always tolerated. Although there are local differences, these customs, on the whole, seem to have much in common. The best early description which I have been able to find is by Langsdorff and concerns the Aleuts of Oonalashka in Alaska: "Boys, if they happen to be very handsome," he says, "are often brought up entirely in the manner of girls, and instructed in the arts women use to please men; their beards are carefully plucked out as soon as they begin to appear, and their chins tattooed like those of women; they wear ornaments of glass beads upon their legs and arms, bind and cut their hair in the same manner as the women, and supply their place with the men as concubines. This shocking, unnatural, and immoral practice has obtained here even from the remotest times; nor have any measures hitherto been taken to repress and restrain it; such men are known under the name of *schopans*."

Among the Konyagas Langsdorff found the custom much more common than among the Aleuts; he remarks that, although the mothers brought up some of their children in this way, they seemed very fond of their offspring. Lisiansky, at about the same period, tells us that: "Of all the customs of these islanders, the most disgusting is that of men, called *schoopans*, living with men, and supplying the place of women. These are brought up from their infancy with females, and taught all the feminine arts. They even assume the manner and dress of the women so nearly that a stranger would naturally take them for what they are not. This odious practice was formerly so prevalent that the residence of one of these monsters in a house was considered as fortunate; it is, however, daily losing ground." He mentions a case in which a priest had nearly married two males, when an interpreter chanced to come in and was able to inform him what he was doing. [. . .]

It is stated by Davydoff, as quoted by Holmberg, that the boy is selected to be a *schopan* because he is girl-like. This is a point of some interest as it indicates that the schopan is not effeminated solely by suggestion and association, but is probably feminine by inborn constitution.

In Louisiana, Florida, Yucatan, etc., somewhat similar customs exist or have existed. In Brazil men are to be found dressed as women and solely occupying themselves with feminine occupations; they are not very highly regarded. They are called *cudinas*: i.e., circumcized. [. . .]

Among all the tribes of the northwest United States sexual inverts may be found. The invert is called a *boté* ('not man, not woman') by the Montana, and a *burdash* ('half-man, half-woman') by the Washington Indians. The *boté* has been carefully studied by Dr. A. B. Holder. Holder finds that the *boté* wears woman's dress, and that his speech and manners are feminine. The dress and manners are assumed in childhood, but no sexual practices take place until puberty. These consist in the practice of *fellatio* by the *boté*, who probably himself experiences the orgasm at the same time. The *boté* is not a pederast, although pederasty occurs among these Indians. Holder examined a *boté* who was splendidly made, prepossessing, and in perfect health. With much reluctance he agreed to a careful examination. The sexual organs were quite normal, though perhaps not quite so large as his *physique* would suggest, but he had never had intercourse with a woman. On removing his clothes he pressed his thighs together, as a timid woman would, so as to conceal completely the sexual organs; Holder says that the thighs 'really, or to my fancy', had the feminine rotundity. He has heard a *boté* "*beg* a male Indian to submit to his caress," and he tells that "one little fellow, while in the agency boarding-school, was found frequently surreptitiously wearing female attire. He was punished, but finally escaped from school and became a *boté*, which vocation he has since followed." [. . .]

These various accounts are of considerable interest, though for the most part their precise significance remains doubtful. Some of them, however, – such as Holder's description of the *boté* [. . .] – indicate not only the presence of esthetic inversion but of true congenital sexual inversion. The extent of the evidence will doubtless be greatly enlarged as the number of competent observers increases, and crucial points are not longer so frequently overlooked.

On the whole, the evidence shows that among lower races homosexual practices are regarded with considerable indifference, and the real invert, if he exists among them, as doubtless he does exist, generally passes unperceived or joins some sacred caste which sanctifies his exclusively homosexual inclinations.

Even in Europe today a considerable lack of repugnance to homosexual practices may be found among the lower classes. In this matter, as folk-lore shows in so many other matters, the uncultured man of civilization is linked to the savage. In England, I am told, the soldier often has little or no objection to prostitute himself to the "swell" who pays him, although for pleasure he prefers to go to women; and Hyde Park is spoken of as a center of male prostitution. [. . .]

This primitive indifference is doubtless also a factor in the prevalence of homosexuality among criminals, although here, it must be remembered, two other factors (congenital abnormality and the isolation of imprisonment) have to be considered. In Russia, Tarnowsky observes that all pederasts are agreed that the common people are tolerably indifferent to their sexual advances, which they call "gentlemen's games." A correspondent remarks on "the fact, patent to all observers, that simple folk not unfrequently display no greater disgust for the abnormalities of sexual appetite than they do for its normal manifestations." He knows of many cases in which men of lower class were flattered and pleased by the attentions of men of higher class, although not themselves inverted. And from this point of view the following case, which he mentions, is very instructive: –

A pervert whom I can trust told me that he had made advances to upward of one hundred men in the course of the last fourteen years, and that he had only once met with a refusal (in which case the man later on offered himself spontaneously) and only once with an attempt to extort money. Permanent relations of friendship sprang up in most instances. He admitted that he looked after these persons and helped them with his social influence and a certain amount of pecuniary support – setting one up in business, giving another something to marry on, finding places for others.

Among the peasantry in Switzerland, I am informed, homosexual relationships are not uncommon before marriage, and such relationships are lightly spoken of as 'Dummheiten' [stupidities, foolishness]. [. . .]

What may be regarded as true sexual inversion can be traced in Europe from the beginning of the Christian era (though we can scarcely demonstrate the congenital element) especially among two classes – men of exceptional ability and criminals; and also, it may be added, among those neurotic and degenerate individuals who may be said to lie between these two classes, and on or over the borders of both. Homosexuality, mingled with various other sexual abnormalities and excesses, seems to have flourished in Rome during the empire, and is well exemplified in the persons of many of the emperors. Julius Caesar, Augustus, Tiberius, Caligula, Claudius, Nero, Galba, Titus, Domitian, Nerva, Trajan, Hadrian, Commodus, and Heliogabalus – many of them men of great ability and, from a Roman standpoint, great moral worth – are all charged, on more or less solid evidence, with homosexual practices. In Julius Caesar – "the husband of all women and the wife of all men" as he was satirically termed – excess of sexual activity seems to have accompanied, as is sometimes seen, an excess of intellectual activity. He was first accused of homosexual practices after a long stay in Bithynia with King Nikomedes, and the charge was very often renewed. Caesar was proud of his physical beauty, and, like many modern inverts, he was accustomed carefully to shave and epilate his body to preserve the smoothness of the skin. Hadrian's love for his beautiful slave Antinoüs is well known; the love seems to have been deep and mutual, and Antinoüs has become immortalized, partly by the romance of his obscure death and partly by the new and strangely beautiful type which he has given to sculpture. Heliogabalus, "the most homosexual of all the company," as he has been termed, seems to have been a true sexual invert, of feminine type; he dressed as a woman and was devoted to the men he loved.

Homosexual practices everywhere flourish and abound in prisons. There is abundant evidence on this point. I will only bring forward the evidence of Dr Wey, formerly physician to the Elmira Reformatory, New York. "Sexuality" (he wrote in a private letter) "is one of the most troublesome elements with which we have to contend. I have no data as to the number of prisoners here who are sexually perverse. In my pessimistic moments I should feel like saying that all were; but probably 80 per cent. would be a fair estimate." And, referring to the sexual influence which some men have over others, he remarks that "there are many men with features suggestive of femininity that attract others to them in a way that reminds me of a bitch in heat followed by a pack of dogs." [. . .]

Prison life develops and fosters the homosexual tendency of criminals; but there can be little doubt that that tendency, or else a tendency to sexual indifference or bisexuality, is a radical character of a very large number of criminals. We may also find it to a considerable extent among tramps, an allied class of undoubted degenerates, who, save for brief seasons, are less familiar with prison life. I am able to bring forward interesting evidence on this point by an acute observer who lived much among tramps in various countries, and largely devoted himself to the study of them. [. . .] It has not, I think, been noted – largely because the evidence was insufficiently clear – that among moral leaders, and persons with strong ethical instincts, there is a tendency toward the more elevated forms of homosexual feeling. This may be traced, not only in some of the great moral teachers of old, but also in men and women of our own day. It is fairly evident why this should be so. Just as the repressed love of a woman or a man has, in normally constituted persons, frequently furnished the motive power for an enlarged philanthropic activity, so the person who sees his own sex also bathed in sexual glamour, brings to his work of human service an ardor wholly unknown to the normally constituted individual; morality to him has become one with love. I am not prepared here to insist on this point, but no one, I think, who studies sympathetically the histories and experiences of great moral leaders can fail in many cases to note the presence of this feeling, more or less finely sublimated from any gross physical manifestation. [. . .]

In this brief glance at some of the ethnographical, historical, religious, and literary aspects of homosexual passion there is one other phenomenon which may be mentioned. This is the alleged fact that, while the phenomena exist to some extent everywhere, we seem to find a special proclivity to homosexuality (whether or not involving a greater frequency of congenital inversion is not usually clear) among certain races and in certain regions. In Europe it would be best illustrated by the case of southern Italy, which in this respect is held to be distinct from northern Italy, although Italians generally are franker than men of northern race in admitting their sexual practices. How far the supposed greater homosexuality of southern Italy may be due to Greek influence and Greek blood it is not very easy to say.

It must be remembered that, in dealing with a northern country like England, homosexual phenomena do not present themselves in the same way as they do in southern Italy today, or in ancient Greece. In Greece the homosexual impulse was recognized and idealized; a man could be an open homosexual lover, and yet, like Epaminondas, be a great and honored citizen of his country. There was no reason whatever why a man, who in mental and physical constitution was perfectly normal, should not adopt a custom that was regarded as respectable, and sometimes as even specially honorable. But it is quite otherwise today in a country like England or the United States. In these countries all our traditions and all our moral ideals, as well as the law, are energetically opposed to every manifestation of homosexual passion. It requires a very strong impetus to go against this compact social force which, on every side, constrains the individual into the paths of heterosexual love. [. . .]

Before stating briefly my own conclusions as to the nature of sexual inversion, I propose to analyze the facts brought out in the histories which I have been able to study.

Race. – All my cases, 80 in number, are British and American, 20 living in the United States and the rest being British. Ancestry, from the point of view of race, was not made a matter of special investigation. It appears, however, that at least 44 are English or mainly English; at least 10 are Scotch or of Scotch extraction; 2 are Irish and 4 others largely Irish; 4 have German fathers or mothers; another is of German descent on both sides, while 2 others are of remote German extraction; 2 are partly, and 1 entirely, French; 2 have a Portuguese strain, and at least 2 are more or less Jewish. Except the apparently frequent presence of the German element, there is nothing remarkable in this ancestry.

'Sexual Inversion Among Primitive Races'
(1902)
C. G. Seligmann

But few details of sexual inversion and perversion are known among savages, and it is commonly and tacitly assumed that abnormalities of the sexual instinct are the concomitants of Oriental luxury or advanced civilization. Too often merely the grosser forms of perversion have been looked for or noted, the condition described by Moll as psycho-sexual hermaphroditism, in which, while the psychical resemblance to the opposite sex colours the whole social life of the individual, there are also present traces of normal hetero-sexual instinct, being unrecognized or ignored. Among American Indians, from Alaska to Brazil, homo-sexual practices occur or occurred. Sodomy was prevalent among the Nahua (Aztec) and Maya nations the latter tolerating if not systematizing its practice. Among savage races Bancroft, speaking of the Isthmian tribes of Cueba and Careba, says: 'The caciques and some of the head men kept harems of youths who were dressed as women, did women's work about the house, and were exempt from war and its fatigues.' Again: 'In the province of Tamaulipa there were public brothels where men enacted the part of women', while the modern Omaha have a special name signifying hermaphrodite for the passive agent, whom they regard with contempt. Among the Aleuts of Alaska certain boys, whom Holmberg states were selected for their girlish appearance, are brought up as girls and decorated as women. Similar instances might be multiplied, but, apart from the last mentioned, which, according to Havelock Ellis, suggests the possibility of congenital inversion, they are all examples of the grossest forms of perversion, and no details suggesting that any of these are cases of congenital inversion are given. Similarly there is reason to believe that the pederasty practiced by certain New Caledonian warriors, which is stated to constitute a relationship more sacred than bloodbrotherhood, is resorted to for convenience and perhaps for Malthusian reasons, as it is among some Papuans of the western district of British New Guinea.

A somewhat different condition of things prevails among the Tupi, a Brazilian tribe in a low stage of civilization to whom Lomonacoll has devoted considerable attention. While noting that sodomy was prevalent in almost every local tribe, and that a class of men were met with whose function it was to lend themselves to the practice, he states that among the Tupi many women took no husbands, devoting themselves for the whole of their lives to perpetual chastity, and quotes Gandavo to the effect that there are some women among those who decide to be chaste who will not consent to know men even under threats of death. They wear their hair cut in the same fashion as the males, go to war with their bows and arrows, and take part in the chase. They frequent the company of men and each one of them has a woman who waits on her, to whom she says she is married and 'with whom she communicates and converses like man and wife'. It seems probable that here, among a people addicted to sodomy and in whom there is no strong feeling against homo-sexual relations, there is an element of true congenital inversion similar to that present in the sporadic cases among Papuans to be immediately described.

While with the Cambridge Anthropological Expedition to Torres Straits and New Guinea several instances were met with in the Rigo district of British New Guinea where, unlike the Fly river district, the habitual practice of pederasty is unknown. These cases occurred among a people practically still in their stone age and so uncontaminated by external influences that even white men's diseases had not yet obtained a footing among them. In the following notes the condition of the genitals is given on what is probably good authority, but in no case would it have been politic to have attempted to verify my informants' descriptions by actual examination. Three of the four cases alluded to were inhabitants of Bulaa, a considerable settlement built for the most part on piles in the sea. One of these had been dead for some time. In her, assuming the native diagnosis of sex to have been correct, there was maldevelopment of the genitalia, while the remaining two Bulaa cases are probably pure instances of psycho-sexual hermaphroditism.

Sex and Character (1903)
Otto Weininger

There are, to wit, nations and races whose men, though they can in no wise be regarded as intermediate forms of the sexes, are found to approach so slightly and so rarely to the ideal of manhood as set forth in my argument, that the principles, indeed the entire foundation on which this work rests, would seem to be severely shaken by their existence. What shall we make, for example, out of the Chinese, with their feminine freedom from internal cravings and their incapacity for every effort? One might feel tempted to believe in the complete effeminacy of the whole race. It can at least be no mere whim of the entire nation that the Chinaman habitually wears a pigtail, and that the growth of his beard is of the very thinnest. But how does the matter stand with the negroes? A genius has perhaps scarcely ever appeared amongst the negroes, and the standard of their morality is almost universally so low that it is beginning to be acknowledged in America that their emancipation was an act of imprudence.

If, consequently, the principle of the intermediate forms of the sexes may perhaps enjoy a prospect of becoming of importance to racial anthropology (since in some peoples a greater share of womanishness would seem to be generally disseminated), it must yet be conceded that the foregoing deductions refer above all to Aryan men and Aryan women. In how far, in the other great races of mankind, uniformity with the standard of the Aryan race may reign, or what has prevented and hindered this; to arrive more nearly at such knowledge would require in the first instance the most intense research into racial characteristics.

The Jewish race, which has been chosen by me as a subject of discussion, because, as will be shown, it presents the gravest and most formidable difficulties for my views, appears to possess a certain anthropological relationship with both negroes and Mongolians. The readily curling hair points to the negro; admixture of Mongolian blood is suggested by the perfectly Chinese or Malay formation of face and skull which is so often to be met with amongst the Jews and which is associated with a yellowish complexion. This is nothing more than the result of everyday experience, and these remarks must not be otherwise understood; the anthropological question of the origin of the Jewish race is apparently insoluble, and even such an interesting answer to it as that given by H.S. Chamberlain has recently met with much opposition. The author does not possess the knowledge necessary to treat of this; what will be here briefly, but as far as possible profoundly analysed, is the psychical peculiarity of the Jewish race.

This is an obligatory task imposed by psychological observation and analysis. It is undertaken independently of past history, the details of which must be uncertain. The Jewish race offers a problem of the deepest significance for the study of all races, and in itself it is intimately bound up with many of the most troublesome problems of the day.

I must, however, make clear what I mean by Judaism; I mean neither a race nor a people nor a recognised creed. I think of it as a tendency of the mind, as a psychological constitution which is a possibility for all mankind, but which has become actual in the most conspicuous fashion only amongst the Jews. Antisemitism itself will confirm my point of view.

The purest Aryans by descent and disposition are seldom Antisemites, although they are often unpleasantly moved by some of the peculiar Jewish traits; they cannot in the least understand the Antisemite movement, and are, in consequence of their defence of the Jews, often called Philosemites; and yet these persons writing on the subject of the hatred of Jews, have been guilty of the most profound misunderstanding of the Jewish character. The aggressive Antisemites, on the other hand, nearly always display certain Jewish characters, sometimes apparent in their faces, although they may have no real admixture of Jewish blood.

The explanation is simple. People love in others the qualities they would like to have but do not actually have in any great degree; so also we hate in others only what we do not wish to be, and what notwithstanding we are partly. We hate only qualities to which we approximate, but which we realise first in other persons.

Thus the fact is explained that the bitterest Antisemites are to be found amongst the Jews themselves. For only the quite Jewish Jews, like the completely Aryan Aryans, are not at all Antisemitically disposed; among the remainder only the commoner natures are actively Antisemitic and pass sentence on others without having once sat in judgment on themselves in these matters; and very few exercise their Antisemitism first on themselves. This one thing, however, remains none the less certain: whoever detests the Jewish disposition detests it first of all in himself; that he should persecute it in others is merely his endeavour to separate himself in this way from Jewishness; he strives to shake it off and to localise it in his fellow-creatures, and so for a moment to dream himself free of it. Hatred, like love, is a projected phenomenon; that person alone is hated who reminds one unpleasantly of oneself.[. . .]

I do not refer to a nation or to a race, to a creed or to a scripture. When I speak of the Jew I mean neither an individual nor the whole body, but mankind in general, in so far as it has a share in the platonic idea of Judaism. My purpose is to analyse this idea.

That these researches should be included in a work devoted to the characterology of the sexes may seem an undue extension of my subject. But some reflection will lead to the surprising result that Judaism is saturated with femininity, with precisely those qualities the essence of which I have shown to be in the strongest opposition to the male nature. It would not be difficult to make a case for the view that the Jew is more saturated with femininity than the Aryan, to such an extent that the most manly Jew is more feminine than the least manly Aryan.

This interpretation would be erroneous. It is most important to lay stress on the agreements and differences simply because so many points that become obvious in dissecting woman reappear in the Jew.[. . .]

The faults of the Jewish race have often been attributed to the repression of that race by Aryans, and many Christians are still disposed to blame themselves in this respect. But the self-reproach is not justified. Outward circumstances do not mould a race in one direction, unless there is in the race the innate tendency to respond to the moulding forces; the total result comes at least as much from the natural disposition as from the modifying circumstances. We know now that the proof of the inheritance of acquired characters has broken down, and, in the human race still more than the lower forms of life, it is certain that individual and racial characters persist in spite of all adaptive moulding. When men change, it is from within, outwards, unless the change, as in the case of women, is a mere superficial imitation of real change, and is not rooted in their natures. And how can we reconcile the idea that the Jewish character is a modern modification with the history of the foundation of the race, given in the Old Testament without any disapprobation of how the patriarch Jacob deceived his dying father, cheated his brother Esau and over-reached his father-in-law, Laban?

The defenders of the Jew have rightly acquitted him of any tendency to heinous crimes, and the legal statistics of different countries confirm this. The Jew is not really anti-moral. But, none the less, he does not represent the highest ethical type. He is rather non-moral, neither very good nor very bad, with nothing in him of either the angel or the devil. Notwithstanding the Book of Job and the story of Eden, it is plain that the conceptions of a Supreme Good and a Supreme Evil are not truly Jewish; I have no wish to enter upon the lengthy and controversial topics of Biblical criticism, but at the least I shall be on sure ground when I say that these conceptions play the least significant part in modern Jewish life. Orthodox or unorthodox, the modern Jew does not concern himself with God and the Devil, with Heaven and Hell. If he does not reach the heights of the Aryan, he is also less inclined to commit murder or other crimes of violence.

So also in the case of the woman; it is easier for her defenders to point to the infrequency of her commission of serious crimes than to prove her intrinsic morality. The homology of Jew and woman becomes closer the further examination goes. There is no female devil, and no female angel; only love, with its blind aversion from actuality, sees in woman a heavenly nature, and only hate sees in her a prodigy of wickedness. Greatness is absent from the nature of the woman and the Jew, the greatness of morality, or the greatness of evil. In the Aryan man, the good and bad principles of Kant's religious philosophy are ever present, ever in strife. In the Jew and the woman, good and evil are not distinct from one another.

Jews, then, do not live as free, self-governing individuals, choosing between virtue and vice in the Aryan fashion. They are a mere collection of similar individuals each cast in the same mould, the whole forming as it were a continuous plasmodium. The Antisemite has often thought of this as a defensive and aggressive union, and has formulated the conception of a Jewish 'solidarity'. There is a deep confusion here. When some accusation is made against some unknown member of the Jewish race, all Jews secretly take the part of the accused, and wish, hope for, and seek to establish his innocence. But it must not be thought that they are interesting themselves more in the fate of the individual Jew than they would do in the case of an individual Christian. It is the menace to Judaism in general, the fear that the shameful shadow may do harm to Judaism as a whole, which is the origin of the apparent feeling of sympathy. In the same way, women are delighted when a member of their sex is depreciated, and will themselves assist, until the proceeding seems to throw a disadvantageous light over the sex in general, so frightening men from marriage. The race or sex alone is defended, not the individual.

It would be easy to understand why the family (in its biological not its legal sense) plays a larger *role* amongst the Jews than amongst any other people; the English, who in certain ways are akin to the Jews, coming next. The family, in this biological sense, is feminine and maternal in its origin, and has no relation to the State or to society. The fusion, the continuity of the members of the family, reaches its highest point amongst the Jews. In the Indo-Germanic races, especially in the case of the more gifted, but also in quite ordinary individuals, there is never complete harmony between father and son; consciously, or unconsciously, there is always in the mind of the son a certain feeling of impatience against the man who, unasked, brought him into the world, gave him a name, and determined his limitations in this earthly life. It is only amongst the Jews that the son feels deeply rooted in the family and is fully at one with his father. It scarcely ever happens amongst Christians that father and son are really friends. Amongst Christians even the daughters stand a little further apart from the family circle than happens with Jewesses, and more frequently take up some calling which isolates them and gives them independent interests.

We reach at this point a fact in relation to the argument of the last chapter. I showed there that the essential element in the pairing instinct was an indistinct sense of individuality and of the limits between individuals. Men who are match-makers have always a Jewish element in them. The Jew is always more absorbed by sexual matters than the Aryan, although he is notably less potent sexually and less liable to be enmeshed in a great passion. The Jews are habitual match-makers, and in no race does it so often happen that marriages are arranged by men. This kind of activity is certainly peculiarly necessary in their case, for, as I have already stated, there is no people amongst which marriages for love are so rare. The organic disposition of the Jews towards match-making is associated with their racial failure to comprehend asceticism. It is interesting to note that the Jewish Rabbis have always been addicted to speculations as to the begetting of children and have a rich tradition on the subject, a natural result in the case of the people who invented the phrase as to the duty of 'multiplying and replenishing the earth'.

The pairing instinct is the great remover of the limits between individuals; and the Jew, *par excellence*, is the breaker down of such limits. He is at the opposite pole from aristocrats, with whom the preservation of the limits between individuals is the leading idea. The Jew is an inborn communist. The Jew's careless manners in society and his want of social tact turn on this quality, for the reserves of social intercourse are simply barriers to protect individuality.

I desire at this point again to lay stress on the fact, although it should be self-evident, that, in spite of my low estimate of the Jew, nothing could be further from my intention than to lend the faintest support to any practical or theoretical persecution of Jews. I am dealing with Judaism, in the platonic sense, as an idea. There is no more an absolute Jew than an absolute Christian. I am not speaking against the individual, whom, indeed, if that had been so, I should have wounded grossly and unnecessarily. Watchwords, such as 'Buy only from Christians', have in reality a Jewish taint; they have a meaning only for those who regard the race and not the individual, and what is to be compared with them is the Jewish use of the

[handwritten marginal note:] now you say so... (yikes)

word 'Goy', which is now almost obsolete. I have no wish to boycott the Jew, or by any such immoral means to attempt to solve the Jewish question. Nor will Zionism solve that question; as H. D. Chamberlain has pointed out, since the destruction of the Temple at Jerusalem, Judaism has ceased to be national, and has become a spreading parasite, straggling all over the earth and finding true root nowhere. Before Zionism is possible, the Jew must first conquer Judaism. [. . .]

Just as Jews and women are without extreme good and extreme evil, so they never show either genius or the depth of stupidity of which mankind is capable. The specific kind of intelligence for which Jews and women alike are notorious is due simply to the alertness of an exaggerated egotism; it is due, moreover, to the boundless capacity shown by both for pursuing any object with equal zeal, because they have no intrinsic standard of value – nothing in their own souls by which to judge of the worthiness of any particular object. And so they have unhampered natural instincts, such as are not present to help the Aryan man when his transcendental standard fails him. [. . .]

The comparison of the Jew with the Englishman fades out much more quickly than that with the woman. Both comparisons first arose in the heat of the conflict as to the worth and the nature of Jews. I may again refer to Wagner, who not only interested himself deeply in the problem of Judaism, but rediscovered the Jew in the Englishman, and threw the shadow of Ahasuerus over his Kundry, probably the most perfect representation of woman in art.

The fact that no woman in the world represents the idea of the wife so completely as the Jewess (and not only in the eyes of Jews) still further supports the comparison between Jews and women. In the case of the Aryans, the metaphysical qualities of the male are part of his sexual attraction for the woman, and so, in a fashion, she puts on an appearance of these. The Jew, on the other hand, has no transcendental quality, and in the shaping and moulding of the wife leaves the natural tendencies of the female nature a more unhampered sphere; and the Jewish woman, accordingly, plays the part required of her, as house-mother or odalisque, as Cybele or Cyprian, in the fullest way.

The congruity between Jews and women further reveals itself in the extreme adaptability of the Jews, in their great talent for journalism, the 'mobility' of their minds, their lack of deeply-rooted and original ideas, in fact the mode in which, like women, because they are nothing in themselves, they can become everything. The Jew is an individual, not an individuality; he is in constant close relation with the lower life, and has no share in the higher metaphysical life.

At this point the comparison between the Jew and the woman breaks down; the being-nothing and becoming-all-things differs in the two. The woman is material which passively assumes any form impressed upon it. In the Jew there is a definite aggressiveness; it is not because of the great impression that others make on him that he is receptive; he is no more subject to suggestion than the Aryan man, but he adapts himself to every circumstance and every race, becoming, like the parasite, a new creature in every different host, although remaining essentially the same. He assimilates himself to everything, and assimilates everything; he is not dominated by others, but submits himself to them. The Jew is gifted, the woman is not gifted, and the giftedness of the Jew reveals itself in many forms of activity, as, for instance, in jurisprudence; but these activities are always relative and never seated in the creative freedom of the will.

The Jew is as persistent as the woman, but his persistence is not that of the individual but of the race. He is not unconditioned like the Aryan, but his limitations differ from those of the woman. [. . .]

Our age is not only the most Jewish but the most feminine. It is a time when art is content with daubs and seeks its inspiration in the sports of animals; the time of a superficial anarchy, with no feeling for Justice and the State; a time of communistic ethics, of the most foolish of historical views, the materialistic interpretation of history; a time of capitalism and of Marxism; a time when history, life, and science are no more than political economy and technical instruction; a time when genius is supposed to be a form of madness; a time with no great artists and no great philosophers; a time without originality and yet with the most foolish craving for originality; a time when the cult of the Virgin has been replaced by that of the Demivierge. It is the time when pairing has not only been approved but has been enjoined as a duty. [. . .]

This woman question is as old as sex itself, and as young as mankind. And the answer to it? Man must free himself of sex, for in that way, and that way alone, can he free woman. In his purity, not, as she believes, in his impurity, lies her salvation. She must certainly be destroyed, as woman; but only to be raised again from the ashes – new, restored to youth – as a real human being.

So long as there are two sexes there will always be a woman question, just as there will be the problem of mankind.

The Sexual Question (1906)
August Forel

A good deal has been said concerning the hot blood of warm climates, and on the whole it appears true that people who inhabit these climates have a more violent and more precocious sexual temperament than those who live in cold regions. But this is not a racial character. The Jews, who have preserved their race unaltered in all climates and under all possible conditions of existence, furnish an object lesson which is particularly appropriate to decide the question. The traits of their character are reflected in their sexual life. Their sexual appetites are generally strong and their love is distinguished by great family attachment. Their sexual life is also influenced by their mercantile spirit, and we find them everywhere connected with the traffic of women and prostitution. They are not very jealous and are much addicted to concubinage, at the same time remaining affectionate to their wife and family. [. . .]

The Conflict of Human Races. – There remains a last postulate, extremely arduous and serious, which we have already mentioned. How is our Aryan race and its civilization to guard against the danger of being passively invaded and exterminated by the alarming fecundity of other human races? One must be blind not to recognize this danger. To estimate it at its proper value, it is not enough to put all "savages" and "barbarians" into one basket and all "civilized" into the other. The question is far more complicated than this. Many savage and semi-savage races become rapidly extinct on account of their comparative sterility. Europeans have introduced among them so much alcohol, venereal disease and other plagues, that they promptly perish from want of the power of resistance. This is the case with the Weddas, the Todas, the Redskins of North America, the Australian aboriginees, Malays and many others.

The question presents itself in another aspect with regard to negroes, who are very resistant and extremely prolific, and everywhere adapt themselves to civilized customs. But those who believe that negroes are capable of *acquiring* a higher civilization without undergoing a phylogenetic cerebral transformation for a hundred thousand years, are Utopians. I cannot here enter into the details of this question. It seems obvious to me, however, that in the already considerable time during which the American negroes have been under the influence of European culture, they ought to have often demonstrated their power of assimilating it and of developing it independently, according to their own genius, if their brains were capable of so doing. Instead of this, we find that negroes in the interior of the island of Haiti, formerly civilized by France, then abandoned to themselves, have, with the exception of a few mulattoes, reverted to the most complete barbarism, and have even barbarized the French language and Christianity, with which they had been endowed.

Compare with this the rapidity with which a civilized or civilizable race, depending on its innate energy, assimilates our culture with or without Christianity! We need only look at what has happened in Japan during the last thirty years, and what the Christian races of the Balkan countries have been doing after delivery from the yoke of the Turks – for example, the Roumanians, Bulgarians and Greeks.

It is by its fruits that we judge the value of the tree. The Japanese are a civilizable and civilized race, and must be treated as such. The negroes, on the contrary, are not so; that is to say, they are only by themselves capable of quite an inferior civilization, and only become adapted to our customs by a superficial veneer of civilization.

Up to what point can the Mongolian, and even the Jewish race, become mixed with our Aryan or Indo-Germanic races without gradually supplanting them and causing them to disappear? This is a question I am incapable of answering. If it were only a question of the Japanese there would be no serious difficulty and the assimilation would be beneficial. But the Chinese and some other Mongolian races constitute an imminent danger for the very existence of the white races. These people eat much less than ourselves, are contented with much smaller dwellings, and in spite of this produce twice as many children and do twice as much work. The connection of this with the sexual question is not difficult to understand.

'A Perversion Not Commonly Noted' (1913)
Margaret Otis

A form of perversion that is well known among workers in reform schools and institutions for delinquent girls, is that of love-making between the white and colored girls. This particular form of the homosexual relation has perhaps not been brought to the attention of scientists. The ordinary form that is found among girls even in high-class boarding-schools is well known, and this feature of school life is one of the many difficulties that presents itself to those in charge of educational affairs. The difference in color, in this case, takes the place of difference in sex, and ardent love-affairs arise between white and colored girls in schools where both races are housed together.

In one institution in particular the difficulty seemed so great and the disadvantage of the intimacy between the girls so apparent that segregation was resorted to. The colored girls were transferred to a separate cottage a short distance from the other buildings. The girls were kept apart both when at work and when at play. The girls were given to understand that it was a serious breach of rules for them to get together, and the white girls were absolutely forbidden to have anything to do with the colored. Yet this separation did not have wholly the desired effect. The motive of "the forbidden fruit" was added. The separation seemed to enhance the value of the loved one, and that she was to a degree inaccessible, added to her charms.

In this particular institution the love of "niggers" seemed to be one of the traditions of the place, many of the girls saying that they had never seen anything of the kind outside; but that on coming here, when they saw the other girls doing it, they started doing the same thing themselves, acting from their suggestion. A white girl on arriving would receive a lock of hair and a note from a colored girl asking her to be her love. The girl sending the note would be pointed out, and if her appearance was satisfactory, a note would be sent in reply and the love accepted. Many would enter into such an affair simply for fun and for lack of anything more interesting to take up their attention. With others it proved to be a serious fascination and of intensely sexual nature. This line from one girl's note shows the feeling of true love: "I do not love for the fun of loving, but because my heart makes me love." One case is on record of a girl, constantly involved in these love affairs with the colored, who afterwards, on leaving the institution, married a colored man. This, however, is unusual, for the girls rarely have anything to do with the colored race after leaving the school.

Opinions differ as to which one starts the affair. Sometimes the white girls write first, and sometimes the colored. "It might be either way," said one colored girl. One white girl, however, admitted that the colored girl she loved seemed the man, and thought it was so in the case of the others. Another white girl said that when a certain colored girl looked at her, she seemed almost to mesmerize her. "It made her feel crazy."

This habit of "nigger-loving" seems to be confined to a certain set of girls. These would congregate in one part of the dormitory to watch at the window for the colored girls to pass by on their way to work. Notes could be slipped out, kisses thrown and looks exchanged. Each of these girls was known to be a "nigger-lover." When questioned on the subject, some insist that they do it just for fun. One said that the girls would wave to the "niggers" just "to see the coons get excited."

The notes when captured show the expression of a passionate love of low order, many coarse expressions are used and the animal instinct is seen to be paramount. The ideal of loyalty is present. A girl is called fickle if she changes her love too often. "I don't like a deceitful girl," appears in one of the letters. That a girl should be true to her love is required by their peculiar moral code. "Fussing" with other girls is condemned. From one of the letters: "This morning when you were going to the nursery you threw a kiss to Mary Smith. If you care for her more than you do for me, why, don't hesitate to tell me. I don't love you because you said you loved me. I could have kept my love concealed if I cared to. I certainly will regret the day I ever wrote or sent my love to you if this downright deceitfulness does not stop."

The penalty for a girl who is fickle or who ceases to care for her lover seems to be a curse from the abandoned forlorn one. "It was not long ago that one of your friends sent me a message saying that you didn't love me, but you didn't want me to know that you didn't, for fear I would curse you. Well, you need have no fear. I never curse any one. I have been so careful over here of every little thing I did, for fear some one might carry something back to you, that I had been deceitful. No, indeed! I am not deceitful."

There is often a reaction from this emotional type of love. Girls formerly lovers abandon each other and hate takes the place of love. The mood will change and not even friendship remains. It is at this moment that the girl may be approached more easily in the way of influencing her to abandon her excessive emotional attitude. At this moment she may be brought to realize that such love is not lasting and does her harm rather than good.

Sometimes the love is very real and seems almost ennobling. On one occasion a girl, hearing that danger threatened her love in another cottage, was inconsolable, quite lost her head and called out: "Oh, my baby! my baby! What will become of my baby!" Her distress was so great that all fear of discovery was lost. She even called her name. The intense emotion dispelled all fear and anxiety for her love alone occupied the field of consciousness. Later, after suffering punishment for her fault, she wrote to a friend: "You can see by this that I am always thinking of you. Oh, sister dear, now this is between you and I. Lucy Jones asks me to give Baby up, for she tries to tell me that Baby does not love me. Don't you see what she is trying to do? To get my love back. Ah! sister darling, I might say I will give my Baby up, but ah, in my heart I love her and always shall." Again: "Ah! I shall never throw Baby down; I don't care what happens, for trouble does not change my mind one bit, and I hope it's not changing yours."

An interesting feature of these love episodes is found in the many superstitious practices, especially among the colored when they wish to win the love of a white girl. Curious love charms are made of locks of hair of their inamoratas. One practice is for a colored girl to bury a lock of hair of the white girl she fancies and this is sure to bring her love. These practices, some of so coarse a nature that they cannot be written down, seem to be part of the system, for system it must be called, so thoroughly ingrained it is in the school life.

When taken to task for their silliness, the girls say: "Well, we girls haven't much else to think about." True enough, they haven't much of the emotional nature that they crave, and it seems they must have the sensational and emotional in some form. One girl says: "When you have been in the habit of having a girl love, and she goes away, you have to get another;

you just can't get along without thinking of one girl more than another." Sometimes, of course, the relation is a perfectly innocent girlish friendship, but even here jealousy enters in.

Some interested in this phase of the school life have asked: "Isn't it true that it is the defective girls who indulge in this low emotional love more than the others?" This is not found to be the case. Many sins are laid at the door of defectiveness, but mental defect does not explain everything. The reverse might rather be said to be the truth. Some of the girls indulging in this love for the colored have, perhaps, the most highly developed intellectual ability of any girls of the school.

One may ask how this phase of indulging the sexual nature is regarded by the girls themselves. The answer will be found in the fact that there are several distinct strata of moral standards in the school. There are some girls who consider themselves a little above the rest. Among these self-considered high-class girls the "nigger-lovers" are despised and condemned. They are held as not good enough to associate with. That water seeks its own level is true even among the delinquent girls themselves. Certain sets and cliques appear, and those who are "high up" scorn the "common kind."

Men and Women (1933)
Magnus Hirschfeld

I would like to ask my readers to read and keep in mind the following; it is a summation of the best knowledge on sex possible to us today; and it will clarify for the reader almost everything he will encounter in this book:

1 No two countries or peoples in the world have identical sex institutions.
2 This dissimilarity is in no way based on differences in sex tendencies, which, taken as a whole, are absolutely alike in all peoples and races and show only individual differences.
3 The variation in sex customs is determined only by the multiplicity of modes of sex expression and of attempts at adjustment.
4 The sexologist ought to avoid the term "savages" with reference to peoples on a low plane of culture, for the sex life of highly cultivated peoples is in many respects freer and more unrestrained than that of primitives.
5 The origin of sex customs is everywhere of a completely *real* nature, though frequently governed by superstitious fear of ghosts and spir-

its. Symbolic and idealistic interpretations are explanations *after* the fact.

6   Every people (and every religion) is convinced that its own morals constitute morality in the *objective* sense. Consequently there is a universal tendency to dismiss all other morals as more or less immoral.

7   Mankind has not yet succeeded in arriving at a uniform solution of sex and love morality which will correspond with the findings of biological and of sociological sex research.

8   Only an objective scientific study of mankind and of sex can prepare the way for the complete realization of human sex rights.

Racism (1938)
Magnus Hirschfeld

Heterosexuals, who regard themselves as 'normal' because they are in the majority, and who (in the prime of life, at any rate) are apt to have an instinctive dislike for homosexuals and their ways – a dislike that is fostered by the suggestive influence of education – hypocritically incline to pretend that homosexual practices cannot have arisen spontaneously in their own happy land and among their own fortunately endowed 'race'. Hence the canting insinuation that homosexuality must have been introduced from without, from the foreign land or by the foreign people with whose name it is associated. Throughout the ages this has been done, for homosexuality and its stigmatisation by heterosexuals are perennial phenomena. I have given a long list of such appellations in my treatise *Homosexualität des Mannes und des Weibes* [*Male and Female Homosexuality*]. Let me briefly recapitulate here, because the subject has a definite bearing upon my central topic of racism.

When the ancient Athenians wished to explain that anyone was addicted to homosexual practices, they said he was inclined to sexual intercourse after the Phoenician, Lacedaemonian, or Cretan manner, the implication being that such ways were not native to Athens. Another locution of the same kind was 'Chalcidian methods', with a reference to the capital of Euboea, where the worship of the 'masculine Venus' was supposed to be much in vogue. A kindred term was siphniazize, from the island of Siphnus in the Aegean; another was phidakize, but in this case the town or country thus decried is not otherwise known to fame.

In the Middle Ages, Florence was in ill repute for the same cause, whence the verb 'florenzen' in the 1422 Zurich legal code. But the Florentines, when they wished to convey the same idea, referred to 'Neapolitan love'.

Again, also during the Middle Ages, homosexuals were said to 'celebrate a shameful Welsh marriage' – the adjective 'Welsh' signifying French, Italian, or simply foreign. To the same period belongs the expression 'mal d'orient', the 'oriental vice', meaning that homosexuality had been imported from the East. This accusation was especially prevalent after the Crusades, and was perhaps in some measure justified because the Crusades, in which celibate semi-monastic orders like the Templars and the Hospitallers played a great part, must, as did monasticism everywhere, have tended to foster homosexuality. Certainly when Philip the Fair coveted the wealth of the Templars, and plotted to destroy them, the accusation of homosexuality in conjunction with that of sorcery was one of the most powerful of his weapons. Both these evil practices were supposed to have been learned in the East.

Such local designations are quite unjustified, but the error is hard to uproot. In a Nazi pamphlet the curious may find a reference to my own studies with a caricature of myself beneath which is written: 'He introduced the oriental vice into Germany.' But for Magnus Hirschfeld, I gather, there would have been no homosexual scandal at the court of the last Hohenzollern emperor of Germany, and no Röhm, Hitler's chief of staff and oldest friend, whose butchery was excused by the chancellor after the blood-bath at the end of June 1934 on the ground of Röhm's 'notorious sexual perversion'.

In the Balkans, when the Rumanians wish to say that a man is homosexually inclined, they call him a Turk. The Turks pass on the accusation by speaking of a Persian with the same meaning; while the Persians use the identical device of a local nomenclature to imply that even if homosexuality does exist in Persia, it is restricted to the border and desert province of Khorassan. [. . .] Returning to the Balkans, we find that a corruption of the folk-name Bulgarian was the origin of the most widely used name for a male homosexual in France and England, and of the English legal term for an offence punishable by a long period of imprisonment. When we go to the Far East we learn (so Suyewo Iwaya tells us) that the Japanese declare the love for boys to have been introduced from China with Buddhism. The same racist predilections must underlie the belief, recorded by Erwin Baelz, for many years professor of medicine at the University of Tokyo, that there is much more 'unnatural vice' in North China than in South China because in the latter region the Chinese blood has been diluted by Malay admixture.

In South America, and especially in Argentina, it is usual to speak of homosexuals as Brasilecos (Brazilians); while in the United States the introduction of homosexual practices is ascribed, now to the Chinese, now to the Italians, and now to some other race of immigrants. We find among primitives the same disinclination to believe that homosexuality can have originated in their own tribe. The Fijians speak of homosexual relations as the 'white man's way'. [. . .]

If I have been somewhat detailed in my discussion of the problems that arise under the heading of the present chapter, it is because there is a lesson to be drawn. The lesson is that it is unwarrantable to call particular localities, peoples, or races to account for attributes that belong to a certain proportion of individuals at all times, in all places, and of whatever stock. A dispassionate humanist will concern himself only with ascertainable facts and actual institutions. The detestation of groups united by locality or by what is termed race, is as prejudiced as hero-worship.

In one of my earlier books I wrote: Everywhere the same passion digs for itself identical channels. Among homosexual men and women, for instance, we encounter everywhere the same main groups, effeminate and virile types, between which stands a third, less strongly characterised group of intermediates. Everywhere, too, we find, in addition to those who are homosexual without qualification, persons whose inclinations or activities are bisexual; in addition to those who are unmistakably homosexual, those whose homosexuality is open to question. Amazingly similar are the types we encounter after nightfall: in Cairo, at the fish Market; in Rome, strolling up and down the Piazza Colonna; in Copenhagen, frequenting the square in front of the Town Hall. They are of the same genus as those who, for the same purpose, visit Pera Street at the Golden Horn or the Friedrichstrasse in Berlin; and we come across like specimens of the intermediate sex, in Hyde Park (London), the Retiro (Madrid), Hibiya Park (Tokyo), the Prater (Vienna), the Champs Elysées (Paris); everywhere they have their haunts; the same sort of people, whether they are Frisians or Basques, on the Seedeich of Cuxhaven, the Concha of San Sebastian, the Molo of Pola, the Water Front of Frisco, seek acquaintances beside the North Sea or the Adriatic, the Bay of Biscay or the Pacific, as the case may be. The uniform aspect of homosexuality in all races and under all skies has been for me a convincing proof of its biological causation. In this matter, beyond question, the sexual type conquers the racial type.

There can be no doubt that, however multifarious sexual customs, conventions, and views may be, from the psycho-biological standpoint there is a general and far-reaching similarity in the sexual behaviour of all peoples. When I say this, I can appeal to an experience which must be almost if not quite unrivalled, so numerous are the men and women from every part of the world who have consulted me about sex matters by word of mouth or by letter. The same tunes, stories of the same passions, sufferings, and difficulties, come from persons belonging to all races. I fully agree with Friedrich Hertz when he writes in *Rasse und Kultur* [*Race and Culture*], p. 232: 'It is not true, as Günther declares, that each race has its own sexual morality, and that reciprocal understanding upon these matters is impossible.'

Sexual peculiarities (abnormalities or perversions, as they are often termed) are so equally distributed among the nations and among every stratum of the population that there can be no excuse for assigning what are merely individual characteristics to groups or races, and to parties or the advocates of specified opinions. [. . .]

We must not, however, fail to recognise that in a predilection for or a detestation and persecution of this race or that, a great part is often played by an unconscious fetishist liking or an unconscious fetishist dislike. (I use the terms fetishist and antifetishist with a sexual connotation.) Other psychosexual temperamental variations, often sublimated or repressed until as far as the conscious is concerned they lie outside the sexual sphere, may be powerful elements in irrational racial preferences and hatreds. I think, for instance, of what may be a powerful masochistic inclination to subserviency, or an aggressiveness which to the dispassionate observer is unmistakably sadistic, or an infantile component which manifests itself in childish delight, malicious joy, or simple playfulness. These examples may help the reader to understand how advantageous may be a study of the depth-psychology of racism. [. . .]

One sexual characteristic which is almost universal among all peoples and in all climes is that a very large proportion of persons are drawn towards those whose temperament contrasts with their own. This is true alike of body and of mind, and underlies the tendency to racial crossings which no power on earth has hitherto been able to hold in check.

The differences between the sexes which make the members of one sex desire caressive and detumescent contacts with those of another have been fostered by natural selection to perpetuate the species. In the last analysis, 'miscegenation' is the mingling of contrasted qualities. This fact shows how groundless is the common dread that racial crossing will lead to the production of a 'homologous racial compost'. The precise opposite is true. In no other way can we secure a greater variety of individual types, achieve more agreeable nonconformity and richer colouring, than by having recourse to the infinitely numerous possibilities of blending that present themselves when we blend assortments of healthy genes from sires and dams of different 'races'.

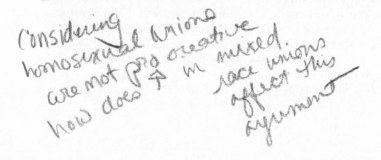

Considering homosexual unions are not pro creative in mixed. how does ↑ race unions affect this argument

Part VIII

Other Sexual Proclivities

Introduction

Lesley Hall

Sexology is often perceived as being the description and classification of bizarre sexual behaviours. Certainly it brings under the rubric of sexuality forms of conduct which many would not immediately identify as even being sexual. In its drive to classify these varied types of behaviour, two principal ways of perceiving such phenomena can be seen to emerge. On the one hand, there are those like Cesare Lombroso and Guglielmo Ferrero, and to a considerable extent Richard von Krafft-Ebing and Iwan Bloch, who define the 'sexual pervert' as a different form of being to the 'normal' person. On the other hand, Havelock Ellis in particular places a great emphasis on the continuity between the normal and the perverse, with the latter defined as an exaggeration of tendencies already present within 'normal' sexuality.

The tendency to define certain sexual types as subhuman is particularly noticeable in the work of Lombroso and Ferrero, who believed that criminals were almost a separate species who could be detected by their physical appearance, which revealed atavistic features. In the passage on prostitutes he draws particular attention to the fact that they, almost uniquely among women, are tattooed, a practice otherwise associated with the male criminal. Ellis, however, while he summarizes the conclusions of other European authorities (including Lombroso and those of his school) who had attempted to define a specific prostitute 'type' of woman, demonstrates his usual scepticism about how far such statements can be trusted or how far they will take the inquirer into this social problem. If prostitutes do differ from the 'normal' woman, he suggests, this difference is very slight, and all the evidence adduced somewhat inconclusive. There was a long tradition of investigation into prostitution as a social problem, which perhaps lies outside sexology proper, to which Ellis alludes in his mention of the 'economic and other conditions' which create prostitutes.

Bestiality had a long history of legal penalization. Krafft-Ebing, while referring to it as 'monstrous and revolting', none the less believed it not necessarily pathological, but due to the rather different causes of 'low morality and great sexual desire', along with 'lack of opportunity for natural indulgence'. Although Krafft-Ebing has been depicted as the great pathologizer, he in fact takes considerable pains to distinguish between the deviations of the 'normal' and those of the pathological case. He cites the case of a man of 'high social position' and 'mentally quite sound' who had been having habitual intercourse with hens for various circumstantial reasons, differentiating this from the case of a man only attracted to animals. In his discussion of fetishism, Krafft-Ebing approaches still more closely to the position that the 'perverse' and the 'normal' are closely allied, although only to move away from this once more, distinguishing the 'preference for certain physical characteristics' from the 'limitation of sexual interest' of the pathological fetishist. His massive study *Psychopathia Sexualis*, however, does query whether sexually unusual behaviour should be judged by those of its practitioners found in the law-courts or the lunatic asylum, or whether these constituted a subset of larger populations just as most criminals or lunatics did.

Bestiality and fetishism were relatively common, but the latter's sexual nature was only fully recognized during the later nineteenth century. A practice probably as old as humanity, masturbation had been defined as sinful by religion, but only subjected to full medico-moral pathologization from the early eighteenth century. By the late nineteenth century it was regarded as a habit leading not only to moral degradation through eroding control over baser instincts, but to deleterious physical and mental consequences. Ellis takes on this stigmatized practice in his usual non-judgemental and urbane style. He redefines the subject as 'auto-erotism', relates it to a wider context, and, far from being a disease of modern civilization, inscribes it as natural and a concomitant of humanity.

Bloch, in *The Sexual Life of Our Time*, strikes a somewhat sensationalist note in his account of voyeurism. One is inclined to feel a little sceptical about the 'societies and secret sexual clubs' he posits. Might these not have been high-minded naturists? The meetings in gardens certainly suggest this. As in the case of Krafft-Ebing's account of the 'secret circle of *roués*' to whom a woman exhibited a sexual act with a bulldog, the evidence seems somewhat anecdotal.

It is often assumed that by the early twentieth century there were two distinct ways in which sexologists understood human sexual deviations, largely hostile to one another. On the one hand, there was the strictly psychoanalytic, which related perversion of the sexual instinct to events in childhood, and on the other, the biologistic school, which believed in certain inborn characteristics leading individuals to become particular sexual 'types'. Wilhelm Stekel (1868–1940) takes a fairly firm psychoanalytic line in his exploration of *Sadism and Masochism*, but concedes that there is an innate 'disposition towards this paraphilia'.

Ellis is even more even-handed in stating the 'need to recognize alike the hereditary and innate factors, the acquired and psychogenetic factors', citing eminent psychoanalytic thinkers who accept both. He points out that both contemporary studies in endocrinology ('internal secretions') and psychoanalysis have a part to play in illuminating problems of sex. In his account of *Eonism* he makes a subtle analysis of cross-dressing. He dismisses the notion that it is necessarily associated with homosexuality, or at least an active and conscious pursuit of homoerotic desires, suggesting that it has a much more complex relationship to the individual's sexual identity.

Magnus Hirschfeld is usually regarded as one of the principal members of the inborn factors school of sexology, with his strong arguments for the biological reality of a 'third sex'. In this account of exhibitionism, however (in a volume posthumously assembled from his writings by Norman Haire and Arthur Koestler), it can be seen that he did not wholly reject ideas of psychogenic causation in at least some anomalous combination of prudish modesty and shameless behaviour in the exhibitionist. In the case of the judge who exposed himself, his severity on the bench is attributed to 'an overcompensated sense of guilt'.

Psychopathia Sexualis [1886] (12th edn 1903)
Richard von Krafft-Ebing

The cases in which sadism and masochism occur simultaneously in one individual are interesting, but they present some difficulties of explanation. [...] From the latter it is evident that it is especially the idea of subjection that, both actively and passively, forms the nucleus of the perverse desires. Traces of the same thing are also to be observed, with more or less clearness, in many other cases. At any rate, one of the two perversions is always markedly predominant.

Owing to this marked predominance of one perversion and the later appearance of the other in such cases, it may well be assumed that the predominating perversion is *original*, and that the other has been *acquired* in the course of time. The ideas of subjection and maltreatment, coloured with lustful pleasure, either in an active or passive sense, have become deeply imbedded in such an individual. Occasionally the imagination is tempted to try the same ideas in an inverted *role*. There may even be realisation of this inversion. Such attempts in imagination and in acts, are, however, usually soon abandoned as inadequate for the original inclination.

Masochism and sadism also occur in combination with contrary sexual instinct, and, in fact, in association with all forms and degrees of this perversion. The individual of contrary sexuality may be a sadist as well as masochist.

Wherever a sexual perversion has developed on the basis of a neuropathic individuality, sexual hyperaesthesia, which may always be assumed to be present, may induce the phenomena of masochism and sadism— now of the one, now of both combined, one arising from the other. Thus masochism and sadism appear as the fundamental forms of psycho-sexual perversion, which may make their appearance at any point in the domain of sexual aberration.

Fetichism [. . .]

In the considerations concerning the psychology of the normal sexual life in the introduction to this work it was shown that, within physiological limits, the pronounced preference for a certain portion of the body of persons of the opposite sex, particularly for a certain form of this part, may attain great psycho-sexual importance. Indeed, the especial power of attraction possessed by certain forms and peculiarities for many men—in fact, the majority—may be regarded as the real principle of individualism in love.

This preference for certain particular physical characteristics in persons of the opposite sex—by the side of which, likewise, a marked preference for certain psychical characteristics may be demonstrated—following *Binet* ('Du Fétischisme dans l'amour', 'Revue Philosophique', 1887) and *Lombroso* (Introduction to the Italian edition of the second edition of this work), I have called 'fetichism'; because this enthusiasm for certain portions of the body (or even articles of attire) and the worship of them, in obedience to sexual impulses, frequently call to mind the reverence for relics, holy objects, etc., in religious cults. This physiological fetichism has already been described in detail.

By the side of this physiological fetichism, however, there is, in the psycho-sexual sphere, an undoubted *pathological, erotic fetichism*, of which there is already a numerous series of cases presenting phenomena having great clinical and psychiatric interest, and, under certain circumstances also, forensic importance. This pathological fetichism does not confine itself to certain parts of the body alone, but it is even extended to inanimate objects, which, however, are almost always articles of female wearing-apparel, and thus stand in close relation with the female person.

This pathological fetichism is connected, through gradual transitions, with physiological fetichism, so that (at least in body-fetichism) it is almost impossible to sharply define the beginning of the perversion. Moreover, the whole field of body-fetichism does not really extend beyond the limits of things which normally stimulate the sexual instinct. Here the abnormality consists only in the fact that the whole sexual interest is concentrated on the impression made by a part of the person of the opposite sex, so that all other impressions fade and become more or less indifferent. Therefore, the body-fetichist is not to be regarded as a *monstrum per excessum* [monster through an aberration], like the sadist or masochist, but rather as a *monstrum per defectum* [monster through a failing]. What stimulates him is not abnormal, but rather what does not affect him,—the limitation of sexual interest that has taken place in him. Of course, this limited sexual interest, within its narrower limits, is usually expressed with a correspondingly greater and abnormal intensity.

It would seem reasonable to assume, as the distinguishing mark of pathological fetichism, the necessity for the presence of the fetich as a *conditio sine qua non* [necessary condition] for the possibility of performance of coitus. But when the facts are more carefully studied, it is seen that this limitation is really only indefinite. There are numerous cases in which, even in the absence of the fetich, coitus is possible, but incomplete and forced (often with the help of fancies relating to the fetich), and particularly unsatisfying and exhausting; and, too, closer study of the distinctive subjective psychical conditions in these cases shows that there are transitional states, passing, on the one hand, to mere physiological preferences, and, on the other, to psychical impotence, in the absence of the fetich.

It is therefore better, perhaps, to seek the pathological criterion of body-fetichism in purely subjective psychical states. The concentration of the sexual interest on a certain portion of the body that has no direct relation to sex (as have the mammae [breasts] and external genitals)—a peculiarity to be emphasised—often leads body-fetichists to such a condition that they do not regard coitus as the real means of sexual gratification, but rather some form of manipulation of that portion of the body that is effectual as a fetich. This perverse instinct of body-fetichists may be taken as the pathological criterion, no matter whether actual coitus is still possible or not.

Fetichism of inanimate objects or articles of dress, however, in all cases, may well be regarded as a pathological phenomenon, since its object falls without the circle of normal sexual stimuli. But even here, in the phenomena, there is a certain outward correspondence with processes of the normal psychical *vita sexualis* [sexual life]; the inner connection and meaning of pathological fetichism, however, are entirely different. In the ecstatic love of a man mentally normal, a handkerchief or shoe, a glove or letter, the flower 'she gave', or a lock of hair, etc., may become the object of worship, but only because they represent a mnemonic symbol of the beloved person – absent or dead – whose whole personality is reproduced by them. The pathological fetichist has not such relations. The fetich constitutes the entire content of his idea. When he becomes aware of its presence, sexual excitement occurs, and the fetich makes itself felt.

According to all observations thus far made, pathological fetichism seems to arise only on the basis of a psychopathic constitution that is for the most part hereditary, or on the basis of existent mental disease.

Thus it happens that it not infrequently appears combined with the other (original) sexual perversions that arise on the same basis. Not infrequently fetichism occurs in the most various forms in combination with inverted sexuality, sadism, and masochism. Indeed, certain forms of body-fetichism (hand- and foot-fetichism) probably have a more or less distinct connection with the latter two perversions. [. . .]

But if fetichism also rests upon a congenital general psychopathic disposition, yet this perversion is not, like those previously considered, essentially of an original nature; it is not congenitally perfect, as we may well assume sadism and masochism to be.

While in the sexual perversions described in the preceding chapters we have met only cases of congenital type, here we meet only *acquired* cases. Aside from the fact that often in fetichism the causative circumstance of its acquirement is traced, yet the physiological conditions are wanting, which in sadism and masochism, by means of sexual hyperaesthesia, are intensified to perversions, and justify the assumption of congenital origin. In fetichism, every case requires an event which affords the ground for the perversion.

As has been said, it is, of course, physiological in sexual life to be partial to one or another of woman's charms, and to be enthusiastic about it; but concentration of the entire sexual interest on such partial impression is here the essential thing; and for this concentration there must be a particular reason in every individual affected. Therefore, we may accept *Binet's* conclusion that *in the life of every fetichist there may be assumed to have been some event which determined the association of lustful feeling with the single impression.* This event must be sought for in the time of early youth, and, as a rule, occurs in connection with the first awakening of the *vita sexualis.* This first awakening is associated with some partial sexual impression (since it is always a thing standing in some relation to woman), and stamps it for life as the principal object of sexual interest. The circumstances under which the association arises are usually forgotten; the result of the association alone is retained. The general predisposition to psychopathic states and the sexual hyperaesthesia of such individuals are all that is original here.

Like the other perversions thus far considered, erotic (pathological) fetichism may also express itself in strange, unnatural, and even criminal acts: gratification with the female person *loco indebito* [in the undue place; i.e., anal intercourse], theft and robbery of objects of fetichism, pollution of such objects, etc. Here, too, it only depends upon the intensity of the perverse impulse and the relative power of opposing ethical motives, whether and to what extent such acts are performed.

These perverse acts of fetichists, like those of other sexually perverse individuals, may either alone constitute the entire external *vita sexualis*, or occur parallel with the normal sexual act. This depends upon the condition of physical and psychical sexual power, and the degree of excitability to normal stimuli that has been retained. Where excitability is diminished, not infrequently the sight or touch of the fetich serves as a necessary preparatory act.

The great practical importance which attaches to the facts of fetichism, in accordance with what has been said, lies in two factors. In the first place, pathological fetichism is not infrequently a cause of *psychical impotence*. Since the object upon which the sexual interest of the fetichist is concentrated stands, in itself, in no *immediate* relation to the normal sexual act, it often happens that the fetichist diminishes his excitability to normal stimuli by his perversion, or, at least, is capable of coitus only by means of concentration of his fancy upon his fetich. In this perversion, and in the difficulty of its adequate gratification, just as in the other perversions of the sexual instinct, lie conditions favouring psychical and physical onanism, which again reacts deleteriously on the constitution and sexual power. This is especially true in the case of youthful individuals, and particularly in the case of those who, on account of opposing ethical and aesthetic motives, shrink from the realisation of their perverse desires.

Secondly, fetichism is of great *forensic importance*. Just as sadism may extend to murder and the infliction of bodily injury, fetichism may lead to theft and even to robbery for the possession of the desired articles.

Erotic fetichism has for its object either a certain portion of the body of a person of the opposite sex, or a certain article or material of wearing apparel of the opposite sex. (Only cases of pathological fetichism in men have thus far been observed, and therefore only portions of the female person and attire are spoken of here.) [. . .]

Violation of Animals (Bestiality)

Violation of animals, monstrous and revolting as it seems to mankind, is by no means always due to psycho-pathological conditions. Low morality and great sexual desire, with lack of opportunity for natural indulgence, are the principal motives of this unnatural means of sexual satisfaction, which is resorted to by women as well as by men.

economic, situation? the men of cows of Beloved

To *Polak* we owe the knowledge that in Persia bestiality is frequently practiced because of the delusion that it cures gonorrhoea; just as in Europe an idea is still prevalent that intercourse with children heals venereal disease.

Experience teaches that bestiality with cows or horses is none too infrequent. Occasionally the acts may be undertaken with goats, bitches, and [. . .] with hens.

The action of Frederick the Great, in a case of a cavalryman who had committed bestiality with a mare, is well-known: 'The fellow is a pig, and shall be reduced to the infantry.'

The intercourse of females with beasts is limited to dogs. A monstrous example of the moral depravity in large cities is related by *Maschka* [. . .]; it is the case of a Parisian female who showed herself in the sexual act with a trained bull-dog, to a secret circle of *roués*, at ten francs a head.

Case 229. In a provincial town a man was caught in intercourse with a hen. He was thirty years old, and of high social position. The chickens had been dying one after another, and the man causing it had been 'wanted' for a long time. To the question of the judge, as to the reason for such an act, the accused said that his genitals were so small that coitus with women was impossible. Medical examination showed that actually the genitals were extremely small. The man was *mentally quite sound*.

South Park's Chicken fucker

There were no statements concerning any abnormalities at the time of puberty, etc. [. . .]

But there is another group of cases falling well within the category of bestiality, in which decidedly a pathological basis exists, indicated by heavy taint, constitutional neuroses, impotence for the normal act, impulsive manner of performing the unnatural act. Perhaps it would serve a purpose to put such cases under the heading of a special appellation; for instance, to use the term 'bestiality' for those cases which are not of a pathological character, and the term 'Zooerasty' for those of a pathological nature. [. . .]

Case 232. X., peasant, aged forty; Greek-Catholic. Father and mother were hard drinkers. Since his fifth year patient had epileptic convulsions – i.e., he would fall down unconscious, lie still two or three minutes, and then get up and run aimlessly about with staring eyes. Sexuality was first manifested at seventeen. The patient had inclinations neither for women nor for men, but for animals (fowls, horses, etc.). He had intercourse with hens and ducks, and later with horses and cows. Never onanism.

The patient painted pictures of saints; was of very limited intelligence. For years, religious paranoia, with states of ecstasy. He had an 'inexplicable' love for the Virgin, for whom he would sacrifice his life. Taken to hospital, he proved to be free from infirmity and signs of anatomical degeneration.

He always had an aversion for women. In a single attempt at coitus with a woman he was impotent, but with animals he was always potent. He was bashful before women; coitus with women he regarded almost as a sin. [. . .]

Whoever seeks and finds sexual gratification exclusively with animals, although the opportunities for the normal act are at hand, must at once be suspected of a pathological condition of the sexual instinct. At any rate more so than the sexually inverted person, for in sexual acts with animals the psychical condition is wanting, i.e., the possibility of the perversion of one part leading to the perversity of the other.

The Female Offender (1893)
Cesare Lombroso and Guglielmo Ferrero

Among male criminals the practice of tattooing is so common as to become a special characteristic; but in female delinquents it is so rare as to be practically non-existent. [. . .]

Among prostitutes, especially those of the lowest class, the case is very different. The proportion of tattooed among them is higher, even setting aside the tattooing of the face with moles, which doubles and even trebles the number of examples.

Segre found 1 in 300 in Milan, De Albertis 28 in 300 at Genoa; I found 7 in 1,561 at Turin—in all, 36 in 2,161, or 2.5 per cent. The principal characteristics of the practice are almost negative. There are few religious symbols (only one in thirty-three cases), but frequent allusions to love mostly illicit, for the instances only include two allusions to parents, while twenty-four out of thirty-three referred to lovers. The small degree of constancy in these attachments is betrayed by the multiplicity of references to lovers, of whom in two cases two were indicated, and in two more, three. The marks consisted:–

In 31   ...   Names and initials.

In 6   ...   Transfixed hearts.
In 3   ...   Men's heads.
In 2   ...   Mottoes.
In 3   ...   Own names.

De Albertis found on the arm of a prostitute, 84 years old, a Genoese, the figure of a zouave between two initials, C. D. One had 'W., my love', and two transpierced hearts on the right forearm. One had caused herself to be tattooed on the breast by an expert practitioner with the figure of her lover, and underneath, the letters 'E. I. M. B.' *(Evvia il mio Bruno* [Long live my Bruno]). This was an allusion to her first lover whom she had known when only fourteen, by whom she had had a child and then been abandoned at the end of two years. She was, nevertheless, a woman of some education.

In Paris also, as a rule, prostitutes are tattooed only with the initials or names of their lovers, followed by the declaration, '*Pour la vie*', flanked sometimes by two flowers or two hearts. The marks are almost always on the shoulders or breast. Only twice was any obscene allusion found.

La Rosny was covered all over with the names and initials of her lovers and the dates of her new attachments.

As to the places chosen for tattooing they are as follows:—

Covered parts	27
Uncovered (face)	1
Right arm	7
Left arm	4
Forearm	19
Thighs	7
Breasts	3

The age at which the tattooing begins is almost always early.

In 1 case	7 years.	
„ 3 „	15 to 17	„
„ 9 „	18 to 24	„
„ 3 „	25 to 28	„
„ 2 „	38 to 44	„

Parent Duchatelet noticed that the tattooing is most frequent in the more degraded girls, who are accustomed to mark themselves with the names of their lovers, effacing always the old with the new, so that in one case there had been 15 names. Old unfortunates prefer to tattoo themselves with the names of women.

De Albertis observed that among prostitutes those who are tattooed are the most depraved.

Out of 28, 15 had been in prison, 10 of them several times, and one 24 times. Nine were covered with scars, 28 were wanting in moral sense, and 20 even in a sense of religion; 25 out of 28 had dulness of touch, and 1 was absolutely wanting in it. All had been precociously depraved, one at 9, another at 10 years—8 between 12 and 14 years. Seven of the number had tattooed themselves, one at the age of 9 out of imitation. Fourteen out of twenty-eight showed anxiety to exhibit the marks. [. . .]

The tattooings are usually always in the same places and of the same colour; and sometimes they are superimposed, an effort being made to cover the name of an old lover with that of the new one. The chief difference seems to be, that while in Copenhagen only male names are found, on Parisian prostitutes there are often female ones. [. . .]

3. *Conclusions.* [. . .] On the whole, therefore, even the peculiarity of tattooing is found to a far smaller degree among criminal women than among men. In females of this class the proportion is as two per thousand, while in young men, especially the military, the proportion rises to 32 and 40 per cent., with a minimum of 14 per cent.

In prostitutes, on the other hand, the average is 2.5 per cent., and has been trebled of late through the recent practice of tattooing the face with moles.

In Denmark, setting moles aside, the proportion is 10 per cent. Still more remarkable is the fact that even among the tattooed female criminals the majority were prostitutes also; and it was the most vicious and the most degraded of the unfortunates themselves who were tattooed, and tattooed more especially on the covered portions of their bodies, such as thighs and breasts. Finally, prostitutes alone, especially in Denmark and France, showed a multiplicity of tattooings, the number amounting to 9, 11, or even 15.

The predominating meaning of all these designs is love; but it is a love which proves the inconstancy of the unfortunate class, since in 26 cases out of 73 the letter E, which constituted a declaration of eternal affection, was followed by the names of 2, 4, 5, and even 6 lovers; while 5 women were tattooed with a funereal cross above the name, or had effaced an old name with a new one.

Studies in the Psychology of Sex, vol. I: *The Evolution of Modesty,* The Phenomena of Sexual Periodicity, Auto- Erotism [1899]
(3rd edn, 1910)
Havelock Ellis

There is no existing word in current use to indicate the whole range of phenomena I am here concerned with. We are familiar with "masturbation," but that, strictly speaking, only covers a special and arbitrary subdivision of the field, although, it is true, the subdivision with which physicians and alienists have chiefly occupied themselves. "Self-abuse" is somewhat wider, but by no means covers the whole ground, while for various reasons it is an unsatisfactory term. "Onanism" is largely used, especially in France, and some writers even include all forms of homosexual connection under this name; it may be convenient to do so from a physiological point of view, but it is a confusing and antiquated mode of procedure, and from the psychological standpoint altogether illegitimate; "onanism" ought never to be used in this connection, if only on the ground that Onan's device was not auto-erotic, but was an early example of withdrawal before emission, or *coitus interruptus.*

While the name that I have chosen may possibly not be the best, there should be no question as to the importance of grouping all these phenomena together. It seems to me that this field has rarely been viewed in a scientifically sound and morally sane light, simply because it has not been viewed as a whole. We have made it difficult so to view it by directing our attention on the special group of auto-erotic facts—that group included under masturbation—which was most easy to observe and which in an extreme form came plainly under medical observation in insanity and allied conditions, and we have wilfully torn this group of facts away from the larger group to which it naturally belongs. The questions which have been so widely, so diversely, and—it must unfortunately be added—often so mischievously discussed, concerning the nature and evils of masturbation are not seen in their true light and proportions until we realize that masturbation is but a specialized form of a tendency which in some form or in some degree normally affects not only man, but all the higher animals. From a medical point of view it is often convenient to regard masturbation as an isolated fact; but in order to understand it we must bear in mind its relationships. In this study of auto-erotism I shall frequently have occasion to refer to the old entity of "masturbation," because it has been more carefully studied than any other part of the auto-erotic field; but I hope it will always be borne in mind that the psychological significance and even the medical diagnostic value of masturbation cannot be appreciated unless we realize that it is an artificial subdivision of a great group of natural facts.

The study of auto-erotism is far from being an unimportant or merely curious study. Yet psychologists, medical and non-medical, almost without exception, treat its manifestations—when they refer to them at all—in a dogmatic and off-hand manner which is far from scientific. It is not surprising, therefore, that the most widely divergent opinions are expressed. Nor is it surprising that ignorant and chaotic notions among the general population should lead to results that would be ludicrous if they were not pathetic. To mention one instance known to me: a married lady who is a leader in social-purity movements and an enthusiast for sexual chastity, discovered, through reading some pamphlet against solitary vice, that she had herself been practicing masturbation for years without knowing it. The profound anguish and hopeless despair of this woman in face of what she believed to be the moral ruin of her whole life cannot well be described. It would be easy to give further examples, though scarcely a more striking one, to show the utter confusion into which we are thrown by leaving this matter in the hands of blind leaders of the blind. Moreover, the conditions of modern civilization render auto-erotism a matter of increasing social significance. As our marriage-rate declines, and as illicit sexual relationships continue to be openly discouraged, it is absolutely inevitable that auto-erotic phenomena of one kind or another, not only among women but also among men, should increase among us both in amount and intensity. It becomes, therefore, a matter of some importance, both to the moralist and the physician, to investigate the psychological nature of these phenomena and to decide precisely what their attitude should be toward them.

I do not purpose to enter into a thorough discussion of all the aspects of auto-erotism. That would involve a very extensive study indeed. I wish to consider briefly certain salient points concerning auto-erotic phenomena, especially their prevalence, their nature, and their moral, physical, and other effects. I base my study partly on the facts and opinions which during the last thirty years have been scattered through the periodical and other medical literature of Europe and America, and partly on the experience of individuals, especially of fairly normal individuals.

Among animals in isolation and sometimes in freedom—though this can less often be observed—it is well known that various forms of spontaneous solitary sexual excitement occur. [...]

In the human species these phenomena are by no means found in civilization alone. To whatever extent masturbation may have been developed by the conditions of European life, which carry to the utmost extreme the concomitant stimulation and repression of the sexual emotions, it is far from being, as Mantegazza has declared it to be, one of the moral characteristics of Europeans. It is found among the people of nearly every race of which we have any intimate knowledge, however natural the conditions under which men and women may live.

The Sexual Life of Our Time (1907)
Iwan Bloch

The psychical element of exhibitionism also plays a part in the practice of the so-called 'voyeurs' and 'voyeuses', that numerous group of male and female individuals who are sexually excited by regarding the sexual acts of other persons (active *voyeurs*), or who allow themselves to be watched by others when themselves performing sexual acts (passive *voyeurs*). In many brothels, apertures in the wall or other arrangements have been made for these *voyeurs* or *gagas*, through which they watch sexual scenes. In fashionable dressmakers' shops, men are also said to watch ladies trying on dresses—at least, so I have been informed by a Parisian. Recently women also have been more and more inclined to see such spectacles. [. . .] Messalina compelled her court ladies to prostitute themselves in her presence. Not infrequently male and female *voyeurs* unite to form societies and secret sexual clubs, in which all the sexual acts are performed in public.

Thus, in the end of September, 1906, in Graz, a 'Secret Society for Immoral Purposes', was discovered by the police. At the head of this club was a merchant, thirty years of age, B—, jun. A number of other persons of good position belonged to this sexual club. They met in the great restaurant 'Zum Königstiger'. Under the title of 'An Assembly of Beauty', festivals were held in the magnificent garden of this restaurant, which were concluded as orgies behind closed doors. The beautiful gardens of the Schlossberg were also the scene of many meetings of the club.

A remarkable category of *voyeurs* is constituted by the so-called 'stercoraires platoniques', individuals who obtain sexual enjoyment by observing the acts of defecation and micturition performed by persons of the other sex, and seek opportunities for such observations in brothels or public lavatories. In the closet of one of the Berlin railway-stations such a *stercoraire* recently made a small artificial opening in the wall, through which he was able to watch other persons when engaged in the act of defecation!

Studies in the Psychology of Sex, vol. VI: *Sex in Relation to Society* (1910)
Havelock Ellis

2. *The Biological Factor of Prostitution.* – Economic considerations, as we see, have a highly important modificatory influence on prostitution, although it is by no means correct to assert that they form its main cause. There is another question which has exercised many investigators: To what extent are prostitutes predestined to this career by organic constitution? It is generally admitted that economic and other conditions are an exciting cause of prostitution; in how far are those who succumb predisposed by the possession of abnormal personal characteristics? Some inquirers have argued that this predisposition is so marked that prostitution may fairly be regarded as a feminine equivalent for criminality, and that in a family in which the men instinctively turn to crime, the women instinctively turn to prostitution. Others have as strenuously denied this conclusion.

Lombroso has more especially advocated the doctrine that prostitution is the vicarious equivalent of criminality. In this he was developing the results reached, in the important study of the Jukes family, by Dugdale, who found that "there where the brothers commit crime, the sisters adopt prostitution;" the fines and imprisonments of the women of the family were not for violations of the right of property, but mainly for offenses against public decency. "The psychological as well as anatomical identity of the criminal and the born prostitute," Lombroso and Ferrero concluded, "could not be more complete: both are identical with the moral insane, and therefore, according to the axiom, equal to each other. There is the same lack of moral sense, the same hardness of heart, the same precocious taste for evil, the same indifference to social infamy, the same volatility, love of idleness, and lack of foresight, the same taste for facile pleasures, for the orgy and for alcohol, the same, or almost the same, vanity. Prostitution is only the feminine side of criminality. And so true is it that prostitution and criminality are two analogous, or, so to say, parallel, phenomena, that at their extremes they meet. The prostitute is, therefore, psychologically a criminal: if she commits no offenses it is because her physical weakness, her small intelligence, the facility of acquiring what she wants by more easy methods, dispenses her from the necessity of crime, and on these very grounds prostitution represents the specific form of feminine criminality." The authors add that "prostitution is, in a certain sense, socially useful as an outlet for masculine sexuality and a preventive of crime" (Lombroso and Ferrero, *La Donna Delinquente,* 1893, p. 571).

Those who have opposed this view have taken various grounds, and by no means always understood the position they are attacking. Thus W. Fischer (in *Die Prostitution*) vigorously argues that prostitution is not an inoffensive equivalent of criminality, but a factor of criminality. Féré, again (in *Dégénérescence et Criminalité*), asserts that criminality and prostitution are not equivalent, but identical. "Prostitutes and criminals," he holds, "have as a common character their unproductiveness, and consequently they are both anti-social. Prostitution thus constitutes a form of criminality." The essential character of criminals is not, however, their unproductiveness, for that they share with a considerable proportion of the wealthiest of the upper class; it must be added, also, that the prostitute, unlike the criminal, is exercising an activity for which there is a demand, for which she is willingly paid, and for which she has to work (it has sometimes been noted that the prostitute looks down on the thief, who "does not work"); she is carrying on a profession, and is neither more nor less productive than those who carry on many more reputable professions. Aschaffenburg, also believing himself in opposition to Lombroso, argues, somewhat differently from Féré, that prostitution is not indeed, as Féré said, a form of criminality, but that it is too frequently united with criminality to be regarded as an equivalent. Mönkemöller has more recently supported the same view. Here, however, as usual, there is a wide difference of opinion as to the proportion of prostitutes of whom this is true. It is recognized by all investigators to be true of a certain number, but while Baumgarten, from an examination of eight thousand prostitutes, only found a minute proportion who were criminals, Ströhmberg found that among 462 prostitutes there were as many as 175 thieves. From another side, Morasso (as quoted in *Archivio di Psichiatria*, 1896, fasc. I), on the strength of his own investigations, is more clearly in opposition to Lombroso, since he protests altogether against any purely degenerative view of prostitutes which would in any way assimilate them with criminals.

The question of the sexuality of prostitutes, which has a certain bearing on the question of their tendency to degeneration, has been settled by different writers in different senses. While some, like Morasso, assert that sexual impulse is a main cause inducing women to adopt a prostitute's career, others assert that prostitutes are usually almost devoid of sexual impulse. Lombroso refers to the prevalence of sexual frigidity among prostitutes. In London, Merrick, speaking from a knowledge of over 16,000 prostitutes, states that he has met with "only a very few cases" in which gross sexual desire has been the motive to adopt a life of prostitution. In Paris, Raciborski had stated at a much earlier period that "among prostitutes one finds very few who are prompted to libertinage by sexual ardor." Commenge, again, a careful student of the Parisian prostitute, cannot admit that sexual desire is to be classed among the serious causes of prostitution. "I have made inquiries of thousands of women on this point," he states, "and only a very small number have told me that they were driven to prostitution for the satisfaction of sexual needs. Although girls who give themselves to prostitution are often lacking in frankness, on this point, I believe, they have no wish to deceive. When they have sexual needs they do not conceal them, but, on the contrary, show a certain *amour-propre* in acknowledging them, as a sufficient sort of justification for their life; so that if only a very small minority avow this motive the reason is that for the great majority it has no existence."

There can be no doubt that the statements made regarding the sexual frigidity of prostitutes are often much too unqualified. This is in part certainly due to the fact that they are usually made by those who speak from a knowledge of old prostitutes whose habitual familiarity with normal sexual intercourse in its least attractive aspects has resulted in complete indifference to such intercourse, so far as their clients are concerned. It may be stated with truth that to the woman of deep passions the ephemeral and superficial relationships of prostitution can offer no temptation. And it may be added that the majority of prostitutes begin their career at a very early age, long before the somewhat late period at which in women the tendency for passion to become strong, has yet arrived. It may also be said that an indifference to sexual relationships, a tendency to attach no personal value to them, is often a predisposing cause of the adoption of a prostitute's career; the general mental shallowness of prostitutes may well be accompanied by shallowness of physical emotion. On the other hand, many prostitutes, at all events early in their careers, appear to show a marked degree of sensuality, and to women of coarse sexual fibre the career of prostitution has not been without attractions from this point of view; the gratification of physical desire is known to act as a motive in some cases and is clearly indicated in others. This is scarcely surprising when we remember that prostitutes are in a very large proportion of cases remarkably robust and healthy persons in general respects. They withstand without difficulty the risks of their profession, and though under its influence the manifestations of sexual feeling can scarcely fail to become modified or perverted in course of time, that is no proof of the original absence of sexual sensibility. It is not even a proof of its loss, for the real sexual nature of the normal prostitute, and her possibilities of sexual ardor, are chiefly manifested, not in her professional relations with her clients, but in her relations with her "fancy boy" or "bully." It is quite true that the conditions of her life often make it practically advantageous to the prostitute to have attached to her a man who is devoted to her interests and will defend them if necessary, but that is only a secondary, occasional, and subsidiary advantage of the "fancy boy," so far as prostitutes generally are concerned. She is attracted to him primarily because he appeals to her personally and she wants him for herself. The motive of her attachment is, above all, erotic, in the full sense, involving not merely sexual relations but possession and common interests, a permanent and intimate life led together. "You know that what one does in the way of business cannot fill one's heart," said a German prostitute; "Why should we not have a husband like other women? I, too, need love. If that were not so we should not want a bully." And he, on his part, reciprocates this feeling and is by no means merely moved by self-interest.

One of my correspondents, who has had much experience of prostitutes, not only in Britain, but also in Germany, France, Belgium and Holland, has found that the normal manifestations of sexual feeling are much more common in British than in continental prostitutes. "I should say," he writes, "that in normal coitus foreign women are generally unconscious of sexual excitement. I don't think I have ever known a foreign woman who had any semblance of orgasm. British women, on the other hand, if a man is moderately kind, and shows that he has some feelings beyond mere sensual gratification, often abandon themselves to the wildest delights of sexual excitement. Of course in this life, as in others, there is keen competition, and a woman, to vie with her competitors, must please her gentlemen friends; but a man of the world can always distinguish between real and simulated passion." (It is possible, however, that he may be most successful in arousing the feelings of his own fellow-country women.) On the other hand, this writer finds that the foreign women are more anxious to provide for the enjoyment of their temporary consorts and to ascertain what pleases them. "The foreigner seems to make it the business of her life to discover some abnormal mode of sexual gratification for her consort." For their own pleasure also foreign prostitutes frequently ask for *cunnilinctus* [sic], in preference to normal coitus, while anal coitus is also common. The difference evidently is that the British women, when they seek gratification, find it in normal coitus, while the foreign women prefer more abnormal methods. There is, however, one class of British prostitutes which this correspondent finds to be an exception to the general rule: the class of those who are recruited from the lower walks of the stage. "Such women are generally more licentious—that is to say, more acquainted with the bizarre in sexualism—than girls who come from shops or bars; they show a knowledge of *fellatio*, and even anal coitus, and during menstruation frequently suggest inter-mammary coitus."

On the whole it would appear that prostitutes, though not usually impelled to their life by motives of sensuality, on entering and during the early part of their career possess a fairly average amount of sexual impulse, with variations in both directions of excess and deficiency as well as of perversion. At a somewhat later period it is useless to attempt to measure the sexual impulse of prostitutes by the amount of pleasure they take in the professional performance of sexual intercourse. It is necessary to ascertain whether they possess sexual instincts which are gratified in other ways. In a large proportion of cases this is found to be so. Masturbation, especially, is extremely common among prostitutes everywhere; however prevalent it may be among women who have no other means of obtaining sexual gratification it is admitted by all to be still more prevalent among prostitutes, indeed almost universal.

Homosexuality, though not so common as masturbation, is very frequently found among prostitutes—in France, it would seem, more frequently than in England—and it may indeed be said that it occurs more often among prostitutes than among any other class of women. It is favored by the acquired distaste for normal coitus due to professional intercourse with men, which leads homosexual relationships to be regarded as pure and ideal by comparison. It would appear also that in a considerable proportion of cases prostitutes present a congenital condition of sexual inversion, such a condition, with an accompanying indifference to intercourse with men, being a predisposing cause of the adoption of a prostitute's career. Kurella even regards prostitutes as constituting a sub-variety of congenital inverts. Anna Rüling in Germany states that about twenty per cent. [of] prostitutes are homosexual; when asked what induced them to become prostitutes, more than one inverted woman of the street has replied to her that it was purely a matter of business, sexual feeling not coming into the question except with a friend of the same sex.

The occurrence of congenital inversion among prostitutes—although we need not regard prostitutes as necessarily degenerate as a class—suggests the question whether we are likely to find an unusually large number of physical and other anomalies among them. It cannot be said that there is unanimity of opinion on this point. For some authorities prostitutes are merely normal ordinary women of low social rank, if indeed their instincts are not even a little superior to those of the class in which they were born. Other investigators find among them so large a proportion of individuals deviating from the normal that they are inclined to place prostitutes generally among one or other of the abnormal classes. [. . .]

The most detailed examinations of ordinary non-criminal prostitutes, both anthropometrically and as regards the prevalence of anomalies, have been made in Italy, though not on a sufficiently large number of subjects to yield absolutely decisive results. Thus Fornasari made a detailed examination of sixty prostitutes belonging chiefly to Emilia and Venice, and also of twenty-seven others belonging to Bologna, the latter group being compared with a third group of twenty normal women belonging to Bologna (*Archivio di Psichiatria*, 1892, fasc. VI). The prostitutes were found to be of lower type than the normal individuals, having smaller heads and larger faces. As the author himself points out, his subjects were not sufficiently numerous to justify far-reaching generalizations, but it may be worth while to summarize some of his results. At equal heights the prostitutes showed greater weight; at equal ages they were of shorter stature than other women, not only of well-to-do, but of the poor class: height of face, bi-zygomatic diameter (though not the distance between zygomas), the distance from chin to external auditory meatus, and the size of the jaw were all greater in the prostitutes; the hands were longer and broader, compared to the palm, than in ordinary women; the foot also was longer in prostitutes and the thigh, as compared to the calf, was larger. It is noteworthy that in most particulars, and especially in regard to head measurements, the variations were much greater among the prostitutes than among the other women examined; this is to some extent, though not entirely, to be accounted for by the slightly greater number of the former.

Ardu (in the same number of the *Archivio*) gave the result of observations (undertaken at Lombroso's suggestion) as to the frequency of abnormalities among prostitutes. The subjects were seventy-four in number and belonged to Professor Giovannini's *Clinica Sifilopatica* [VD Clinic] at Turin. The abnormalities investigated were virile distribution of hair on pubes, chest, and limbs, hypertrichosis on forehead, left-handedness, atrophy of nipple and tattooing (which was only found once). Combining Ardu's observations with another series of observations on fifty-five prostitutes examined by Lombroso, it is found that virile disposition of hair is found in fifteen per cent. as against six per cent. in normal women; some degree of hypertrichosis in eighteen per cent.; left-handedness in eleven per cent. (but in normal women as high as twelve per cent. according to Gallia); and atrophy of nipple in twelve per cent.

Giuffrida-Ruggeri, again (*Atti della Società Romana di Antropologia*, 1897, p. 216), on examining eighty-two prostitutes found anomalies in the following order of decreasing frequency: tendency of eyebrows to meet, lack of cranial symmetry, depression at root of nose, defective development of calves, hypertrichosis and other anomalies of hair, adherent or absent lobule, prominent zygoma, prominent forehead or frontal bones, bad implantation of teeth, Darwinian tubercle of ear, thin vertical lips. These signs are separately of little or no importance, though together not without significance as an indication of general anomaly.

More recently Ascarilla, in an elaborate study (*Archivio di Psichiatria*, 1906, fasc. VI, p. 812) of the finger prints of prostitutes, comes to the conclusion that even in this respect prostitutes tend to form a class showing morphological inferiority to normal women. The patterns tend to show unusual simplicity and uniformity, and the significance of this is indicated by the fact that a similar uniformity is shown by the finger prints of the insane and deaf-mutes (De Sanctis and Toscano, *Atti Società Romana Antropologia*, vol. viii, 1901, fasc. II).

In Chicago Dr. Harriet Alexander, in conjunction with Dr. E.S. Talbot and Dr. J.G. Kiernan, examined thirty prostitutes in the Bridewell, or House of Correction; only the "obtuse" class of professional prostitutes reach this institution, and it is not therefore surprising that they were found to exhibit very marked stigmata of degeneracy. In race nearly half of those examined were Celtic Irish. In sixteen the zygomatic processes were unequal and very prominent. Other facial asymmetries were common. In three cases the heads were of Mongoloid type; sixteen were epignathic, and eleven prognathic; five showed arrest of development of face. Brachycephaly predominated (seventeen cases); the rest were mesaticephalic; there were no dolichocephals. Abnormalities in shape of the skull were numerous, and twenty-nine had defective ears. Four were demonstrably insane, and one was an epileptic (H.C.B. Alexander, "Physical Abnormalities in Prostitutes," Chicago Academy of Medicine, April 1893; E.S. Talbot, *Degeneracy*, p. 320; *Id., Irregularities of the Teeth*, fourth edition, p. 141).

It would seem, on the whole, so far as the evidence at present goes, that prostitutes are not quite normal representatives of the ranks into which they were born. There has been a process of selection of individuals who slightly deviate congenitally from the normal average and are, correspondingly, slightly inapt for normal life. The psychic characteristics which accompany such deviation are not always necessarily of an obviously unfavorable nature; the slightly neurotic girl of low class birth—disinclined for hard work, through defective energy, and perhaps greedy and selfish—may even seem to possess a refinement superior to her station. While, however, there is a tendency to anomaly among prostitutes, it must be clearly recognized that that tendency remains slight so long as we consider impartially the whole class of prostitutes. Those investigators who have reached the conclusion that prostitutes are a highly degenerate and abnormal class have only observed special groups of prostitutes, more especially those who are frequently found in prison. It is not possible to form a just conception of prostitutes by studying them only in prison, any more than it would be possible to form a just conception of clergymen, doctors, or lawyers by studying them exclusively in prison, and this remains true even although a much larger proportion of prostitutes than of members of the more reputable professions pass through prisons; that fact no doubt partly indicates the greater abnormality of prostitutes.

It has, of course, to be remembered that the special conditions of the lives of prostitutes tend to cause in them the appearance of certain professional characteristics which are entirely acquired and not congenital. In that way we may account for the gradual modification of the feminine secondary and tertiary sexual characters, and the appearance of masculine characters, such as the frequent deep voice, etc. But with all due allowance for these acquired characters, it remains true that such comparative investigations as have so far been made, although inconclusive, seem to indicate that, even apart from the prevalence of acquired anomalies, the professional selection of their avocation tends to separate out from the general population of the same social class, individuals who possess anthropometrical characters varying in a definite direction. The observations thus made seem, in this way, to indicate that prostitutes tend to be in weight over the average, though not in stature, that in length of arm they are inferior though the hands are longer (this has been found alike in Italy and Russia); they have smaller ankles and larger calves, and still larger thighs in proportion to their large calves. The estimated skull capacity and the skull circumference and diameters are somewhat below the normal, not only when compared with respectable women but also with thieves; there is a tendency to brachycephaly (both in Italy and Russia); the cheek-bones are usually prominent and the jaws developed; the hair is darker than in respectable women though less so than in thieves; it is also unusually abundant, not only on the head but also on the pudenda and elsewhere; the eyes have been found to be decidedly darker than those of either respectable women or criminals.

So far as the evidence goes it serves to indicate that prostitutes tend to approximate to the type which, as was shown in the previous volume, there is reason to regard as specially indicative of developed sexuality. It is, however, unnecessary to discuss this question until our anthropometrical knowledge of prostitutes is more extended and precise.

Sadism and Masochism (1924)
Wilhelm Stekel

An erroneous conception of the sadomasochistic complex makes pain the central factor for consideration and occupies itself with the phenomenon of gratification derived from pain. The expression *algolagnia*, coined by Schrenck-Notzing, accords with this idea. We have ascertained, however, that the decisive thing in the phenomenon of sadomasochism is the affect, which is fed from two sources: in the sadist, from his own sense of power in overcoming the resistance of another and from his feeling himself into the humiliation of his partner; in the masochist, from the overcoming of his own resistances (power over himself!) and the feeling of himself into the partner who humbles him, in which we were able to show that we have to do not with separate events, but with polar expressions of a single complex.

Many authors see in sadomasochism only a quantitative heightening of the normal sexual impulse, whereby sadism corresponds to the masculine, masochism to the feminine component of the sexual instinct. But it will not do simply to compare with each other the ideas masculine–sadistic and feminine–masochistic, although this point of view apparently gains support through many manifestations of the sexual life.

The problem will have to be solved through a large number of analytic investigations of relevant cases. It will thus be shown that the problem of bisexuality bears a large part in the psychogenesis of sadomasochism, not, to be sure, in so simple a sense as the older authors believed. If 'masculine' were identical with 'aggressive', all individuals with strong amounts of M, to use Weininger's expression, would necessarily be sadistically oriented, while the preponderance of F would lead to masochism. This in no way agrees with the facts. The sadistic disposition is found in women *and* in men and is in no way connected with the accentuation of one component of the sexual impulse.

Conditions are much more complicated than to permit of solution with so simple a key. One fact alone should give us thought, that in the animal world the female is sometimes the aggressive member. Aggressiveness may reach such a degree in certain of the arachnoids that the female devours the male during copulation. In the struggle between the sexes, which can be demonstrated also in the animal kingdom, the active role often belongs to the female.

It is not correct to accept sadomasochism merely as a congenital disposition, as Julius Schuster tries to do. He comes to these conclusions: 'Algolagnia is the quantitatively heightened specific impulse to sexual pleasure; it is a genotypically conditioned disposition. It can therefore only be evolved, not acquired. Very complex factors in its development from the day of birth on may be demonstrated: the oral and the anal zone as well as the other erogenous zones of the pregenital phase; further, the erogenicity of the skin and muscles, the affective processes, the Oedipus complex and the castration complex, in general all psychic experiences.'

This comprehensive statement contains about everything which the old and the new school have been able to say thus far concerning sadomasochism.

I take the stand, however, that sadomasochism is a disorder of the environment, to be referred therefore to definite influences in childhood. Of course, a disposition toward this paraphilia exists; it is the same disposition which all parapathies have in common: a strong impulsive life. The parapathic is a phenomenon of reversion. On this basis, the sadism is more strongly accentuated; it persists beyond the infantile period which belongs to all people; it is frequently turned into masochism as a result of the consciousness of guilt; but it remains anchored in the unconscious. The psychogenesis of this paraphilia goes back to the earliest years of childhood and appears to one who does not know as a native disposition, since the precipitating causes have fallen under repression.

I repeat: Sadomasochism is a form of psychosexual infantilism. The impulse shows an obsessive character and manifests itself as repetition compulsion. In all cases of sadomasochism we shall find the entire instrumentarium of infantilism and with it a well-developed fetishism accompanied by its most important phenomenon, flight from the partner. Careful analysis shows that all these cases are obsessive parapathies. The obsessive parapathy seeks to overcome the inner resistances through a compulsion; it binds the impulse, as a result of the displacement of affect, through an obsessive symptom. [. . .]

It is characteristic that sadists and masochists are very sensitive to pains if they occur without affect; that is, if they lie beyond the zone of their sexual life. I know masochists who apparently submit to the greatest pain, but tremble before the dentist and cannot bear toothache. Schuster admits this fact when he remarks: 1. Pain is felt as pleasurable only when it is bound with sexual pleasure; at the moment when the thoughts stray from sexual pleasure, pain appears. 2. In sexually pleasurable sensations of pain, it is a matter merely of drowning out the pain through a sexually toned idea.

Schuster confuses cause and effect. It is not the sexuality that drowns out the pain; it is only that with the help of the affect the pain is changed to pleasure.

All sadomasochists are affect-hungry individuals. They are in constant need of an affective spectacle. It is solely to be proved how and why they have come precisely to the specific affect. We shall see from many examples that it concerns a definite repressed affect, a specific attitude of hate toward a person of the environment. The hatred then turns itself against substitute objects or against one's own person. It is, however, withdrawn from its original object. On this account the descriptive portrayal of sadomasochists, as we know it from innumerable clinical histories, will never lead to investigation of the problem.

Studies in the Psychology of Sex, vol. VII: *Eonism* (1928)
Havelock Ellis

Those investigators who concentrate on the constitutional foundations of psycho-sexual anomalies, and those investigators who explore the mechanisms revealed by psycho-analysis are alike performing necessary tasks. Nothing is now more certain than the influence of the varying balance of the internal secretions in building up the psycho-sexual constitution. Nothing also is more illuminating than the mechanisms which the masters of psycho-analysis have revealed in unravelling the varied experiences of the individual. Both are essential to a complete interpretation of the varied cases that arise. Evil only ensues when, in one party or the other party, there is a failure to realize the immense services which the opposite party is rendering.

Realization of the need to recognize alike the hereditary and innate factors, the acquired and psycho-genetic factors, in the constitution of this anomaly may be noted among the most recent investigations. Thus Dr. Ernest Jones clearly assumes the existence of both sets of factors in all psycho-analytic investigations. Dr. Lothar Goldmann of New York (though his observations seem to have been made chiefly in Berlin) is quite ready to accept both, as regards transvestism. He points out that in many cases the subject shared the room of a sister in childhood, the period to which the aberration may so often be traced back, but as we know that the close association of brothers and sisters is commonly without significance for later life we are compelled to seek for a congenital predisposition. Goldmann sees in transvestism "a variety of sexual disposition of high biological and cultural significance." He is inclined to regard it as a form of auto-erotism, but seeks to distinguish between an erotic and a more permanent psychic form of the anomaly. He points out, like other investigators, its comparative rarity in women, and finds that in men when it is homosexual it tends to become less marked with years or with gratification of the homosexual impulses, but in the more prevalent heterosexual cases it became pronounced with age; this distinction seems just. He also remarks how, in the case of a distinguished musical composer, the bisexual constitution involved by the anomaly aided him to reach his highest musical possibilities. On the whole, he concludes that the hormonic explanation of this peculiar and many-sided anomaly is often, without question, the signpost pointing to the right road, but that there are also numerous cases where we need psychology in order to attain a completely satisfying answer to the thousandfold questions involved.

It was by Hirschfeld's important work in this field that I was stimulated to return to the subject and to bring forward my own small contribution. In a study published in the *Alienist and Neurologist* (May and August, 1913), describing four cases of the anomaly, I proposed for it the term "Sexo-Aesthetic Inversion," which I used as the title of the study, and I also suggested as an alternative the name "Eonism" after the Chevalier d'Eon, the most famous historical subject of this anomaly, to be used as comparable to the terms "sadism" and "masochism." ("Aesthetic inversion," I should say, was the name suggested to me by a man of scientific and scholarly distinction who was himself the subject of this anomaly in a pronounced form.) I pointed out the propriety of involving aesthetic emotion in this connection since the main characteristic of these people— the impulse to project themselves by sympathetic feeling into the object to which they are attracted, or the impulse of inner imitation—is precisely the tendency which various recent philosophers of aesthetics have regarded as the essence of all aesthetic feeling. It now, however, seems to me undesirable to use the word "inversion" in this connection as it is too apt to arouse suggestions of homosexuality, which may be quite absent, though it remains true that the phenomenon we are concerned with is one of erotic empathy, of a usually heterosexual inner imitation, which frequently tends to manifest itself in the assumption of the habits and garments of the desired sex; for the important point is that this impulse springs out of admiration and affection for the opposite sex, therefore the subject of it is not usually tempted to carry the inner imitation so far as to imitate the sexual desires of that sex and so to become unlike it by being homosexual; that is how it is that, to superficial view, he seems less logical, less thorough-going, than the sexual invert.

Moreover, "sexo-aesthetic inversion," even if acceptable as a descriptive term, still remains one of those hybrid Graeco-Latin compounds which it is best if possible to avoid. "Aesthetic sexual inversion" is misleading, since it would apparently be equivalent to "aesthetic homosexuality." The same subject of the anomaly who suggested "aesthetic inversion" also independently proposed Laurent's term, "psychical hermaphroditism"; but that is not accurate since these people are not always conscious of possessing the psychic disposition of both sexes, but sometimes only of one, the opposite sex, the sex to which they are attracted. Hirschfeld regretted that the difficulty cannot be solved by adopting the name of some well-known subject of the condition as in the terms "sadism" and "masochism," but thought none sufficiently well-known. He overlooked the well-known Chevalier d'Eon who exhibited this impulse very definitely, and I am now inclined to think best the term I had more tentatively suggested in my first contribution to the subject and to call this anomaly "Eonism."

Some years ago a man was found drowned off the Cornish coast dressed in women's clothes and with his hands fastened together. Among his effects at the hotel he was staying at were numerous refinements of the feminine toilette and feminine articles of dress. He was a lawyer, practising as a solicitor near London, and regarded by his acquaintances (of whom one is known to me) as an ordinary and normal man of quiet habits. There was no suggestion that his death was due to violence. It was evident that he had sought what was from the point of view of the Eonist (apparently with masochistic tendencies) the most voluptuous death possible.

Such a case reveals some of the peculiarities of Eonism. It tends to occur among people who are often educated, refined, sensitive, and reserved. It is for the most part successfully concealed from the subject's friends and acquaintances, even from the nearest members of his own family. It is sometimes associated with manifestations which recall masochism or passive algolagnia. Thus it is in some aspects a form of erotic symbolism which, while it might be classified under inversion, in the wider sense of that term, yet has resemblances to erotic fetichism, and occurs in the kind of people who tend to be subject to fetichism. It also resembles, in some of its features, the kind of auto-erotism called Narcissism or erotic self-admiration. Aesthetic inversion cannot, however, be identified either with fetichism or with Narcissism; the subject is not really in love either with a fetich or, except in one special type, with himself.

Although this psychic peculiarity is so difficult both to name and to define, it is, strange as that may seem, the commonest of all sexual anomalies to attain prominence in the public newspapers. There are several reasons why that should be. There is not only the real frequency of the condition, but the fact that it is so striking and so intriguing a violation of our most obvious conventional rules and regulations of social life. There is the further consideration that, since in its simple uncomplicated form it constitutes no violation of our moral feelings and laws, it is easily possible to discuss it plainly in the most reputable public prints.

Sexual Anomalies and Perversions (1936)
Magnus Hirschfeld

Exhibitionism is a pathological urge to obtain sexual satisfaction by exposing the sexual organs or other intimate parts of the body in the presence of persons who are erotically attractive to the subject. This anomaly occurs far more frequently in men than in women, and is comparatively widespread, as evidenced by the fact that exhibitionism accounts for approximately one-third of all sexual crime.

The literature on the subject is accordingly very extensive, and contains hundreds of accurately described clinical cases; yet [. . .] it has not been possible so far to clear up the precise nature of this anomaly. The majority of the available cases are court cases, as exhibitionists usually only consult a doctor when they have come into conflict with the law. As a rule, they are timid people of exaggerated modesty, whose prudery contrasts strangely and significantly with the shamelessness of their actions.

In the majority of cases it is the masculine member, in the erect or normal state, that is exposed, though exposure of other parts, such as the buttocks, also occurs.

An essential feature in the behaviour of the exhibitionist is his eager enjoyment of his victim's reaction. The reaction is, in fact, the source of his erotic pleasure, and the exhibitionist's satisfaction is complete or incomplete according to whether the victim's reaction is intense (fear, blushing, escape), or whether they deliberately ignore the exposure. All the exhibitionist wants is to evoke strong emotions, so that other acts accompanying the exposure are only of a secondary character. When, as often happens, the exhibitionist uses obscene words, or invites the victim to 'take hold', etc., his sole purpose is to call attention to the exposed part. Some exhibitionists achieve this by coughing or whistling during the act of exposure, while others throw sweets or coins to children.

In the majority of cases the exhibitionist executes various movements with the exposed member, such as shaking or rubbing it, or he moves his body in imitation of the coital act. These accompanying acts frequently lead to ejaculation, but ejaculation may occur without them, though in very many cases it does not occur at all.

But whereas obscene words used by an exhibitionist during the act of exposure are only of a secondary character, such talk may constitute the sole act of exhibitionism. Since, as we have said, the exhibitionist's enjoyment essentially consists in the reaction he evokes, it is possible for an exhibitionist to indulge his urge by merely saying obscene words to women or young girls. This type of exhibitionist is called a *verbal exhibitionist*, and is, of course, far more rare than the ordinary type. The verbal exhibitionist sometimes uses the telephone for this purpose, in which case the victim's indignant tone is sufficient to produce the desired effect in the exhibitionist.

The exhibitionist generally haunts parks and open spaces—Hyde Park in London, the Bois de Boulogne in Paris, etc. Sometimes an exhibitionist will take up a position along a railway line and expose himself to travellers in passing trains. Such acts are also committed in the trains themselves. Some years ago the case of a Berlin judge who acted in cases of sexual crime created a considerable scandal.

The judge in question showed no mercy for sexual criminals, and was accordingly feared by them. Then one day he himself was arrested in a suburban train for exposing his erect member to a girl with whom he was alone in a compartment. His sternness on the bench was probably due to an overcompensated sense of guilt.

Exhibitionists also haunt doorways, staircases, and the precincts of girls' schools, and acts of exposure further occur at theatres and even churches. During a performance of 'Parsifal' at the Viennese Opera House, a man stepped to the front of a box completely naked, having undressed at the back of the box.

Many exhibitionists dress in such a manner as to facilitate exposure. *Disire cloaked in a Trenchcoat* There is the 'exhibitionist overcoat'. Many exhibitionists go for a walk with their member hanging out under their overcoat.

In addition to ordinary and verbal exhibitionists there are also psychological exhibitionists, whose exaggerated urge for frankness causes them to reveal to all the world weaknesses which other people endeavour to conceal. Classic examples of psychological exhibitionism are the confessions of Rousseau and the memoirs of Frank Harris. *otherwise known as BIG MOUTHS!*